Spatial Working Memory

Current Issues in Memory
Series Editor: Robert Logie
Professor of Human Cognitive Neuroscience, University of Edinburgh, UK

Current Issues in Memory is a series of edited books that reflect the state-of-the-art in areas of current and emerging interest in the psychological study of memory. Each volume is tightly focused on a particular topic and consists of seven to ten chapters contributed by international experts. The editors of individual volumes are leading figures in their areas and provide an introductory overview. Example topics include: binding in working memory, prospective memory, memory and ageing, autobiographical memory, visual memory, implicit memory, amnesia, retrieval, memory development.

Other titles in this series:

Forgetting
Edited by Sergio Della Sala

The Visual Word in Memory
Edited by James R. Brockmole

Current Issues in Applied Memory Research
Edited by Graham M. Davies & Daniel B. Wright

Spatial Working Memory

Edited by André Vandierendonck &
Arnaud Szmalec

Psychology Press
Taylor & Francis Group
HOVE AND NEW YORK

First published 2011
by Psychology Press
27 Church Road, Hove, East Sussex BN3 2FA

Simultaneously published in the USA and Canada
by Psychology Press
711 Third Avenue, New York NY 10017

www.psypress.com

Psychology Press is an imprint of the Taylor & Francis Group, an informa business

Typeset in Times by
RefineCatch Limited, Bungay, Suffolk
Printed and bound in Great Britain by TJ International Ltd, Padstow, Cornwall
Cover design by Lisa Dynan

British Library Cataloguing in Publication Data
A catalogue record for this book is available from the British Library

Library of Congress Cataloging-in-Publication Data
Spatial working memory / edited by André Vandierendonck & Arnaud Szmalec.
p. cm.
Includes bibliographical references and index.
ISBN 978-1-84872-033-6 (hb)
1. Short-term memory. 2. Space perception. I. Vandierendonck, André. II. Szmalec, Arnaud.
BF378.S54S63 2011
153.1′3—dc22 2010053316

ISBN: 978-1-84872-033-6

Contents

List of contributors vi
Preface vii

1 **Progress in spatial working memory research** 1
ANDRÉ VANDIERENDONCK AND ARNAUD SZMALEC

2 **The visual and the spatial of a multicomponent working memory** 19
ROBERT H. LOGIE

3 **Spatial information in (visual) working memory** 46
HUBERT D. ZIMMER & HEINRICH R. LIESEFELD

4 **Exploring the determinants of memory for spatial sequences** 67
FABRICE B. R. PARMENTIER

5 **What underlies the ability to guide action with spatial information that is no longer present in the environment?** 87
BRADLEY R. POSTLE

6 **The organization of visuospatial working memory: Evidence from the study of developmental disorders** 102
CESARE CORNOLDI AND IRENE C. MAMMARELLA

7 **The nature of visuospatial representation within working memory** 122
COLIN HAMILTON

8 **What can symmetry tell us about working memory?** 145
LAURA PIERONI, CLELIA ROSSI-ARNAUD, AND ALAN D. BADDELEY

9 **The role of spatial working memory in understanding verbal descriptions: A window onto the interaction between verbal and spatial processing** 159
VALÉRIE GYSELINCK AND CHIARA MENEGHETTI

Author index 181
Subject index 192

Contributors

Alan D. Baddeley is in the Department of Psychology at the University of York, UK.

Cesare Cornoldi is in the Department of General Psychology at the University of Padua, Padova, Italy.

Valérie Gyselinck is in the Laboratory of Cognitive Psychology and Neuropsychology, University Paris Descartes & CNRS.

Colin Hamilton is in the Department of Psychology at Northumbria University, Newcastle upon Tyne, UK.

Heinrich R. Liesefeld is in the Department of Psychology, the Brain & Cognition Unit at Saarland University, Saarbrücken, Germany.

Robert H. Logie is in the Department of Psychology at the University of Edinburgh, UK.

Irene Mammarella is in the Department of Developmental Psychology at the University of Padua, Padova, Italy.

Chiara Meneghetti is in the Department of General Psychology at the University of Padua, Padova, Italy.

Fabrice B. R. Parmentier is in the Department of Psychology at the University of the Balearic Islands, Palma, Spain.

Laura Pieroni is in the Dipartimento di Psicologia at Sapienza Università di Roma, Italy.

Bradley R. Postle is in the Department of Psychology and Psychiatry at the University of Wisconsin, Madison, USA.

Clelia Rossi-Arnaud is in the Dipartimento di Psicologia at Sapienza Università di Roma, Rome, Italy.

Arnaud Szmalec is in the Department of Experimental Psychology at Ghent University, Belgium.

André Vandierendonck is in the Department of Experimental Psychology at Ghent University, Belgium.

Hubert D. Zimmer is in the Department of Psychology, the Brain & Cognition Unit at the Saarland University, Saarbrücken, Germany.

Preface

The idea for this book arose during an international psychology conference that took place in 2008 in Berlin. During the course of the conference one of us (A.V.) enjoyed a drink in the sunshine with Robert Logie. The discussion wandered over many ideas and topics and came to that of working memory. It resulted in us agreeing that the pace of recent evolutions in research on visual and spatial working memory warranted a book taking stock of the current situation. It was not clear at that stage how broad the focus of the book was going to be. However, 6 weeks later, at the fourth European Working Memory Symposium (EWOMS-4) the idea was discussed further with several colleagues attending this small conference in rainy Bristol and this led to the decision that we would invite colleagues to contribute a chapter on *spatial working memory*, as distinct from *visual* working memory and visual object memory. This book is about how we are able to remember at which place in space something was perceived and how we are able to recall in which order we visited a series of locations.

Although the capacity to remember spatial information is biologically of utmost importance, in our modern society, this ability is completely overpowered by the verbal world, as if something that cannot be expressed verbally has no reason for existence and is possibly not in our minds. This verbal dominance has for a long time governed research on all kinds of memory, and still continues to do so. Whereas most publications address verbal memory, only a small minority are devoted to visual and/or spatial processes. This verbal dominance existed when Alan Baddeley and Graham Hitch (1974) first formulated their ideas about working memory: a short-term information storage system that also allows operations on the stored information. In their conception of working memory, dedicated modality-specific storage systems were included for verbal (phonologically coded) information and for visual and spatial information. After an initial strong research focus on verbal working memory, which continues even today, visual and spatial working memory appeared more and more in the picture. While in the last two or three decades, the amount of research on working memory has expanded, the number of publications on visual and spatial working memory has also tremendously increased in an attempt to catch up with the verbal tradition. The trends observable in the web of science are ostensively clear on this. In the 1980s only 26 articles were published on the topic of spatial working memory; in the 1990s this increased to 551, and in the first decade of the twenty-first century, 2291 articles appeared. In other words, in the last decade, four times as many articles addressed spatial working memory compared with two decades before. However, the trend in working memory research in general has expanded similarly. Nevertheless, in view of this strong growth of research regarding spatial working memory, a book like the present one can help readers find their way through the vast number of findings and theories.

The book tries to achieve this goal by providing a forum for top researchers in the domain of spatial working memory to review and discuss findings in relation to their own views and the hypotheses of colleagues about the processes and the memory structures underlying the ability to store and to operate on spatial information. Our general idea is that spatial working memory concerns the storage and manipulation of information that refers to locations in space irrespective of the modality of the receptors (visual, auditory, kinesthetic, etc.) that provided the information. The core characteristic of spatial information is location in space; it can be specified in an egocentric or an allocentric frame of reference. In an egocentric reference, a location is expressed in relation to the perceiver, whereas an allocentric reference specifies a location in relation to environmental features or to other objects in space, independently from the position of the perceiver. In some situations, one type of reference must be translated into the other type, the most extreme example of which is a translation from a verbal description to a spatial layout.

A thread throughout the volume concerns the specification of the kind of system that allows spatial working memory abilities. Is working memory a modality-free system for temporary maintenance that can operate on different kinds of memory content, or is it composed of several functionally separable systems that are each dedicated to one particular input modality? In a similar vein, are there specializations for processing simultaneous and sequential information, or is the working memory system a general purpose system that can cope with dynamic as well as static information? How does the system bind information from different modalities into a unitary representation? Broadly, the book consists of two parts. Chapters 1–5 deal with the question of what kind of system working memory is. On the basis of available data, these chapters elucidate behavioural limitations and regularities of working with (visuo)spatial information and how these constrain our hypotheses of the working memory system. Part of this problem concerns the basic architecture of the working memory system and its specialized subsystems. These chapters also address methodological questions, such as how the research method can ensure that the observed data are informative about underlying structures. In the second part, Chapters 6–9 do not ignore these theoretical background issues but rather focus on specific problems of spatial working memory, such as how our views on working memory can be used to better understand the development of particular skills in children with developmental deficiencies, or how the working memory system can handle individual differences in the representation of spatial information, or how the visuospatial system can support and interact with the environment or with the verbal system.

In the first chapter, 'Progress in spatial working memory research', André Vandierendonck and Arnaud Szmalec focus on the theoretical question of which kind of architecture is needed to explain the extant data on spatial working memory. The multicomponent view of working memory is the oldest one and was for a long time the only available view. More recently, other researchers have proposed models in which long-term memory receives a prominent place. Inevitably, the question arises of which kind of architecture is the best one to summarize the existing data and is the most productive one to generate new predictions. In this context, the authors focus on a series of findings regarding the representation of spatial order. They also discuss the utility of the interference and dissociation methodology that is typically used to distinguish between subsystems of the proposed working memory architectures.

In Chapter 2, 'The visual and the spatial of a multicomponent working memory', Robert H. Logie reviews the vast amount of evidence in support of the multicomponent working memory architecture. This review reveals support for dissociable storage systems for verbal/phonological information on the one hand and visuospatial information on the other. Moreover, visual and spatial storage are also shown to be dissociable, and at the same time, the author shows that these two systems have a common basis. This review also addresses dissociations between domain-specific (verbal, visual, spatial, ...) and domain-general process (the central executive in the multicomponent model). It is stressed how all these components work together in specific tasks and situations. A consequence of this is that it is important to carefully apply the dissociation methodology in order to ensure that a particular task setting is not achieved by other working memory components than the ones intended.

Hubert D. Zimmer and Heinrich R. Liesefeld expand on the representation of 'Spatial information in (visual) working memory' in the third chapter. These authors also adhere to a multicomponent view of working memory. Based on a distinction between different types of tasks, these authors discuss the role of eye movements and of covert attention shifts as spatial rehearsal mechanisms, and the role of sequential and visual information in tasks that require remembering the order of a sequence of locations or positions. They go on to discuss the role of spatial information in tasks where visual distinctions between objects are possible and how several underlying processes (visual, spatial, executive, ...) may each contribute to different tasks.

In Chapter 4, 'Exploring the determinants of memory for spatial sequences', Fabrice B. R. Parmentier reviews the literature regarding the support for modality-specific specializations within working memory. The review shows that there is an impressive amount of evidence in favour of separate storage systems for verbal and visuospatial information. The review also shows, however, that specifically when memory for sequence order is involved, many studies failed to find modality-based dissociations and, on the contrary, showed cross-modal interference. The author explores the consequences of these findings for our views on working memory, in particular, spatial working memory.

Although all these chapters (1–4) focus on behavioural studies, occasionally they refer to patient data or to data that have been obtained using neurophysiological methods. Nevertheless, neuroscience-based approaches (e.g., event-related potentials, functional magnetic resonance imaging, transcranial magnetic stimulations, etc.) are very informative with respect to brain regions and brain pathways involved in all kinds of cognitive tasks. Chapter 5 by Bradley R. Postle addresses these issues under the title 'What underlies the ability to guide action with spatial information that is no longer present in the environment?'. The author reviews a selection of studies that address working memory for spatial information and shows how working memory systems can be specified as emergent properties of particular processing stages.

In Chapter 6, 'The organization of visuospatial working memory: Evidence from the study of developmental disorders', Cesare Cornoldi and Irene C. Mammarella explore cases in which the functioning of spatial working memory is deficient or suboptimal. On the one hand, the existing knowledge and models of working memory can be used to better understand cases of impaired cognitive development; on the other hand, information obtained in the study of children with developmental dysfunction also provides constraints on theory development. In addition to a review of relevant evidence, these authors discuss in more depth the characteristics of spatial working memory in children with Down syndrome, Williams syndrome, spina bifida, and children with nonverbal learning deficiencies.

Chapter 7, 'The nature of visuospatial representation within working memory', by Colin Hamilton provides an extensive review of the popular spatial and visual task protocols. It is argued that a clear separation between visual and spatial working memory processing is difficult to operationalize. The author goes on to summarize evidence for a multicomponent view on spatial and visual working memory from experimental research and individual differences within both a neuropsychological and developmental context, including some of the author's own work. The chapter ends with an attempt to integrate the reviewed findings in Baddeley's (2000) working memory model and Cornoldi and Vecchi's (2003) continuity model, while remaining open to alternative (e.g., single resource) views and discussing ways to proceed in future research.

In Chapter 8, 'What can symmetry tell us about working memory?', Laura Pieroni, Clelia Rossi-Arnaud, and Alan D. Baddeley explore the role of environmental properties such as pattern and path symmetries. Research has shown that all kinds of similarities and redundancies in a to-be-memorized stimulus affect memory performance. Regularities in memory performance based on similarities or dissimilarities are very informative about the underlying structure. For example, the observation that phonological similarities in visually presented words affect short-term memory recall was at the basis of the hypothesis that verbal short-term memory strongly relies on phonological codes. Similarly, within the visuospatial modality, stimulus similarity and stimulus structure have been found to play an important role. One of these is symmetry, not only within a set of simultaneously presented elements that constitute an object or a shape, but also in sequentially presented elements at different locations, the symmetry in a spatial sequential path affects memory performance. Interestingly, only vertical symmetry seems to be relevant in spatial paths and the question is why this, and only this, kind of symmetry affects performance.

What can this specific finding tell us about the underlying working memory mechanisms?

The final chapter, 'The role of spatial working memory in understanding verbal descriptions: A window onto the interaction between verbal and spatial processing', addresses the interaction of spatial and verbal working memory. Valérie Gyselinck and Chiara Meneghetti review a range of studies in which the main question is how verbal descriptions of spatial organizations, such as a route through a city or a description of a spatial layout or situation, are handled by the working memory system. They review an accumulation of evidence showing that this kind of verbal information is preferentially stored and operated on by means of visual and spatial codes. This work shows that the human working memory system is refined, specialized, and flexible. The chapter also shows how working memory intertwines with all kinds of cognitive processes and skills and in that respect it takes on the role of a concluding and overarching chapter.

This book presents a representative but not an exhaustive review of the literature on spatial working memory. We hope it is of value to all researchers working on cognitive skills in relation to spatial representations and working memory more generally. We also believe it is useful for students interested in spatial working memory in that it provides a short route to the literature. Finally, we hope that many other readers find in this book an interesting overview of the state of the art regarding working memory for spatial information, which will provoke some debate and thus stimulate further development in (spatial) working memory theory.

In closing, we would like to thank everyone who helped us in the different stages of the realization of this book.

André Vandierendonck
Arnaud Szmalec
Ghent, 30 June 2010

References

Baddeley, A. (2000). The episodic buffer: A new component of working memory? *Trends in Cognitive Sciences, 4,* 417–423.

Baddeley, A. D., & Hitch, G. (1974). Working memory. In G. H. Bower (Ed.), *The psychology of learning and motivation* (Vol. 8, pp. 47–89). New York: Academic Press.

Cornoldi, C., & Vecchi, T. (2003). *Visuo-spatial working memory and individual differences.* Hove, UK: Psychology Press.

1 Progress in spatial working memory research

André Vandierendonck and Arnaud Szmalec

Introduction

Working memory concerns the temporary maintenance of information needed for other cognitive activities. Working memory typically maintains and updates information while this information is worked on to achieve other goals, such as solving a problem, drawing a conclusion, comprehending a text, etc. The specificity of working memory is that it must maintain information for direct access while attention is needed to process information for other purposes. Within working memory, a distinction is made between verbal and visuospatial working memory. Whereas verbal working memory operates on verbal representations, visuospatial working memory operates on visual and spatial representations.

In the last half century, much research effort has focused on verbal working memory, whereas research on working memory for visual and spatial information has been rather sparse. Nevertheless, in many situations, human behaviour requires the ability to mentally represent the *location* of objects in space in addition to other information such as the objects' *visual features*. For both location and visual features, verbal coding of the information is often not efficient, let alone biologically adaptive. This chapter focuses on the characteristics and the specificity of spatial working memory and the methods used to detect functional differences between visual and verbal working memory.

Location in space is the core characteristic of spatial information, irrespective of whether the position of an object in space or the position of a particular feature within an object is concerned. Although the spatial location of an object is often expressed in visual terms, gestural movements and auditory information are also used to indicate a location or a sound source. For sighted people, a visual representation is, however, indispensable to think of a collection of objects in space as a structure or a form. For example, four identical objects may be seen to form a square, even though the objects that constitute this form each occupy a particular location in space. No doubt such a visualized or imagined structure can support memory for the spatial locations of the constituting objects. Strictly speaking, a memory representing four identical objects as a square is a *visual memory*, even if it is used to support spatial information. In a similar vein, verbal representations can also support spatial information. Chess coding yields an example in point: e3 would then refer to a pawn in column e, row 3. For the sake of the present chapter, we will restrict the use of the term *spatial* to refer to the location in space of one or more objects irrespective of whether visual information is involved. Nevertheless, specific memory tasks have been developed that address the spatial and the visual focus of the coding of objects in space. We will briefly introduce these tasks.

In fact, a broad variety of tasks have been used to study the human ability to maintain visual and spatial information over a short period. Characteristic of these tasks is that visual information is presented either simultaneously or sequentially for later recall or recognition while taking care that verbal recoding strategies cannot easily be used to improve task performance. Most of these tasks are modelled in a similar way to verbal span tasks, where the amount to be remembered is stepwise increased until the individual's performance limit (the memory span) is reached. One of the oldest and most popular tasks is the Corsi Blocks Task (CBT; Corsi, 1972). In the original version it consists of a wooden board with nine identical blocks in a fixed random configuration. The experimenter taps a sequence of blocks at a rate of one per second. Immediately after the sequence is completed, the participant has to tap the same blocks in the same order as presented. Starting with sequences of three blocks, the task is continued until the participant fails to reproduce two out of three attempted sequences. The task is very popular as a neuropsychological test and is nowadays used in different variants, including two-dimensional variations (Berch, Krikorian, & Huha, 1998). Some variants change the configuration of the blocks and in computerized applications it is possible to see the blocks only while they are highlighted. The Dots Task (Jones, Farrand, Stuart, & Morris, 1995) is a well-known variant in which dots are briefly shown one at a time, and at the end all dots reappear simultaneously on their positions. The subject now has to reproduce the order in which the dot position occurred at presentation. Typically, the dot positions are selected randomly for each trial. This has the advantage that it is more difficult to develop strategies based on the configuration of the dots. Common to all variations of these Corsi-like tasks is that identical elements are shown in a series of spatial locations and that the order of the locations has to be remembered.

A rather different kind of task is the Visual Pattern Test (VPT; Della Sala, Gray, Baddeley, Allamano, & Wilson, 1999; Wilson, Scott, & Power, 1987). It consists of a two-dimensional matrix in which half of the squares are black and the other half are white. The matrix is briefly shown to the participant, who is then asked to indicate on a blank grid which cells were filled. This test was designed to measure visual memory while excluding, as much as possible, sequential and spatial task aspects. Nevertheless, participants indicate one cell at a time, which makes recall sequential along a spatial path, even though there is no explicit requirement to remember sequential information. Although the test mainly addresses visual working memory, for reasons such as the one mentioned, the test is often considered to overlap with spatial working memory.

Abilities to process information presented in different modalities or encoding systems (such as verbal, arithmetic, visual, spatial, …) are clearly distinct. An important question is whether a difference must be made in working memory with regard to these presentation modalities. In our present day technical environment we are confronted with computers that code everything (texts, formulas, photographs, maps, …) in binary codes. Some theorists have defended the claim that memory for text and for images uses the same underlying abstract coding system (see e.g., Anderson, 1978, for an explicit position on this). Meanwhile, a large body of evidence has been collected to support the view that the human memory system uses different encoding formats as a function of the information being processed. Studies have shown (e.g., Baddeley, Grant, Wight, & Thomson, 1975; Brooks, 1968) that maintenance of verbal information is more impaired when a simultaneously executed task requires verbal processing (e.g., verbal judgement or production of verbal responses) than when it requires visual or spatial processing (e.g., decisions about visual or spatial features). Similarly, maintenance of spatial information is impaired more when the concurrent task is spatial than when it is verbal (e.g., Brooks, 1968; Logie, Zucco, & Baddeley, 1990). Although, most if not all researchers to date seem to agree that memory uses different encoding formats, views differ with respect to the question of whether there are working memory subsystems that are specialized for processing particular encoding formats. In fact, working memory theories differ from each other in a number of important assumptions regarding working memory functioning and structure (see Miyake & Shah, 1999). In the present chapter, we will focus on the issue of specializations in working memory based on information-modality and on the validity of the methodology used to collect evidence in support of such a view.

Working memory architecture

Although the short-term memory model of Atkinson and Shiffrin (1968, 1971) was the first model that claimed to explain the function of working memory, Baddeley and Hitch (1974) were the first to elaborate the concept of working memory into an influential framework. Based on a series of experiments focusing on variants of span tasks, these investigators proposed a working memory architecture with two slave systems, namely, the phonological loop for handling verbal/phonological materials and the visuospatial sketchpad for maintenance of visual and spatial information, both controlled by a general purpose attentional control system, called the central executive. This framework was later updated to cope with new research findings (Baddeley, 1986, 2000). Nowadays, the model also contains a so-called episodic buffer that interfaces the two slaves with each other and with (episodic) long-term memory. An impressive series of studies have reported evidence that by and large supports the basic assumptions of the model. Nevertheless, the framework has as yet not been very successful in explaining how perceived elements (form, location, colour, temporal position in a sequence) are bound together. Although the addition of the episodic buffer was meant to facilitate such an explanation thus far the binding mechanism remains underspecified in the framework. Yet, specific formal models have been developed on the basis of the phonological loop that are able to explain at least temporal binding (e.g., Brown, Neath, & Chater, 2007; Brown, Preece, & Hulme, 2000; Burgess & Hitch,

1999; Henson, 1998; Page & Norris, 1998, 2009). Being developed within a verbal context, it is not clear whether these models can also explain spatial serial recall, although this is, in principle, possible.

A related problem with this multicomponent conceptualization of working memory is that the chain of processing from perception to long-term memory always passes through the slave systems. This way information arrives in the slaves before the meaning and the relevance for further processing has been assessed (for an exception with respect to this assumption within a multicomponent architecture, see Baddeley & Logie, 1999; Logie, 1995). Other working memory models prefer to assume that the primary link goes from perception to long-term memory, where the currently activated part is believed to constitute working memory (e.g., Barrouillet, Bernardin, & Camos, 2004; Cowan, 2005; Engle, Kane, & Tuholski, 1999; Oberauer, 2009). In these conceptualizations, activation in long-term memory also provides the basis for explaining binding.

Simplifying, it can be said that there are two categories of views about working memory. One category defines working memory as a subset of long-term memory. These views account for meaning, interference, and binding in working memory, but they do not consider the content or the modality in which the information is coded as particularly relevant. The other category contains models that are somehow related to the Baddeley–Hitch model (but for another multicomponent view, see e.g., Cornoldi & Vecchi, 2003). They propose a multicomponent architecture for working memory with separate components for modality-specific storage.

This situation cannot be reduced to the simple question of who is right. As already indicated, there is an important body of evidence showing that modality makes a difference, but there is also a growing number of studies in favour of unitary views. We shall not review all the evidence in this chapter, as it is addressed in several other chapters in this book. The proponents of a multicomponent view argue that the available evidence supports the hypothesis that working memory comprises several structurally distinct components dedicated to storage of information coded in a particular way. If it is accepted that the working memory system comprises specialized stores that are able to maintain information for a brief period of time (but see Parmentier, Chapter 4, this volume; Postle, Chapter 5, this volume; and Zimmer & Liesefeld, Chapter 3, this volume), two questions need more consideration. First, are these specialized stores necessary for the operation of working memory? In other words, is a working memory without these slave systems possible? Second, are these specialized stores sufficient to explain working memory? To put it differently, do they contain everything that has to be maintained for a successful later retrieval of the information or are other memory components also involved? The phonological loop, for example, contains phonologically coded information, but not semantic codes. Does this mean that semantic and episodic information is not part of working memory? Several answers seem to be possible. A minimalist answer could be that the phonological codes provide access to the corresponding information in long-term memory. In practice, this means that in order to access semantic information, a phonological code in the phonological loop is used as a cue to retrieve the semantic code from long-term memory. A more intermediate position is that the semantic codes are in an activated state in long-term memory simultaneously with the phonological code. Access is possible by activating the link between the phonological and the semantic code. In the latter view, the phonological loop and activated long-term memory (in the sense of the unitary models) together constitute verbal working memory. This excursion into verbal working memory is useful, as visuospatial working memory in the multicomponent model is completely analogical. For example, Logie's (1995) inner scribe maintains spatial movement information. Is this information restricted to motor codes or does the system allow access to spatial memory representations? Is this kind of information somehow backed by an activated spatial memory?

In order to bridge the unitary and multicomponent views, research is needed that helps in finding answers to questions like these. As maintenance of serial order information is at the basis of instruments for measuring working memory capacity (cf. Complex Span Tests; Case, Kurland, & Goldberg, 1982; Daneman & Carpenter, 1980; Turner & Engle, 1989), an explanation of how working memory deals with order information may give some clues about the kind of storage devices that are needed. It is well-known that processing of serial order plays a crucial role in cognition because many skills, such as language (Conway & Pisoni, 2008; Szmalec, Duyck, Vandierendonck, Mata, & Page, 2009), arithmetic (Campbell, 2005), and motor planning (Rosenbaum, Cohen, Jax, Weiss, & van der Wel, 2007) are sequential in nature.

The role of order coding

The study of serial order processing in working memory was initially focused on the sequencing of verbal information. Several models have been developed to describe how humans represent serial order among verbal working memory contents (e.g., Brown et al., 2007; Burgess & Hitch, 2006; Henson, 1998; Page & Norris, 2009). As the research into the visual and spatial aspects of working memory always lagged behind research into verbal aspects, recall of spatial serial order information has thus far not been modelled. In view of the analogy between verbal and visuospatial working memory within the multicomponent architecture, a simple solution could be to apply these models in the spatial domain. However, because most of these serial memory models explicitly address the maintenance of verbal serial memory, it is not clear how well they generalize to visual and spatial working memory. Some of these models, such as the primacy model (Page & Norris, 1998) and its successor (Page & Norris, 2009), represent serial order as an emergent property of the representation of the individual elements in the sequence. On the assumption that spatial order memory can be modelled in the same way within spatial storage, it follows that the representation of the order of a list of verbal elements cannot interfere with the representation of the order of a list of spatial elements.

A study by Depoorter and Vandierendonck (2009) reports findings that are relevant to this issue. These authors tested whether interference occurred between two memorized sequences of events. To that end two short-term memory tasks were combined in an ABBA sequence, where the first occurrence of a letter refers to the presentation of the items for memorization and the second occurrence refers to the recognition test of that information. Within this design, these researchers varied the kind of information presented and recalled in the A-task and in the B-task. Both tasks could either be a serial order memory task or an item memory task. The two tasks were also tested in single-task conditions, i.e., in an AABB sequence. Dual-task interference was measured as the memory performance on a particular task under dual-task conditions (ABBA) relative to the memory performance of the same task under single-task conditions (AABB). The lower this performance index, the more performance suffered from the presence of the imbedded memory task.

When both A and B were verbal tasks, serial memory performance on the A-task was more impaired when the B-task was also a serial memory task, than when the B-task was an item memory task. This shows that order interference occurs within the verbal modality. When the A- and B-tasks were both spatial tasks, the same result was observed, showing order interference within the spatial modality. Thus far, these findings are completely consistent with the multicomponent view of working memory. However, in subsequent experiments, Depoorter and Vandierendonck (2009) combined verbal and spatial tasks. Serial memory performance of a verbal A-task was impaired when the imbedded B-task was a spatial serial memory task compared with when it was a memory task for individual locations occurring in the test. Likewise, serial memory performance of a spatial A-task was impaired when the imbedded task was a verbal serial memory task. The latter two findings show the existence of cross-modal order interference both from the verbal to the spatial modality and from the spatial to the verbal modality. Moreover, the degree of interference was similar to that observed in within-modal conditions.

This finding of similar degrees of within- and cross-modal interference may be because of procedural overlaps between the verbal and the spatial memory tasks. More specifically, the item presentation was visual in both tasks, and the recognition procedure required recognition of the order in which items had been presented by a manual choice response. To check whether these overlaps, which were also present in the item tasks, could account for the findings, Vandierendonck and Suardi (2011) replicated the cross-modal interference conditions by using aural presentation and oral serial recall in the verbal task and visual presentation with serial recall by pointing to the object locations in the spatial task. The cross-modal order interference in both directions was confirmed.

This set of findings contrasts with the findings of Saito, Logie, Morita, and Law (2008), who used memory for kanji characters that varied in terms of phonological and visual similarity. They observed that serial recall was affected by both phonological and visual similarity and that the phonological similarity effect disappeared under articulatory suppression. Although this study provides clear evidence that participants process the information in the modalities available and also shows that the visual similarity effect manifests itself in order memory, the study does not provide direct evidence for the conclusion that order is coded in the modality-specific subsystems of the multicomponent model. In fact, if these findings are taken to imply that order is coded in the slave systems, the question remains which one of the two slaves is used for storing the order, and if both slaves are used simultaneously to store order, how are occasional conflicts between the two ordered sequences resolved? This issue evidently deserves further follow-up. Nevertheless, the finding that memory for one series of elements interferes with memory for another series of elements, irrespective of the modality of the elements (Depoorter & Vandierendonck, 2009) strongly suggests that item order is not part of the modality-specific storage of the sequences of words and locations. These findings are difficult to account for by present day models of serial recall. Models that assume that order is an emergent property of a modality-specific trace do not predict cross-modal order interference. Similarly, models with position coding for the order, postulate that each element in the sequence is linked to position information. As the second memory task (B) follows the first task, the positions to which the items of both tasks are linked would be different, and such a model would not seem to predict even within-modality order interference. However, in our view, the most challenging implication of these findings is not that the findings are difficult to explain by serial recall models, but rather the implication that *order interference behaves differently than item interference*. In other words, these findings suggest that order coding is represented in a *different memory system* that is used for both the verbal and the spatial modality. Within the multicomponent view, the central executive does not seem to be a candidate for maintenance of this information, because it has always been claimed that this system has no memory storage (Baddeley, 1986, 2000). The recently added episodic buffer is a possibility. However, as this component is not very well elaborated, it is also difficult to see how it could work. A final possibility is that episodic long-term memory is an appropriate medium for order encoding. One way to allow the multicomponent view to explain the order interference findings would be to recognize that the working memory system also encompasses activated long-term memory representations. Clearly, further research will be needed to specify how any of these suggestions can account precisely for cross-modal order interference.

Further work using the Hebb learning paradigm may be helpful to achieve this. Hebb (1961) asked participants to perform an immediate verbal serial recall task in which one particular sequence of digits was repeated every third trial. He observed that serial recall for repeating sequences increased substantially compared with non-repeating sequences, a phenomenon that is known as the Hebb repetition effect. In essence, the Hebb repetition effect is a serial order learning phenomenon that shows that a sequence of events maintained briefly in short-term memory gradually develops into a stable long-term memory trace. A number of studies have used the Hebb repetition paradigm to compare short- and long-term memory for serial order across verbal and visuospatial representations. Couture and Tremblay (2006), for example, found a comparable Hebb repetition effect across verbal and visuospatial item modalities. In a study on the role of serial order learning in language acquisition, Mosse and Jarrold (2008) observed that the magnitude of Hebbian learning correlates with performance on a nonword learning task. Interestingly, this correlation was observed for Hebbian learning with verbal materials, but also with visuospatial materials, suggesting that the ability of representing serial order in working memory is domain-general. Comparable findings were reported in a recent study on Hebbian learning in dyslexia (Szmalec, Loncke, Page, & Duyck, In press). This study revealed that adults with dyslexia show impaired Hebbian learning for verbal sequences, but also for visuospatial sequences (in the dots task), on the basis of which Szmalec et al. concluded that dyslexia might reflect a general impairment in long-term serial order learning. Taken together, the findings on Hebbian learning all point in the direction of an abstract representation of sequential information in long-term memory, which is shared among the different verbal and spatial encoding formats.

The observation that Hebb repetition learning works equally well for verbal as for spatial materials and the finding that short-term serial recall of one list interferes with short-term serial recall of any other list both point in the direction of a role for long-term memory in relation to working memory. If this hypothesis, that order coding involves long-term memory, is replicated in further research, it follows that the modality-specific storage systems are used for *maintenance of identity information* rather than for serial order information.

A similar picture seems to arise from research using neuroscience methods. Going back to the work of Goldman-Rakic (1987, 1990), the cognitive neuroscientific view on working memory initially showed that the short-term retention and manipulation of information correlates with neural activity in the human prefrontal cortex (e.g., Miller & Cohen, 2001; Smith & Jonides, 1999). The precise contribution of prefrontal cortex (PFC) to working memory has been the subject of extensive research. Early neuroimaging studies revealed hemispheric specialization for the different types of information held in working memory, with the left hemisphere mainly responsible for the verbal working memory system and the right hemisphere for the spatial working memory system (Smith & Jonides, 1997). Also the proposed distinction between the two principal functions of working memory, namely the passive storage of information on the one hand, and the active manipulation of working memory contents on the other hand, converges with findings from neuroanatomical localization. Neuroimaging data showed more posterior activation when experimental protocols targeted the storage function, whereas activity in more frontal brain regions appeared to be associated with active manipulation of information.

The exact contribution of frontal and posterior brain areas to working memory has been further specified in recent years. First, it is a well-replicated finding that short-term retention and manipulation of information is associated with sustained activity in the dorsolateral part of the PFC (e.g., D'Esposito & Postle, 1999; Leung, Gore, & Goldman-Rakic, 2002). However, it has been clearly demonstrated that the patterns of activity in the PFC do not depend on the modality of the working memory contents. For these reasons, it is nowadays assumed that, in contrast to what was initially thought, the PFC does not seem to fulfil the storage function of working memory, but rather can be held responsible for biasing attention to the brain regions that are involved in the temporary storage of information (e.g., Postle, 2006). With respect to this storage function itself, recent studies indicate that, in fact, the temporary retention of information seems to be supported by the same brain areas that have evolved to encode sensory representations (e.g., Hamidi, Tononi, & Postle, 2008). In the light of these findings, several representatives of the neuroscience view on working memory adhere to a working memory architecture that shows some important differences from the view advocated in the behavioural research tradition. More precisely, the neuroscience view essentially proposes that if the brain is able to maintain a sensory representation of information, it is also able to show working memory for this information, by directing attention to these sensory regions through PFC connections (e.g., Postle, 2006). From this perspective, working memory is an emergent property of the brain, and there is no need to define different memory systems for verbal, visual, or spatial information. Although this view has primarily evolved from functional neuroimaging work, it is also supported by recent behavioural evidence for domain-general working memory resources (Vergauwe, Barrouillet, & Camos, 2009, 2010). The idea of working memory as an emergent property of the brain does, however, not reduce temporary maintenance of information to be merely that of a prolonged state of perception. Obviously, patients with working memory impairments do not experience perceptual difficulties, which suggests that the direction of attention towards domain-specific information remains one essential function of working memory that is not achieved at the level of those sensory brain regions. Finally, it is also important to keep in mind that discovering common brain activation in working memory maintenance and encoding of sensory information does not necessarily point towards shared functions or processes, an assumption that is often too easily made within the neuroimaging research tradition. So in summary, although working memory may have emerged from the ability to retain sensory information, there is no doubt that the brain hosts a temporary memory system. But whether this system is shared across perceptual or storage modalities or whether domain-specific memory systems exist remains an issue of debate.

Methodological considerations

Although the working memory research traditions in behavioural and neuroscience initially both assumed a working memory architecture that comprises several specialized memory systems, the incorporation into a multicomponent view of novel neuroscience findings is not always straightforward. It is therefore particularly important to remain critical about the methodological approaches that led to the evolution of existing and to the development of new theoretical viewpoints on the architecture of working memory. Because the structure of memory has to be inferred from observations in neuroimaging as well as in behavioural studies, the role of the methods used to infer features of memory storage is of paramount importance. The question must be considered whether the evidence really supports the claims that are made. Although the body of evidence in support of separate modality-specific storage systems in working memory is impressive, it is not completely evident from these studies whether the observed within-modality interference is a purely content-based effect or whether order information is also involved, as suggested by some of the findings already discussed.

In order to answer this question we must have a closer look at the methods used to test the role of specific modalities so that we can judge whether such a strong conclusion is supported by the findings. In behavioural research, typically, dual-task methods have been used for these tests. The dual-task method (e.g., Baddeley & Hitch, 1974; Wickens, 1984) has stimulated countless studies in experimental (neuro)psychology and not least in the working memory research tradition. The paradigm has proven very useful over the last 30 years, and it remains highly influential to this day (see Gyselinck & Meneghetti, Chapter 9, this volume; Pieroni, Rossi-Arnaud, & Baddeley, Chapter 8, this volume). Notwithstanding its attractiveness in terms of clear rationale and ease of use, it is important also to be aware of its limitations. The rationale for using dual-task methods is that each component in the working memory system has a *limited capacity*. If a particular task (e.g., retaining a sequence of dot locations) consumes most of this capacity, concurrent execution of another task that requires the same storage unit would result in a performance cost. Depending on the priority assigned to both concurrent tasks, it may even be expected that performance of both tasks will be impaired. Although the reasoning is sound and relatively easy to apply, in practice it is very difficult to be sure that two simultaneously executed tasks tax the same underlying storage system *and only this one*. There are several caveats that must be considered.

A first concern is that even simple tasks involve several processes and underlying cognitive structures. A task set specifies task control parameters that specify how this goal can be achieved; these parameters include orientation of perceptual attention, biasing of activation towards the relevant stimulus categorization, biasing of responding towards the instructed output modality, etc. (Logan & Gordon, 2001). Moreover, control processes are involved to shield the task from interference due to irrelevant information. In other words, when executing two non-automatic tasks concurrently, there is a dual-task cost that is not due to storage capacity limits, but rather to the need to control appropriate task execution. This implies that concurrent task execution will always result in a performance cost. In order to cope with this problem, *selective interference* methodology has been introduced (Salthouse, 1974). Using this method, Vandierendonck, Kemps, Fastame, and Szmalec (2004), for example, investigated whether spatial memory in the CBT involves spatial processing. Spatial serial recall was tested in five conditions: control (single task), spatial tapping, articulatory suppression, random-, and fixed-interval generation. Immediate serial recall in the spatial tapping condition was dramatically impaired compared with both the control condition and the articulatory suppression condition. These findings show selective interference due to a concurrent spatial task but not a concurrent verbal task. This same study also showed that encoding of a spatial path in the CBT requires executive control. From previous research it is known that random generation of time intervals taxes executive control processes whereas fixed-interval generation does so to a much lesser extent or not at all (Stuyven, Van der Goten, Vandierendonck, Claeys, & Crevits, 2000; Vandierendonck, 2000; Vandierendonck, De Vooght, & Van der Goten, 1998). By comparing CBT recall performance in the conditions with random- and fixed-interval generation, it was found that recall was impaired under random- but not under fixed-interval generation. In sum, by using the selective interference methodology, this study showed that encoding of a spatial path calls on executive control as well as on spatial processing.

A second concern of using selective interference is that the method is relatively sensitive to strategic adjustments in the sense that participants do not always prioritize both tasks according to the instructions or that they do not perform the tasks in the same way as the experimenter assumes. In particular, on some occasions participants recode the information in order to improve performance; they do this in the belief that performance will be better if such a recoding is used or in order to avoid the interference imposed by a secondary task. In the CBT task, for example, participants may try to attach a verbal label, like a number, to the Corsi blocks and hence try to recall the sequence of spatial block positions as a verbal sequence of numbers. This strategy can be particularly useful when spatial memory is taxed by a secondary task. Such strategies can be discouraged by changing the positional configuration of the blocks on each consecutive trial so that verbal labelling of the blocks becomes virtually impossible. Modern Corsi-like spatial serial recall tasks, like the dots task, have clearly taken such strategic aspects into consideration and are therefore nowadays believed to be more valid measures of spatial working memory (e.g., Parmentier, Elford, & Maybery, 2005; Parmentier, Chapter 4, this volume).

A third issue is more technical. Application of the selective interference method requires knowledge about the processes and the structures involved in executing each of the tasks. Obviously, this knowledge is not present or is at best incomplete for the primary task (the recall task); the fact that a test is designed to find out whether a particular memory task (e.g., CBT) calls on storage of spatial codes means that this knowledge is not present. For a correct usage of the selective interference method, however, this knowledge must be available for the other tasks used. Tasks such as spatial tapping and articulatory suppression are well-known to focus on a specific modality and to be low-attention demanding. That is also the reason why they are often used in selective interference designs. In many cases, however, the need arises to use other tasks. In the older literature, very often pursuit tracking (following a moving target) or deciding whether the corners of a block letter are internal or external are used to tax spatial processing (Brooks Task; e.g., Baddeley et al., 1975; Brooks, 1968). It is quite obvious that both tasks are attention demanding, particularly the Brooks Task (e.g., Salway & Logie, 1995). To the extent that the primary memory task is also attention demanding, there may be at least two sources of overlap, namely spatial processing and attentional or cognitive control. In addition, many of the popular secondary tasks involve some kind of response selection, i.e., a choice reaction about the identity of a required response. Knowing that even the most basic forms of response selection (like choosing a left/right response based on the pitch of a sound) involve attentional control (Szmalec, Vandierendonck, & Kemps, 2005), it can be questioned how selective secondary task interference can actually be.

Because of these difficulties, proper application of the selective interference method requires the inclusion of controls. In such a case, it can be said that a dissociation of processing is observed; this means that of two possible processes, A and B, only one (A) is involved in performing a particular task. It may also be possible to show the reverse, namely that in another task, only the other one (B) of the two possible processes is required. Both cases together form a double dissociation. It is often argued that observation of a double dissociation is a necessary condition to conclude that two qualitatively separable cognitive systems/processes, rather than two quantitatively differing versions of the same process, underlie performance.

Neuropsychological double dissociations have also proven to be very useful for investigating functional separability among cognitive processes. Darling, Della Sala, Logie, and Cantagallo (2006), for example, described two patients, one who demonstrated a selective impairment of memory on a visual task, but not on a spatial task, and a second patient who showed exactly the opposite, i.e., a deficit of memory on the spatial task, but not on the visual task. Clearly, such patterns of results provide strong evidence for the functional separability between visual and spatial working memory, and similar examples can be found in large numbers across different research areas of cognitive neuropsychology. Notwithstanding the attractiveness of the technique, the question remains whether the observation of a double dissociation is sufficient to support the conclusion that two different systems underlie such observations. Because this is an issue of tremendous importance in deciding between componential and unitary structures, we consider it further in the following paragraphs.

It is clear that the success of the selective interference paradigm, and also of the double-dissociation approach, largely depends on choosing appropriate tasks to measure the working memory components of interest. The construct validity of these working memory tasks has been heavily debated (e.g., the Task Purity Problem), but, so far, there is not much consensus when it comes to choosing an appropriate task from the various alternatives. One theoretical framework that may be useful for classifying working memory tasks is the continuity framework of Cornoldi and Vecchi (2003; see also Cornoldi & Mammarella, Chapter 6, this volume). Within this framework, working memory tasks are defined using two dimensions. The first one, which is called the horizontal continuum, is used to define the types of materials that are involved in a task (e.g., spatial, visual, verbal). The second dimension, i.e., the vertical continuum, represents the amount of attentional control that is involved in a particular task. Each working memory task can thus be positioned relative to both these dimensions, and the distance between two tasks in this two-dimensional space reflects the degree of independence between the tasks. Within the continuity framework, the tasks that have proven most useful in yielding selective interference and in producing dissociations are those that are low on the vertical dimension, or in other words the ones that involve minimal attentional control. Conversely, tasks that require more attentional control (higher on the vertical dimension) are often less efficient when applied in a dual-task setting (cf. Hegarty, Shah, & Miyake, 2000). The continuity framework thus offers a classification of working memory tasks that may prove to be useful for differentiating working memory systems.

It is beyond doubt that working memory theory has been mainly developed through the demonstration of double dissociations between tasks that are assumed to operationalize different memory systems, such as the distinction between short- and long-term memory (e.g., Glanzer & Cunitz, 1966). In working memory research for example, Logie (1995) provided strong empirical evidence for the functional separability of a verbal and a visuospatial working memory system, also using the double-dissociation logic (see also Hamilton, Chapter 7, this volume; Logie, Chapter 2, this volume). In a similar vein, Klauer and Zhao (2004) more recently presented a series of double dissociations that support the separability of the visual and the spatial working memory system. The fact that the double-dissociation approach has led to a working memory architecture that does in some important aspects differ from the views derived from other approaches (e.g., functional magnetic resonance imaging (fMRI), transcranial magnetic stimulation (TMS): see also Postle, Chapter 5, this volume) has led some researchers to question what exactly can be inferred from double dissociations. Dunn and Kirsner (1988, 2003), for example, cast serious doubts on the assumption that dissociations between tasks provide strong evidence for the existence of separate cognitive processes underlying the two tasks. They argue that the double-dissociation logic is trivial because no two tasks recruit exactly the same mental processes and therefore any two tasks can eventually produce a double dissociation. In this context, it is important to remark that double dissociations are not a *conditio sine qua non* for increasing our knowledge of working memory. Recent studies on spatial working memory have shown for example that stringent manipulations of visuospatial stimulus characteristics can also enable significant advances in our knowledge about the function and structure of working memory, without necessarily relying on a double-dissociation or dual-task logic (e.g., Parmentier et al., 2005; Parmentier, Chapter 4, this volume).

Conclusions

In this chapter, we have considered the contemporary views of spatial working memory in terms of the architecture they propose, and we evaluated the evidence in favour of these conceptualizations. On the one hand, there is strong support for a multicomponent view as expressed in the models of Baddeley and colleagues (Baddeley, 1986, 2000; Baddeley & Hitch, 1974; Baddeley & Logie, 1999; Logie, 1995) from findings of dissociations and double dissociations between verbal and visuospatial working memory and between visual and spatial working memory (see also Klauer & Zhao, 2004). On the other hand, there is also evidence that is more difficult to accommodate within this view. In the present chapter, we paid attention to the maintenance of serial order information and reviewed evidence from within- and cross-modal order interference in working memory (e.g.,

Depoorter & Vandierendonck, 2009) and from Hebbian learning. All these findings can easily be accommodated by models that either propose that working memory is the activated part of long-term memory (e.g., Cowan, 2005; Oberauer, 2009) or that consider working memory to be an emergent property of information processing (Postle, 2006), or even by a multicomponent working memory model that also includes activated long-term memory (e.g., Baddeley & Logie, 1999; Logie, 1995).

We also discussed the methodological approaches that have led to those differences in conceptualization. It is clear that, as new techniques become available for studying human cognition, different approaches develop and novel theoretical insights are acquired. Throughout the last decades, the double-dissociation logic has played a significant role in the development of a multicomponent view on working memory and it will probably remain influential for several more years to come. At the same time, this view is now constantly challenged, in part by findings that originate from rapidly progressing neuroimaging research. It is important to realize that each methodological approach has its advantages and drawbacks and deserves to be critically assessed. Earlier in this chapter, we have critically evaluated the use of dissociation logic. However, that does not imply that behavioural work should be replaced with brain imaging studies. A number of authors (e.g., Page, 2006) have made a critical analysis of functional imaging techniques and argued that these techniques can tell which brain region is responsible for supporting a particular cognitive process (the 'where' question), whereas they do not tell us much about how these processes are performed (the 'how' question). In this sense, just like the fact that a double dissociation between visual and spatial tasks may not provide conclusive evidence for differentiating visual and spatial working memory, one could equally question whether common neural activation for visual and spatial working memory tasks unequivocally points towards functional unity.

It is often the evaluation of the convergences and diversities between different approaches that allows us to make significant progress. With respect to working memory, there is consensus that the human brain can represent information in different encoding formats or modalities and that the brain is also able to show working memory for these different kinds of information. While it is clear that in recent decades research in spatial working memory has made important progress, some questions remain under debate, such as whether the short-term retention of information presented in different modalities relies on separable (dissociable) working memory systems and whether this separability applies to object, location, and order information.

References

Anderson, J. R. (1978). Arguments concerning representations for mental imagery. *Psychological Review, 85,* 249–277.

Atkinson, R. C., & Shiffrin, R. M. (1968). Human memory: A proposed system and its control processes. In K. W. Spence & J. T. Spence (Eds.), *The psychology of learning and motivation* (Vol. 2, pp. 89–195). New York: Academic Press.

Atkinson, R. C., & Shiffrin, R. M. (1971). The control of short-term memory. *Scientific American, 225,* 82–90.

Baddeley, A. (1986). *Working memory*. Oxford: Oxford University Press.

Baddeley, A. (2000). The episodic buffer: A new component of working memory? *Trends in Cognitive Sciences, 4,* 417–423.

Baddeley, A. D., Grant, S., Wight, E., & Thomson, N. (1975). Imagery and visual working memory. In P. M. A. Rabbitt & S. Dornic (Eds.), *Attention and performance* (pp. 205–217). London: Academic Press

Baddeley, A. D., & Hitch, G. (1974). Working memory. In G. H. Bower (Ed.), *The psychology of learning and motivation* (Vol. 8, pp. 47–89). New York: Academic Press.

Baddeley, A. D., & Logie, R. H. (1999). Working memory: The multiple-component model. In A. Miyake & P. Shah (Eds.), *Models of working memory. Mechanisms of active maintenance and executive control* (pp. 28–61). Cambridge: Cambridge University Press.

Barrouillet, P., Bernardin, S., & Camos, V. (2004). Time constraints and resource sharing in adults' working memory spans. *Journal of Experimental Psychology: General, 133,* 83–100.

Berch, D. B., Krikorian, R., & Huha, E. M. (1998). The Corsi-block tapping task: Methodological and theoretical considerations. *Brain and Cognition, 38,* 317–338.

Brooks, L. R. (1968). Spatial and verbal components in the act of recall. *Canadian Journal of Psychology, 22,* 349–368.

Brown, G. D. A., Neath, I., & Chater, N. (2007). A temporal ratio model of memory. *Psychological Review, 114,* 539–576.

Brown, G. D. A., Preece, T., & Hulme, C. (2000). Oscillator-based memory for serial order. *Psychological Review, 107,* 127–181.

Burgess, N., & Hitch, G. J. (1999). Memory for serial order: A network model of the phonological loop and its timing. *Psychological Review, 106,* 551–581.

Burgess, N., & Hitch, G. J. (2006). A revised model of short-term memory and long-term learning of verbal sequences. *Journal of Memory and Language, 55,* 627–652.

Campbell, J. I. D. (2005). *Handbook of mathematical cognition*. New York: Psychology Press.

Case, R., Kurland, D. M., & Goldberg, J. (1982). Operational efficiency and the growth of short-term-memory span. *Journal of Experimental Child Psychology, 33,* 386–404.

Conway, C. M., & Pisoni, D. B. (2008). Neurocognitive basis of implicit learning of sequential structure and its relation to language processing. In G. F. Eden & D. L. Flower (Eds.), *Learning, skill acquisition, reading, and dyslexia* (Vol. 1145, pp. 113–131). Oxford: Blackwell Publishing.

Cornoldi, C., & Vecchi, T. (2003). *Visuo-spatial working memory and individual differences*. Hove, UK: Psychology Press.

Corsi, P. M. (1972). *Human memory and the medial temporal region of the brain.* Unpublished Doctoral dissertation, McGill University, Montreal, Canada.

Couture, M., & Tremblay, S. (2006). Exploring the characteristics of the visuospatial Hebb repetition effect. *Memory & Cognition, 34,* 1720–1729.

Cowan, N. (2005). *Working memory capacity*. Hove, UK: Psychology Press.

D'Esposito, M., & Postle, B. R. (1999). The dependence of span and delayed-response performance on prefrontal cortex. *Neuropsychologia, 37,* 1303–1315.

Daneman, M., & Carpenter, P. A. (1980). Individual differences in working memory. *Journal of Verbal Learning and Verbal Behavior, 19,* 450–466.

Darling, S., Della Sala, S., Logie, R., & Cantagallo, A. (2006). Neuropsychological evidence for separating components of visuo-spatial working memory. *Journal of Neurology, 253,* 176–180.

Della Sala, S., Gray, C., Baddeley, A., Allamano, N., & Wilson, L. (1999). Pattern span: A tool for unwelding visuo-spatial memory. *Neuropsychologia, 37,* 1189–1199.

Depoorter, A., & Vandierendonck, A. (2009). Evidence for modality-independent order coding in working memory. *Quarterly Journal of Experimental Psychology, 62,* 531–549.

Dunn, J. C., & Kirsner, K. (1988). Discovering functionally independent mental processes: The principle of reversed association. *Psychological Review, 95,* 91–101.

Dunn, J. C., & Kirsner, K. (2003). What can we infer from double dissociations? *Cortex, 39,* 1–7.

Engle, R. W., Kane, M. J., & Tuholski, S. W. (1999). Individual differences in working memory capacity and what they tell us about controlled attention, general fluid intelligence, and functions of the prefrontal cortex. In A. Miyake & P. Shah (Eds.), *Models of working memory. Mechanisms of active maintenance and executive control* (pp. 102–134). Cambridge: Cambridge University Press.

Glanzer, M., & Cunitz, A. R. (1966). Two storage mechanisms in free recall. *Journal of Verbal Learning and Verbal Behavior, 5,* 351–360.

Goldman-Rakic, P. S. (1987). Circuitry of the prefrontal cortex and the regulation of behavior by representational memory. In V. B. Mountcastle, F. Plum, & S. R. Geiger (Eds.), *Handbook of neurobiology* (pp. 373–417). Bethesda, MA: American Physiological Society.

Goldman-Rakic, P. S. (1990). Cellular and circuit bais of working memory in prefrontal cortex of nonhuman primates. *Progress in Brain Research, 85,* 325–336.

Hamidi, M., Tononi, G., & Postle, B. R. (2008). Evaluating frontal and parietal contributions to spatial working memory with repetitive transcranial magnetic stimulation. *Brain Research, 1230,* 202–210.

Hebb, D. O. (1961). Distinctive features of learning in the higher animal. In J. F. Delafresnaye (Ed.), *Brain mechanisms and learning* (pp. 37–46). Oxford: Blackwell.

Hegarty, M., Shah, P., & Miyake, A. (2000). Constraints on using the dual-task methodology to specify the degree of central executive involvement in cognitive tasks. *Memory & Cognition, 28,* 376–385.

Henson, R. N. A. (1998). Short-term memory for serial order: The start-end model. *Cognitive Psychology, 36,* 73–137.

Jones, D., Farrand, P., Stuart, G., & Morris, N. (1995). Functional equivalence of verbal and spatial information in serial short-term memory. *Journal of Experimental Psychology: Learning, Memory, and Cognition, 21,* 1008–1018.

Klauer, K. C., & Zhao, Z. M. (2004). Double dissociations in visual and spatial short-term memory. *Journal of Experimental Psychology: General, 133,* 355–381.

Leung, H. C., Gore, J. C., & Goldman-Rakic, P. S. (2002). Sustained mnemonic response in the human middle frontal gyrus during on-line storage of spatial memoranda. *Journal of Cognitive Neuroscience, 14,* 659–671.

Logan, G. D., & Gordon, R. D. (2001). Executive control of attention in dual-task situations. *Psychological Review, 108,* 393–434.

Logie, R. H. (1995). *Visuo-spatial working memory.* Hillsdale, NJ: Lawrence Erlbaum Associates, Inc.

Logie, R. H., Zucco, G. M., & Baddeley, A. D. (1990). Interference with visual short-term memory. *Acta Psychologica, 75,* 55–74.

Miller, E. K., & Cohen, J. D. (2001). An integrative theory of prefrontal cortex function. *Annual Review of Neuroscience, 24,* 167–202.

Miyake, A., & Shah, P. (1999). *Models of working memory. Mechanisms of active maintenance and executive control.* Cambridge: Cambridge University Press.

Mosse, E. K., & Jarrold, C. (2008). Hebb learning, verbal short-term memory, and the acquisition of phonological forms in children. *Quarterly Journal of Experimental Psychology, 61,* 505–514.

Oberauer, K. (2009). Design for a working memory. In B. H. Ross (Ed.), *Psychology of learning and motivation: Advances in research and theory* (Vol. 51, pp. 45–100). San Diego, CA: Elsevier Academic Press Inc.

Page, M. P. A. (2006). What can't functional neuroimaging tell the cognitive psychologist? *Cortex, 42,* 428–443.

Page, M. P. A., & Norris, D. (1998). The primacy model: A new model of immediate serial recall. *Psychological Review, 105,* 761–781.

Page, M. P. A., & Norris, D. (2009). A model linking immediate serial recall, the Hebb repetition effect and the learning of phonological word forms. *Philosophical Transactions of the Royal Society B-Biological Sciences, 364,* 3737–3753.

Parmentier, F. B. R., Elford, G., & Maybery, M. (2005). Transitional information in spatial serial memory: Path characteristics affect recall performance. *Journal of Experimental Psychology: Learning, Memory, and Cognition, 31,* 412–427.

Postle, B. R. (2006). Working memory as an emergent property of the mind and brain. *Neuroscience, 139,* 23–38.

Rosenbaum, D. A., Cohen, R. G., Jax, S. A., Weiss, D. J., & van der Wel, R. (2007). The problem of serial order in behavior: Lashley's legacy. *Human Movement Science, 26,* 525–554.

Saito, S., Logie, R. H., Morita, A., & Law, A. (2008). Visual and phonological similarity effects in verbal immediate serial recall: A test with kanji materials. *Journal of Memory and Language, 59,* 1–17.

Salthouse, T. A. (1974). Using selective interference to investigate spatial memory representations. *Memory & Cognition, 2,* 749–757.

Salway, A. F. S., & Logie, R. H. (1995). Visuospatial working memory, movement control and executive demands. *British Journal of Psychology, 86,* 253–269.

Smith, E. E., & Jonides, J. (1997). Working memory: A view from neuroimaging. *Cognitive Psychology, 33,* 5–42.

Smith, E. E., & Jonides, J. (1999). Neuroscience – Storage and executive processes in the frontal lobes. *Science, 283,* 1657–1661.

Stuyven, E., Van der Goten, K., Vandierendonck, A., Claeys, K., & Crevits, L. (2000). Saccadic eye movements under conditions of cognitive load. *Acta Psychologica, 104,* 69–85.

Szmalec, A., Duyck, W., Vandierendonck, A., Mata, B., & Page, M. P. A. (2009). The Hebb repetition effect as a laboratory analogue of novel word learning. *Quarterly Journal of Experimental Psychology, 62,* 435–443.

Szmalec, A., Loncke, M., Page, M. P. A., & Duyck, W. (In press). Order or dis-order? Impaired Hebb learning in dyslexia. *Journal of Experimental Psychology: Learning, Memory, and Cognition.*

Szmalec, A., Vandierendonck, A., & Kemps, E. (2005). Response selection involves executive control: Evidence from the selective interference paradigm. *Memory and Cognition, 33,* 531–541.

Turner, M. L., & Engle, R. W. (1989). Is working memory capacity task dependent? *Journal of Memory and Language, 28,* 127–154.

Vandierendonck, A. (2000). Is judgment of random time intervals biased and capacity limited? *Psychological Research, 63,* 199–209.

Vandierendonck, A., De Vooght, G., & Van der Goten, K. (1998). Does random time interval generation interfere with working memory executive functions? *European Journal of Cognitive Psychology, 10,* 413–442.

Vandierendonck, A., Kemps, E., Fastame, C., & Szmalec, A. (2004). Working memory components in the Corsi blocks task. *British Journal of Psychology, 95,* 57–79.

Vandierendonck, A., & Suardi, A. (2011). How is order coded in working memory? Manuscript in preparation.

Vergauwe, E., Barrouillet, P., & Camos, V. (2009). Visual and spatial working memory are not that dissociated after all: A time-based resource-sharing account. *Journal of Experimental Psychology: Learning Memory and Cognition, 35,* 1012–1028.

Vergauwe, E., Barrouillet, P., & Camos, V. (2010). Do mental processes share a domain-general resource? *Psychological Science, 21,* 384–390.

Wickens, C. D. (1984). Processing resources in attention. In R. Parasuraman & D. R. Davies (Eds.), *Varieties of attention* (pp. 63–102). New York: Academic Press.

Wilson, J. T. L., Scott, J. H., & Power, K. G. (1987). Developmental differences in the span of visual memory for pattern. *British Journal of Developmental Psychology, 5,* 249–255.

2 The visual and the spatial of a multicomponent working memory

Robert H. Logie

Our experience of the visual world is driven by external stimulus input combined with acquired lifetime knowledge. Understanding of how this is accomplished is spread across multiple lines of research ranging from visual psychophysics through visual perception and attention, visual short-term memory, mental imagery, object recognition, episodic visual memories, and semantic visual knowledge. Visuospatial working memory might be seen as a possible interface between these diverse topic areas; it is not quite visual attention because it deals with current visuospatial mental representations of the world not direct stimulus input, but it is fed by the products of visual attention. It is not episodic or semantic memory, but its contents are influenced by prior experiences at least as much as they are by visual perception. As such visuospatial working memory supports online cognition in that it holds, manipulates, and updates our current interpretation of the external visual world as well as holding and manipulating temporary reactivations of past experiences (e.g., Byrne, Becker, & Burgess, 2007; Logie & van der Meulen, 2009; van der Meulen, Logie, & Della Sala, 2009; Wolbers, Hegarty, Büchel, & Loomis, 2008). The properties of manipulation and updating here are crucial, because it is through manipulation of our current mental representations that visuospatial working memory can generate novel representations to support problem solving and creative thinking, navigation, planning future actions, and learning (see reviews in Cornoldi, Logie, Brandimonte, Kaufmann, & Reisberg, 1996; Helstrup & Logie, 1999; Logie, 2003; Roskos-Ewoldsen, Intons-Peterson, & Anderson, 1993). This mental workspace could be seen as the virtual world of our experience, while the external world is real in the sense that it is relatively stable and predictable most of the time, and it also acts as the external input for the diverse virtual mental worlds across individuals.

Given that this book is focused on spatial cognition, it would be important first to consider the operational definition of 'spatial'. This could refer to the relative locations of several different objects in an array, or even the relative locations of individual features within an object. Spatial could refer to the order in which a series of locations is identified, or it could refer to a series of arm or body movements. In this chapter I will try to be clear as to which sense of the concept 'spatial' is being discussed. The discussion will centre on experimental and neuropsychological evidence regarding the debate as to how visual and spatial aspects of temporary mental representations are handled in online cognition, and whether both are separate from online cognition for verbal aspects of temporary representations. This will lead on to a discussion as to whether there are domain-specific cognitive resources to support respectively verbal, spatial, and visual working memory.

Visual, spatial, and verbal divisions

The case for dissociating visuospatial from verbal processing and temporary storage was supported through a wide range of studies starting in the 1960s, demonstrating both experimental and neuropsychological double dissociations. This literature tends not to be considered in more contemporary studies of the topic. Extensive reviews of that earlier literature have been published previously (Logie, 1995, 2003; Logie & van der Meulen, 2009), and so I shall not reiterate that material in detail here. However, more recent theoretical arguments should consider how to account for the earlier as well as the more contemporary findings in this area. Therefore, given the limited inclusion of the earlier experimental and neuropsychological evidence in current debates, I will summarize here some of the main earlier findings to set the scene for the remainder of this chapter.

One of the first demonstrations of a verbal/visuospatial dissociation in working memory was a study by Brooks (1968) in which participants were asked to imagine scanning clockwise around a block capital letter, and to indicate 'yes' for each corner that comprised an outside angle, and 'no' if the corner comprised an inside angle. For example with the block letter 'E', starting at the top left, the correct sequence of responses would be 'yes, yes, yes, no, no, yes, yes, no, no, yes, yes, yes'. In one condition, participants had to speak aloud their responses while imagining the block letter. In the other case, participants had to point to the words 'yes' and 'no' that were printed randomly on a sheet of paper. Brooks found that participants performed more poorly when they had to point to the responses than to say them. In other words, holding and scanning a visual mental image is more difficult when selecting items from a visual array than when generating a oral response. In contrast, when participants were asked to think about phrases such as 'A bird in the hand is not in the bush', then to classify each word in the phrase as a noun (respond yes) or not (respond no), the opposite pattern was found: responding orally resulted in poorer performance than selecting responses from a visual array. Brooks (1967) reported a similar result for a task in which participants had to imagine a sequence of movements around an imagined 4×4 square matrix. In this case, a description of the path (up-right-down-down-right-down-left etc.) was either read or was heard. Participants performed much more successfully when they listened to the description of the path than when they were required to read it. These and similar results (e.g., Baddeley & Lieberman, 1980; Farmer, Berman, & Fletcher, 1986) suggested that verbal output disrupts verbal working memory but not visuospatial working memory, whereas visual selection and reading memory instructions disrupt visuospatial working memory but not verbal working memory. Logie, Zucco, and Baddeley (1990) also used dual-task methodology to show that memory for visually presented matrix patterns was disrupted by a concurrent task that involved mental construction of a block pattern with the visual appearance of one of the digits one to nine. Matrix patterns were not disrupted by concurrent mental arithmetic. In the same study, memory for visually presented letter sequences was disrupted by mental arithmetic, but not by imagining block images of number symbols.

Baddeley and Lieberman (1980) demonstrated that a concurrent spatial tracking task disrupted performance of the Brooks Spatial Task. However, a less well-known aspect of that study is that they also showed that a concurrent visual task (brightness judgements) did not disrupt spatial memory, and that concurrent spatial tracking did not disrupt use of the peg word mnemonic that requires generation of bizarre mental images of scenes or objects without reference to spatial location. From this extended pattern of results, Baddeley and Lieberman concluded that the immediate memory system that they were investigating was primarily spatial in nature and was also involved in motor control for tracking, whereas visual immediate memory was rather less dependent on this system. This suggestion was explored in more detail by Logie (1986) who focused on the use of the peg word visual imagery mnemonic to aid recall of a list of words. Use of this mnemonic was shown to be disrupted by concurrent presentation of a series of irrelevant pictures, but not by a series of aurally presented irrelevant words. In contrast, recall of lists of words based on the memory strategy of rote rehearsal was disrupted by the aurally presented irrelevant words but not by the irrelevant pictures. This form of double dissociation in the results confirmed the previous suggestions that visual/spatial immediate memory might rely on a different cognitive system than verbal immediate memory. However, when taken together with the Baddeley and Lieberman findings, the results were consistent with the suggestion that immediate memory for primarily visual material such as with the peg word mnemonic was dependent on a different set of cognitive functions than was retaining a spatial sequence such as for the Brooks tasks.

In all of the studies described, the interference observed could not be interpreted as simply the result of high cognitive demand from the requirement to perform two concurrent tasks. The double dissociations observed indicated that it was the nature of the tasks that was important, not the overall cognitive load. Neither could there be an account based on simple overlap of sensory features, because aural presentation was used for one of the tasks and visual presentation was used for the concurrent task (Logie, 1986; Logie et al., 1990), or mentally imaged materials based on aural presentation were combined with arm movement for pointing or with oral output (Baddeley & Lieberman, 1980; Brooks, 1967, 1968; Farmer et al., 1986). What was important was the nature of the cognitive processing required to undertake the task, not the modality of input or output.

Additional early evidence came from dissociations found in a range of single case studies of patients with focal brain damage. For example, Ross (1980) described a patient with completely intact recall of object names (e.g., could correctly recall that a pen had been presented among a range of distractor objects), but who was severely impaired in remembering the visual appearance of objects (could not select a particular pen that had been presented from among a range of distractor pens). The converse pattern has been shown by patients with short-term verbal memory deficits. For example, patient K.F. (Shallice & Warrington, 1970; Warrington & Shallice, 1972) could recall only one or two digits from an aurally presented sequence, but could reliably recall four digits if they were presented visually. When making recall errors with visually presented letters, K.F. tended to make visual confusions rather than phonological confusions, suggesting that he was attempting to remember the letters visually rather than as a set of phonological codes. These patterns of sparing and impairment suggest that verbal working memory can be damaged while leaving intact the ability to remember visual characteristics of stimuli, and vice versa. This points further to separate memory systems for short-term storage of phonological and visual codes. Similar dissociations between patients have been reported over subsequent decades (see reviews in Logie & Della Sala, 2005; Vallar & Shallice, 1990).

More recent evidence has come from studies of patients with unilateral spatial neglect. This results from a brain injury, typically a stroke in the right hemisphere, and is associated with the patient being unable to report details from their left side (e.g., Kinsbourne, 2006). In some cases this involves an inability to report from memory details on the left side of an imagined familiar environment such as the inside of their house or the main square in their home town (Beschin, Cocchini, Della Sala, & Logie, 1997; Bisiach & Luzzatti, 1978; Guariglia, Padovani, Pantano, & Pizzamiglio, 1993), or even to report details on the left side of a spatial array that the patients have heard described to them (Logie, Beschin, Della Sala & Denis, 2005). Despite their severe impairment in forming and holding temporary representations of spatial arrays, these patients nevertheless have completely intact immediate verbal memory. This again points to rather different resources underlying immediate verbal and immediate visuospatial memory. Notably these patients have no difficulty with visual memory as such; they are just unable to process and remember material in particular spatial positions, most commonly the left side of physical or mentally represented space (Beschin et al., 1997; Denis, Beschin, Logie, & Della Sala, 2002; Robertson & Halligan, 1999). This strengthens the case that spatial representations and visual representations in working memory might be dissociated.

A very recently reported phenomenon helps build on this case. Della Sala, Darling, and Logie (2010) reported a study of over 60,000 healthy individuals who were asked to recall the colour, shape, and location of up to four stimuli shown briefly on the computer screen. What was striking about these data was the fact that when errors in recall occurred, they were much more likely to be for stimuli that had appeared on the right side of the screen rather than the left. This lateralized bias in recall could not be explained by the order in which items were recalled, nor by biases in attention or perceptual processing. This kind of result not only points to the suggestion that spatial location is handled differently by the cognitive system than are colour and shape but it also suggests that there are lateralized biases in the way in which spatial mental representations are formed, held, or accessed. A similar phenomenon has been reported for long-term memory in which healthy participants tend to omit details on the right when recalling familiar scenes from memory (McGeorge, Beschin, Colnaghi, Rusconi, & Della Sala, 2007). Detailed theoretical discussion of the lateralized bias in patients with unilateral spatial neglect and in healthy participants is beyond the remit and scope of this chapter. However, the empirical demonstrations described above set the challenge to theories of working memory to explain not only the evidence for a separation between visual and spatial memory. They also have to start considering why it might be that visuospatial mental representations can be subject to lateralized biases that are found in patients with lateralized brain damage and in healthy participants.

Contemporary critiques of domain specificity

Over the last decade, the concept of domain-specific resources in working memory has met with some criticism from studies that fail to demonstrate the dissociations that might be predicted from a multicomponent model (see also Vandierendonck & Szmalec, Chapter 1, this volume). The alternative models assume that working memory is constrained by limited capacity, domain-general attention (e.g., Barrouillet, Bernardin, & Camos, 2004; Cowan, 2005a). So where selective interference occurs, this is because the memory codes are similar, not because those memory codes overlap, or because there is competition for limited capacity attention that switches rapidly between concurrent task demands. These approaches tend not to consider the experimental and neuropsychological double dissociations reported over the last few decades, some of which are described above. However, there are also difficulties in interpreting the lack of a difference between conditions as the basis for undermining the idea that the cognitive system comprises a collection of domain-specific resources acting together for successful online cognition. I will illustrate the contrast first by describing a study that demonstrates the presence of multiple resources that can operate in parallel and then discussing some of the subsequent criticisms of that and related studies.

In a series of studies of healthy adults, Cocchini, Logie, Della Sala, MacPherson, and Baddeley (2002) showed that participants could retain aurally presented digit sequences, at their own maximum capacity or span, successfully while encoding and recalling visually presented matrix patterns, the complexity of which was also set at the maximum capacity for each participant. A summary of the basic procedure is shown in Figure 2.1. This technique involved giving the participant a preload on Task 1 that they retained for a period of 15 s while performing encoding and retrieval for interpolated Task 2. Then material for Task 1 was retrieved. Performance under these dual-memory load conditions was compared with performing each of the memory tasks alone either with immediate recall or with an unfilled delay of 15 s. Crucially, the sequence length for the digit recall task and the pattern complexity (number of squares in the matrix) were set at the span level for each participant, and this was true for both the single tasks and the dual-task conditions. This ensured that under single-task conditions, participants were all performing at the limits of their own individual ability, thus the lack of dual-task disruption observed could not be explained by ceiling or floor effects in

Digits + Patterns

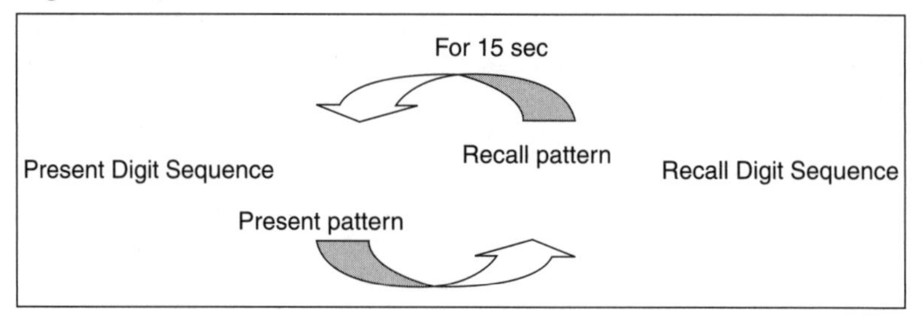

Patterns + Digits

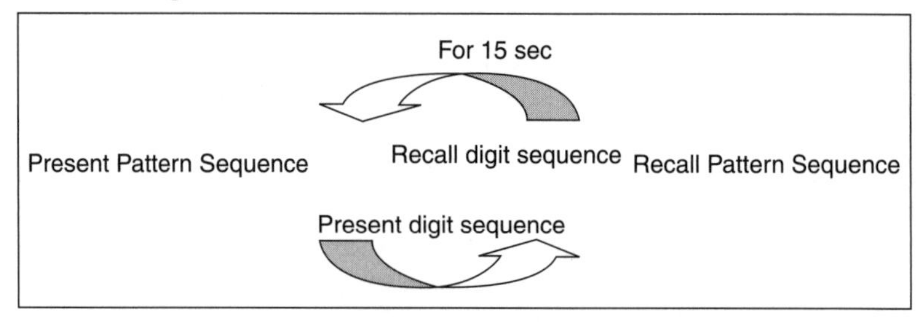

Figure 2.1 Preload procedure for combining verbal (digit sequence recall) and visuo-spatial (square matrix pattern recall) memory tasks. In both cases, performance is compared with immediate and delayed (unfilled delay) recall for pattern memory only or digit memory only. Modified from Cocchini, G., Logie, R. H., Della Sala, S., MacPherson, S. E., Baddeley, A. D. (2002). Concurrent performance of two memory tasks: Evidence for domain specific working memory systems. *Memory and Cognition*, 30, 1086–1095. Reprinted with permission.

the data. Moreover, performance on both tasks was assessed, and there was no evidence of a trade-off with participants protecting performance on one task at the expense of the other.

Morey and Cowan (2004) criticized the Cocchini et al. (2002) study on two grounds. One was that performance levels were in the region of 90%, which Morey and Cowan interpreted as a possible ceiling effect. However, this was a misinterpretation of the procedure because, as noted above, the demand levels of the tasks were adjusted for the span of each individual participant, and so the 90% performance reflects the fact that each participant was performing at the limits of their own individual ability. As such, this was not a ceiling effect. Morey and Cowan also criticized the Cocchini et al. study for failing to consider whether trials that resulted in poor performance of one task were accompanied by higher performance on the other task. It is true that the Cocchini et al. data were not analysed on a trial by trial basis. However, there was no indication in the overall data patterns that participants consistently favoured one task at the expense of the other, and the reported results were driven by considering the overall changes in performance on both tasks between single- and dual-task conditions. Moreover, in a further study, Logie, Cocchini, Della Sala, and Baddeley (2004) systematically varied demand of one task (digit recall) while fixing the demand of the second task (visuomotor tracking) at the span for each individual participant. A second manipulation was to vary the demand of visuomotor tracking while fixing the demand for digit recall at the span sequence length for the individual. With healthy volunteers, varying demand of one task had no impact on the performance of the other task for both types of manipulation (see Figures 2.2 and 2.3, see p. 32). This gives strong evidence that there is no trade-off between tasks that are driven by overall task demand. It reinforces the idea that different memory systems are required for each task, and that these memory systems each have their own resources allowing concurrent performance in parallel rather than dependence on a single attentional system switching between tasks.

In their study, Morey and Cowan (2004) combined a digit memory load with memory for the location of coloured squares in a visual array. They found that increasing the verbal (digit) load had a substantial disruptive effect on memory for the colours. However, they used colours that were easy to name, and the colour array task could effectively have been performed by participants encoding the colour names rather than the visual appearance of the array. The results could then be interpreted as demonstrating dual-task interference between two verbal memory loads rather than, as the authors suggest, an attentional load that was common to a verbal and a visual memory task. A similar problem arose in a later series of experiments by Saults and Cowan (2007), which again combined nameable colours with a verbal memory load. The authors used visual masking to reduce the impact of sensory contributions to the memory task. However, by doing so, they would have actually increased the likelihood that participants were using verbal codes to retain the colours. So, when confronted by a secondary verbal load, this would have interfered with the use of verbal labels for the colours, resulting in poorer performance in the dual-task condition.

Evidence that participants use names of items that are assumed to involve visual processing was reported by Brandimonte, Hitch, and Bishop (1992) who showed that participants spontaneously use verbal codes when presented with pictures of nameable items (as was the case for the studies by Cowan and colleagues). This was true even when instructed to process the visual features of the depicted objects. When participants were prevented from using verbal codes through concurrent articulatory suppression, and they had to rely on a cognitive strategy that involved purely visual processing, their performance on the visuospatial processing task actually improved.

A range of other studies have shown that participants use a range of memory codes to support performance (e.g., Paivio, 1971; 1986), and it is misleading to suggest that the stimulus modality will necessarily dictate the kind of memory codes or the cognitive processing involved in task performance. For example, Logie, Della Sala, Laiacona, Chalmers, and Wynn (1996) tested 252 adults on immediate verbal serial recall tasks to investigate the extent to which individual participants show well-established short-term memory phenomena such as phonological similarity effects and word length effects. A substantial minority of participants did not show poorer recall of phonologically similar compared with phonologically different lists, or poorer recall of lists of long words compared with lists of short words. This was despite the fact that these classic effects were highly significant in the analysis of the aggregate data across all participants. In an analysis of self-reported strategies, it appeared that some participants were using the visual appearance of the words or mental images of the meanings of the words to aid recall. The appearance of phonological similarity and word length effects was associated with participants who reported using the strategy of subvocal rehearsal to remember the word lists.

The use of visual codes in remembering verbal material was shown more systematically by Logie, Della Sala, Wynn, and Baddeley (2000) who presented sequences of words or letters that were visually similar or visually distinct, for example *guy*, *sigh*, *lie*; *who*, *blue*, *ewe* (visually distinct) or *fly, cry, dry; hew, new, few* (visually similar). In the case of the words, items within lists were phonologically similar, so phonological similarity did not differ between the visually similar and visually distinct lists. Participants recalled fewer items from lists that were visually similar than from lists that were visually distinct, suggesting that they were using visual codes to remember the words. The same result was found when participants were asked to recall the letter and the letter case of visually presented letters in that sequences comprising letters that are similar in upper and lower case, for example WcKm, were more difficult to recall than sequences in which upper and lower case versions are visually different, such as gRQb. A follow-up study by Saito, Logie, Morita, and Law (2008) used Japanese Kanji characters, with Japanese speakers, to manipulate phonological similarity and visual similarity within the same lists. Results showed that participants were using both visual and phonological codes to support their memory performance and that these were independent. For example articulatory suppression removed the effect of phonological similarity but had no effect on the presence of visual similarity. That is, articulatory suppression disrupted the use of phonological codes in memory but not the use of visual codes. This kind of result is difficult to explain in terms of a single, limited capacity focus of attention. Therefore, despite arguments to the contrary, there appear to be separate capacities for visual codes and for phonological codes.

Visual and spatial divisions

Given the evidence for a dissociation between visuospatial and verbal components of working memory, the next obvious step in the context of the current chapter is to consider the extent to which the cognitive resources supporting visual and spatial processing and storage might overlap (see also Hamilton, Chapter 7, this volume). As noted earlier, one early hint that they might not completely overlap was reported by Baddeley and Lieberman (1980) who showed that memory for an imagined pathway around a square matrix pattern (Brooks, 1967) was disrupted by concurrent unseen arm movement, but not by concurrent judgements of the brightness of patches of light. Participants were blindfolded in the arm movement condition, suggesting that it was control of the movement itself rather than observing one's own arm movement that was causing the disruption of memory for the imagined pathway. Quinn and Ralston (1986; Quinn, 1994) confirmed the result that the Brooks Task (1967) is disrupted by concurrent arm movement. Logie (1986) argued that the memory task used by Baddeley and Lieberman (1980) was a spatial task involving memory for a sequence of movements, and this was the reason that it was disrupted by concurrent movements. Therefore a visual memory task should be more susceptible to disruption from irrelevant visual input than was the spatial memory task used by Baddeley and Lieberman. This then led to the Logie (1986) study showing that the peg word mental imagery mnemonic was disrupted by presenting a series of irrelevant pictures. This was not just because participants had to perform two tasks concurrently, because presentation of irrelevant pictures had no effect on recall of words based on rote rehearsal. So taking the Baddeley and Lieberman (1980) result together with the results from Logie (1986), it appeared that memory for an imagined pathway (spatial as a movement sequence) shared cognitive resources with control of arm movement, whereas retaining static images of objects (peg word mnemonic) shared cognitive resources with visual perceptual input.

In a series of experiments, Quinn and McConnell (e.g., 1996, 1999, 2006) followed up on the Logie (1986) result by showing that use of the peg word mnemonic was also disrupted by a pattern of flickering dots similar to the screen on a poorly tuned analogue television. This reinforces the conclusion that the visual processing involved in generating and retrieving visual mental images overlaps with aspects of visual perception. In contrast, Smyth and Pendleton (1989, 1990) showed that memory for a sequence of body movements was unaffected by irrelevant visual input, but was disrupted by interpolated arm movements. Together, again, these studies point to the notion that memory for a sequence of movements through space is supported by different cognitive mechanisms than is memory for visual representations that have no particular spatial location.

One study to directly compare visual and spatial working memory was reported by Logie and Pearson (1997) in which they tested three groups of children aged respectively 6, 9, and 12 on memory for visually presented square matrix patterns, referred to as the Visual Patterns Test (VPT, Wilson, Scott, & Power, 1987), and for sequences of movements around a set of randomly arranged wooden blocks known as the Corsi Blocks Task (CBT, Milner, 1971). Results showed that the two tasks correlated poorly within each age group of children, and the changes in performance with age followed very different trajectores. This suggested that visual immediate memory for the matrix patterns developed with age somewhat independently of spatial memory for movement sequences. A similar dissociation was reported in a follow-up developmental study reported by Pickering, Gathercole, Hall, and Lloyd (2001).

The dissociation was reinforced by neuropsychological evidence from Della Sala, Gray, Baddeley, Allamano, and Wilson (1999) who described two brain injured patients, with one demonstrating specific deficits on the CBT with preserved performance on the VPT, and the other showing impairment on the VPT with no corresponding impairment on the CBT. If the cognitive systems supporting performance on these two tasks substantially overlap, then we should find that impairments on one task accompany impairments on the other. These studies of contrasting patients show very clearly that this is not necessarily the case. Darling, Della Sala, Logie, and Cantagallo (2006) described two further patients, one of whom was found to have an impairment in remembering spatial locations but had no difficulty remembering the visual appearance of a stimulus. The second patient showed the converse, with an impairment in memory for what a stimulus looked like but no difficulty in remembering where stimuli had appeared. A more recent study of healthy young adults (Darling, Della Sala, & Logie, 2009) showed a similar dissociation using experimental dual-task methods. Concurrent arm movement (tapping) was shown to disrupt memory for spatial location, whereas irrelevant visual input disrupted memory for the visual appearance of stimuli. Dissociations were not dependent on having sequential presentation for the spatial task and simultaneous presentation for the visual task. It was the nature of the material for recall (location versus appearance) that was crucial for the dissociation, rather than the mode of presentation (sequential or simultaneous). Analogous results using dual-task methods have been reported by Hecker and Mapperson (1997) and by Tresch, Sinnamon, and Seamon (1993).

The above studies suggest that memory for visual appearance and memory for location might be separable. However, this leaves open whether the other interpretation of ‘spatial’ as a sequence of locations might behave in the same way. Rudkin, Pearson, and Logie (2007) showed that memory for a sequence of movements seems to involve greater general purpose attentional resources than does remembering a set of locations that are presented simultaneously. A similar reliance on domain-general resources was reported by Salway and Logie (1995) who showed that memory for the sequence of imagined movements in the Brooks (1967) matrix task was very substantially disrupted by concurrent verbal random generation, a task thought to draw heavily on domain-general attention (Baddeley, 1966; Evans, 1978). Salway and Logie (1995) found much less disruption of rote memory for a verbal sequence by concurrent random generation, so the effect of random generation on the Brooks matrix imagery task cannot easily be interpreted by suggesting that participants were actually relying on verbal codes for this spatial sequential task. Further support comes from Vandierendonck, Kemps, Fastame, and Szmalec (2004) who showed that memory for Corsi block sequences was disrupted by concurrent random-interval generation, a task in which participants are required to randomly vary the inter-tap interval for a series of finger taps on a single key. The advantage to the random-interval task is that it has neither verbal nor spatial requirements, and so is a purer call on domain-general resources, sometimes called executive functions.

The suggestion that retaining sequences of locations might involve domain-general resources that are not required for retaining arrays of locations, would offer an account of the patterns of results just described. This interpretation raises the question as to what it is about remembering a sequence of locations that would draw on domain-general rather than domain-specific resources. One possibility is that memory for location and memory for appearance rely on separable resources, but that memory for sequences of movements relies on both memory for locations and also memory for the order of the sequence of locations. The requirement to remember order of locations as well as the locations themselves might therefore draw on domain-general resources simply because two different features of the stimuli have to be encoded and retrieved, namely order and location rather than just location alone. However, this seems an unconvincing account of the neuropsychological evidence given that there was no overall difference in executive functioning between otherwise contrasting patients in the Della Sala et al. (1999) study of neuropsychological dissociations between Corsi block and visual matrix pattern performance. So, the question remains open as to whether or not remembering the sequential order of locations requires general attentional resources.

Klauer and Zhao (2004) presented what is probably the most systematic set of studies to date demonstrating spatial and visual dissociations. Across six experiments, they found clear double dissociations between memory for spatial location and memory for visual appearance.They further showed that these dissociations could not be interpreted by suggesting that some tasks draw more heavily than others on general purpose attentional resources. This kind of conclusion creates difficulties for theories of working memory that assume that the capacity of working memory is heavily influenced by a single, general purpose focus of attention (e.g., Barrouillet, Bernadin, & Camos, 2004; Cowan, 2005).

A recent critique of one of the experiments reported by Klauer and Zhao (2004) and of their conclusions was presented by Vergauwe, Barrouillet, and Camos (2009) who described two experiments exploring the idea that retention of visually presented material is primarily constrained by general purpose, time-dependent cognitive resources rather than being specific to visual, spatial, or verbal domain-specific resources. Tasks chosen by the authors to represent spatial or visual working memory were equally disrupted by tasks performed during a retention interval that were labelled as involving respectively spatial or visual processing. The authors argue that disruption appears to be related more to the amount of time that rehearsal is disrupted by the interpolated attention-demanding tasks rather than the specific nature of the tasks that are being combined. This is suggested to undermine the visual–spatial distinction, reported by Klauer and Zhao (2004).

One difficulty with the Vergauwe et al. (2009) paper and subsequent arguments (e.g., Vergauwe, Barrouillet, & Camos, 2010) is that, like the Morey and Cowan (2004, 2005) and Saults and Cowan (2007) papers, there is little consideration of the wide range of evidence for the visual–spatial distinction from studies of healthy adults or of brain damaged patients, some of which are reviewed earlier in the chapter. Any theory of visuospatial cognition would have to account for this earlier body of evidence as well as the more recent studies. There are also several methodological problems with the Vergauwe et al. (2009) experiments. For example, one task labelled as 'spatial' involved presenting a set of independent linear movements each of a single target, with each starting from one of eight different positions around a square (the four corners and the four mid-points of each side), and moving to the complementary position on the other side of the square. Participants were asked to remember the order in which each of the movements was presented. However, there was no control for verbal labelling or verbal rehearsal, and the task could have been performed by remembering each starting point as a set of number labels, and would not require memory for the movement itself. For example, the verbal codes 3, 5, 8, 4 could be used at the retrieval stage to reconstruct starting points at top right, bottom right, left middle, and right middle of the square respectively. Alternatively, the task could be accomplished by remembering a visual pattern of starting points without remembering any of the movements across the screen. So, there is no guarantee that participants actually used any spatial coding for the movements to retain the items. The task could equally be described as a visual memory task for starting points or a verbal memory task for a sequence of numbered locations.

The task labelled as 'visual memory' by Vergauwe et al. (2009) involved retaining a sequence of 2 × 3 matrix patterns, with increasing sequence length. Sequential presentation of a series of visual patterns typically results in single item recency effects (Broadbent & Broadbent, 1981; Phillips & Christie, 1977a, 1977b), and is a very unusual technique for studying visual memory. A more common method is to increase complexity of a single pattern for subsequent recall on the grounds that visual immediate memory retains a single pattern and its limits are based on pattern complexity, not on the length of a sequence of different patterns. Requiring the retention of sequences of patterns could well make this task more spatial than visual and using such simple square patterns leads to the possibility of reliance on verbal coding, for example squares 2, 5, 6 were filled in array one, whereas squares 1, 3, 4 were filled in array two, squares 2, 3, 5 in array three, and so on. At recall, participants could then recall chunks of 3-digit sequences to reconstruct the arrays. A number of the patterns could also have resembled letter shapes, for example an 'L' or 'T'. These strategies would have been enough to support quite high performance levels without relying on visual coding (for a similar argument see Broadbent & Broadbent, 1981), and there was no attempt to verify the strategies that participants had adopted.

There are similar as well as additional problems with the second experiment in the paper. The overall difficulty is that the processing and memory requirements of the chosen tasks are assumed without providing any evidence that those assumptions are justified. The work also takes arguments that have been developed in studying verbal working memory and attempts to apply these to visuospatial working memory, but without adequate consideration of previous evidence in the latter area.

A further difficulty with this kind of critique that is illustrated by the Vergauwe et al. (2009) paper is that they report a lack of a dissociation among the tasks that they have chosen to employ. However, this merely reflects the fact that participants happen to use the same cognitive resource to perform the chosen tasks. In principle, it only requires a demonstration that the systems are separate with appropriately chosen tasks, or a demonstration of double dissociations in patients to make the case, and several such studies are described earlier in this chapter.

Any theory suggesting that there are no such dissociations has to offer a convincing explanation for the prior evidence to the contrary.

Domain-general and domain-specific resources

The findings discussed above make the case for domain-specific resources being available to support respectively verbal, visual, and spatial aspects of online cognition and temporary storage in working memory. However, this does not eschew the use of domain-general resources in addition to these domain-specific resources. The literature on visuospatial working memory has consistently recognized that there is some contribution of domain-general resources to performance in dual-task conditions. In many of the dual-task studies cited above there was a small main effect of dual task compared with single task. For example, in the Logie et al. (1990) study the authors were quite explicit in noting a small main effect of dual versus single task in addition to the specific effects shown in the theoretically important interaction. This small dual-task cost is amplified in the case of people suffering from Alzheimer's disease. Specifically, when asked to listen to and recall digit sequences at individual span levels of demand, healthy younger and older people are unaffected in recall when asked concurrently to follow a moving target around a computer screen at their maximum possible speed. Target tracking likewise is unaffected by concurrent digit recall (Baddeley, Logie, Bressi, Della Sala, & Spinnler, 1986; Logie et al., 2004; MacPherson, Della Sala, Logie, & Willcock, 2007). This offers additional evidence for domain-specific resources shown in other dual-task studies described earlier (e.g., Cocchini et al., 2002).

However, the Baddeley et al. (1986) and Logie et al. (2004) studies and others (e.g., Alberoni, Baddeley, Della Sala, Logie, & Spinnler, 1992; MacPherson et al., 2007; Sebastian & Menor, 2006) have shown that people suffering from Alzheimer's disease are very severely impaired when required to undertake two tasks at the same time. This dual-task impairment is insensitive to the demands of each of the individual tasks, and is in addition to any impairment shown for each of the tasks performed on their own. Figures 2.2 and 2.3 show that there is an overall difference in dual-task performance between the patients and younger and older healthy participants, but the patients show exactly the same pattern with regard to changing task demands as do the participants in both single- and dual-task conditions. That is, for all three groups, performance on one task is affected by increasing demand on that task (Figures 2.2a, 2.2b, 2.3a, and 2.3c), but is not affected by changes in demand of a contrasting task that is performed concurrently (Figures 2.2c and 2.3b). So, there is no impact of dual-task demand on the healthy participants, suggesting that the two tasks rely on separate resources that can operate in parallel. Moreover, the patients show an impairment when performing two tasks that are designed to be simple for each individual (well below their individual span) as well as when the two individual tasks are very demanding (Logie et al., 2004), but demand does not interact with single versus dual task. It is the requirement to carry out two tasks (regardless of individual task demand) at the same time that causes difficulty for the patients, not the overall cognitive

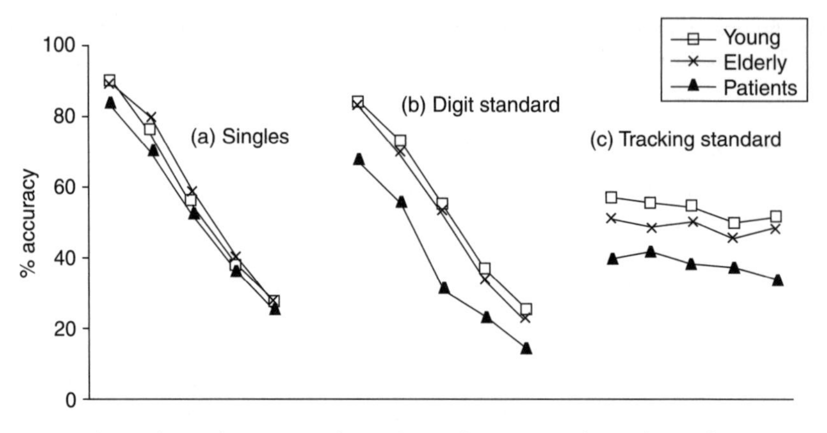

Figure 2.2 Mean percentage time on target for tracking with (a) tracking performed alone and tracking demand varied; (b) tracking demand varied concurrently with recall of fixed length sequences of digits; and (c) tracking demand fixed concurrently with recall of varied length sequences of digits for younger and older healthy participants and Alzheimer's patients. Note in (c) that tracking performance is unaffected by variations in demand for the concurrent digit recall task in all three groups. From Logie et al. (2004). Reprinted with permission.

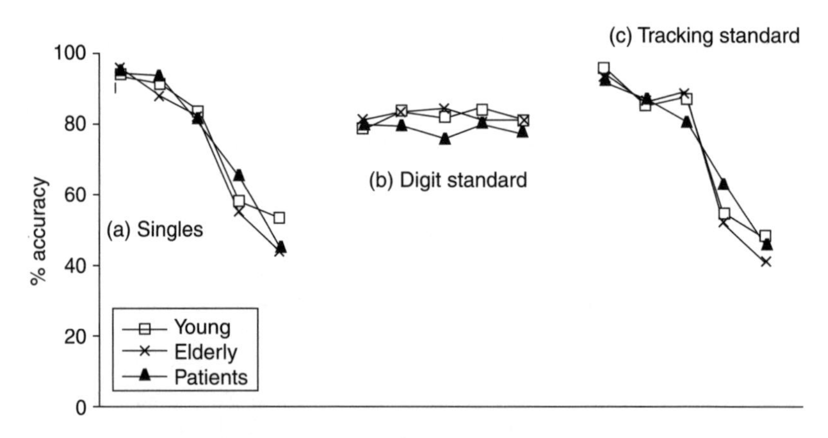

Figure 2.3 Mean percentage digit recall with (a) recall performed alone and sequence length varied, (b) recall of fixed length sequences of digits concurrently with tracking demand varied, and (c) recall of varied length sequences of digits concurrently with tracking demand fixed for younger and older healthy participants and Alzheimer's patients. Note in (b) that digit recall is unaffected by variations in demand for the concurrent tracking task in all three groups. From Logie et al. (2004). Reprinted with permission.

demand on their damaged cognitive system. This points to some form of domain general cognitive function that supports concurrent task performance in the healthy brain, and that is specifically damaged in Alzheimer's disease. However, this dual-task function is not explained by reference to general purpose, limited capacity attention. That is, the ability to perform two diverse tasks concurrently relies on domain-general as well as domain-specific resources, but this ability is not driven by a domain general limited capacity attentional system.

A further approach to considering whether verbal, visual, and spatial working memory rely on domain-general or domain-specific resources has been to consider individual differences in performance on tasks that are assumed to rely on each of these different forms of memory or processing (e.g., Kane, Hambrick, Tuholski, Wilhelm, Payne, & Engle, 2004; Shah & Miyake, 2006). In part that literature has been driven by the question of why measures of working memory appear to correlate highly with measures of fluid intelligence (e.g., Friedman, Miyake, Young, DeFries, Corley, & Hewitt, 2008; Kane & Engle, 2002; Unsworth, Redick, Heitz, Broadway, & Engle, 2009). This is an important and interesting question, but is orthogonal to the question of whether there are domain-specific resources available within a multiple component working memory system. More crucially, an individual differences approach might actually be completely uninformative regarding whether working memory is domain-general or comprises a range of domain-specific systems. The argument for this follows.

The general assumption underlying individual differences studies is that the maximum scores that an individual can achieve on any particular test reflect the capacity of that individual on the test. Capacities vary from one individual to another on the same test, and a given individual varies in their capacity to perform different tests. In individual difference studies, those maximum capacities are used to assess whether they reflect common variance that could be explained by a single factor or by multiple factors. If a single factor can explain most of the variance across tests in a large number of individuals, then it is assumed that there is a single cognitive function that generates that variance. However, there are some problems with this assumption. First, a given individual might draw on a range of cognitive abilities to achieve their maximum score on a single test. Therefore, we cannot be sure that a single test reflects the operation of a single cognitive function. For example, Cowan (Cowan et al., 2005) has argued that the core capacity of the focus of attention within working memory is four items, but that the score on a particular test might be enhanced beyond that basic capacity to reflect the deployment of mnemonic strategies. So, subvocal rehearsal can increase the score on serial-ordered recall of a random word list (i.e., verbal span) to seven items rather than four. Chunking in groups of three words can increase span to 9 items or more, whereas the peg word mnemonic can increase the span to 15 or more with very little practice on the technique. On the basis of Cowan's assumptions, the score that a participant achieves on an immediate verbal serial-ordered recall task could reflect the capacity of focused attention, as well as the efficiency with which the participant can use subvocal rehearsal, chunking, and other mnemonics to support performance. Moreover, a given score could be achieved by any combination of these strategies. So, we cannot assume that the maximum score obtained reflects the operation of a single cognitive system. The same argument could apply to a wide range of cognitive tests, and earlier in the chapter, I illustrated how reported findings could be interpreted as reflecting the operation of visual memory, verbal memory, or spatial memory unless the researchers undertake systematic studies to test their assumptions about the cognitive requirements of novel paradigms that they devise.

An illustration comes from a functional magnetic resonance imaging (fMRI) study (Rypma, Prabhakaran, Desmond, Glover, & Gabrieli, 1999) that examined the impact on brain activation patterns of increasing the number of items to be retained in an immediate memory task. Requiring participants to retain three letters resulted in activation of the left caudal inferior frontal gyrus, compared with storing only one letter. However, asking participants to retain six letters resulted in additional, bilateral activation in the prefrontal areas, notably the middle and superior frontal gyri. Retaining six items would be getting close to standard letter span for many healthy adults, and scores might range between five and nine in an individual differences study. However, Rypma et al. (1999) showed that storing six items recruits more brain networks than does remembering three items, and so it seems reasonable to conclude that the maximum test score reflects the operation of multiple cognitive systems. As such, variance between individuals in their maximum scores on a digit span test would be completely insensitive to the presence of multiple cognitive systems contributing to task performance. A similar argument can be made from the behavioural data in the Saito et al. (2008) study showing that participants spontaneously used both phonological and visual codes to remember visually presented verbal material. Taking an overall score reflecting individual variation in memory capacity for that material would not have told us anything about the nature of the memory codes contributing to performance. A logical conclusion from this argument is that the variance in maximum test scores on any test will be very insensitive to the contribution of each of a range of individual cognitive systems to performance on the test. That is, we cannot rely on individual differences in test performance to draw conclusions about whether there are domain-general or domain-specific systems supporting cognitive performance.

A corollary of this argument is that an individual cognitive system might be necessary but not sufficient to perform a test. For example, in order to read the text of this chapter, the reader must have some minimum level of eyesight. However, if we were to measure the variance in visual acuity across a large number of readers of this book, the correlation with a measure of reading ability would be very poor. This does not mean that vision does not make an important contribution to reading success – it is simply that reading by sighted people under normal lighting conditions and with a reasonable size of font does not require the maximum acuity available to most individuals, and so a measure of the limits of acuity for each individual will not be a strong predictor of reading. So too a test involving spatial and visual processing might well involve contributions from a range of cognitive systems, but variance across individuals in their maximum possible score on the test will not be informative about the contribution from these different systems. For example, a system that specializes in temporary retention of spatial location might be required to retain the visual appearance of a stimulus in some hypothetical task. However, the demands on the spatial memory systems might be very low and well within the capacity of all of the individuals that take part. Therefore it would make no contribution to individual differences in task performance. In contrast, the demand of the task on a visual memory system might be rather high and could be at the limit of capacity of that domain-specific system for one individual, above the capacity for another, but well below the capacity of a third. So, the difference in scores between individuals on this hypothetical test would suggest that there is just a single, possibly domain-general memory system involved. There would be no variation in the scores resulting from the use of the domain specific spatial memory system, and so there would be no evidence for its contribution to task performance. The misleading conclusion would be that there is a single, domain-general cognitive system that is the sole contributor to variance in task performance.

However, if we use an experimental approach, then dissociations might become evident. For example, we could prevent the use of each hypothesized domain-specific system one by one, through a secondary task technique, or observe the impact on task performance of domain-specific impairment as a result of focal brain damage. It would then become very clear whether each system can be separately identified as contributing to task performance. In the reading example given above, if we were to use a very small font size for the text, then variations in visual acuity in our participant sample would become important and would contribute to variation in reading ability, whereas this was not been the case when using a larger font. A concrete example within the core topic for this book comes from a range of studies that demonstrated substantial interference with memory for spatial sequences, such as the Brooks (1967) matrix task or Corsi blocks, from concurrent arm or hand movement (e.g., Baddeley & Lieberman, 1980; Brooks, 1967; Quinn & Ralston, 1986; Quinn, 1994; Smyth & Pendleton, 1989, 1990). These experimental studies suggest that the cognitive systems necessary for controlling arm or hand movement are important in remembering a sequence of locations. However, a number of studies have shown that variation between participants in their arm movement speed or efficiency does not predict performance on these tests of spatial memory (e.g., Logie & Vecchi, 2006; Smyth & Scholey, 1994). So, using an individual differences approach, we would conclude that arm movement control systems are not involved in sequential, spatial memory. However, using an experimental approach, it is very clear that arm movement control is very important. That is, the movement control system contributes to memory for spatial sequences, but that system does not have to operate at its maximum capacity to do so, and therefore individual variation in that maximum capacity is uninformative with regard to the nature of underlying cognitive systems. Individual difference approaches can be extremely useful, for example in predicting successful ageing (e.g., Deary, Whiteman, Whalley, Fox, & Starr, 2004), or scholastic achievement and other cognitive abilities such as language comprehension (e.g.,

Caplan & Waters, 1999; Daneman & Hannon, 2007). They are much less useful when debating whether working memory comprises multiple specialized components or general purpose control of attention.

Multiple domain specific components of working memory

The original multiple component framework for working memory proposed by Baddeley and Hitch (1974) and modified by Logie (1995), Baddeley and Logie (1999), and Logie (2003) suggested that there are multiple, domain-specific temporary memory systems: a phonological store coupled with a subvocal rehearsal for retaining phonological and articulatory codes, a visual cache for retention of the visual appearance of scenes or objects, a spatial rehearsal system for retaining pathways and sequences of movements, and a range of executive functions that support, for example, memory updating, task switching, inhibition, and dual-task performance. Baddeley (2000) proposed an additional component, the episodic buffer, which was thought to retain integrated representations of material drawn from different sensory modalities and from stored knowledge in long-term memory. It was also thought to require attention for forming and retaining its contents. This did not replace the domain-specific memory stores but was considered to draw on the contents of those stores.

Baddeley and colleagues have used feature binding paradigms to explore the characteristics of the hypothesized episodic buffer. In a series of experiments, Allen, Baddeley, and Hitch (2006; Allen, Hitch, & Baddeley, 2009) demonstrated that a concurrent, attention-demanding task had no more effect on memory for bindings between features, such as combinations of colours and shapes, than it did on memory for those individual features such as sets of shapes or sets of colours. Gajewski and Brockmole (2006) showed that a visual distractor between the study and test display in memory had no greater negative impact on memory for individual features than it did on memory for bindings between features in object representations. Brockmole, Parra, Della Sala, and Logie (2008) showed that healthy older people show no poorer performance than younger people in memory for feature bindings than they do in memory for individual visual features, despite the reduction in general mental ability that is associated with cognitive ageing. These findings build on an earlier study by Luck and Vogel (1997) showing that there is no additional cognitive cost associated with retaining bound features within integrated objects compared with retaining individual features. These findings suggest that domain-general attention is not required to form bindings within integrated object representations or retain them on a temporary basis as was assumed in the original proposal for an episodic buffer.

If indeed there are multiple domain-specific memory systems in working memory, there is clearly a logical need to account for the way in which participants can retain integrated representations that, for example, incorporate visual, spatial, verbal, and semantic information. If domain-general attention is not required to do so, then how might this be achieved and how can the evidence for an integrated temporary memory system be reconciled with the evidence for domain-specific systems reviewed earlier in the chapter? One possible resolution is to suggest that there is hippocampal involvement in the binding or integration process. The hippocampus has been strongly implicated in learning of associations, but it is less clear as to whether or not it has a role in temporary memory for novel bindings of visual features. Some initial suggestions on this issue arose from Hannula and Ranganath (2008) who used fMRI techniques to demonstrate hippocampal involvement in tasks that involve relational binding of objects. However, Piekema, Kessels, Mars, Petersson, and Fernandez (2006) showed that the hippocampus was only involved if the task required temporary binding of objects to locations. The Hannula and Ranganath (2008) finding also contrasts sharply with a recent case study (Baddeley, Allen, & Vargha-Khadem, 2010) of an individual with congenital hippocampal damage and a dense developmental amnesia, who has no difficulty with short-term binding tasks that involve colour and shape combinations, or even verbal temporary binding.

Another recent case study was reported by Parra, Della Sala, Logie, and Abrahams (2010) of a patient with acquired focal damage in the anterior pole of the left temporal lobe but without hippocampal damage. This patient had a specific deficit in short-term binding of colour and shape, suggesting that a binding deficit is not necessarily linked to hippocampal damage. Moreover, this patient was completely normal when undertaking temporary binding tasks in which she could use verbal labels or semantic associates. That is, she had a visual binding deficit without an impairment in verbal binding or semantic binding. Other studies with healthy older adults have shown that when the bindings involve spatial location (e.g., colour–location or shape–location combinations), then older healthy people show impairments in binding over and above the reduction in memory for individual features (e.g., Olson, Zhang, Mitchell, Johnson, Bloise, & Higgins, 2004; Parra, Abrahams, Logie, & Della Sala, 2009), even if, as noted earlier, this is not true for colour-shape bindings that do not involve location (Brockmole et al., 2008). These recent findings are consistent with a body of evidence suggesting that features such as shape and colour that identify an object are processed via a different neuroanatomical pathway than is location (e.g., Carlesimo, Perri, Turriziani, Tomaiuolo, & Caltagirone, 2001; Funahashi, Takeda, & Watanabe, 2004; Ruchkin, Johnson, Grafman, Canoune, & Ritter, 1997; Smith & Jonides, 1995, 1999; Ungerleider & Mishkin, 1982).

Taken together the findings from these studies suggest that short-term binding of features of objects draws on different neural systems from those supporting short-term retention of the location of those objects in space, and on different systems from those that retain verbal and semantic properties of stimuli. That is, the results are consistent with the hypothesis that visual and spatial processing and storage in working memory draw on separate cognitive systems, which are in turn different from the system supporting verbal immediate memory. With regard to the episodic buffer, the results suggest that it might not include location of stimuli. It also appears not to rely on domain-general attentional resources. It does appear to retain integrated representations, but the neuropsychological case studies suggest that visual binding problems can arise without problems in binding verbal or semantic information, and there is, as yet, no strong evidence pointing to a single system that has the characteristics suggested for an episodic buffer.

The evidence for separation of these different aspects of working memory function does not help with regard to understanding how integrated object representations can be formed and retained. One possibility is that, instead of thinking of the episodic buffer as a coherent system that is different from the other components within working memory, the integration could be considered an emergent property of communication between domain-specific representation systems. Suggestions that this might be the case come from studies of individuals with neurodegenerative diseases. Diffusion tensor imaging techniques have confirmed that Alzheimer's disease is associated with loss of brain connectivity as a result of white matter loss (e.g., Bozzali & Cherubini, 2007; Chua, Wen, Slavin, & Sachdev, 2008; Morris, 2004). Some recent studies have shown that individuals with Alzheimer's disease have a specific deficit in forming and retaining temporary bindings between features (Parra, Abrahams, Fabi, Logie, Luzzi, & Della Sala, 2009; Parra, Abrahams, Logie, Méndez, Lopera, & Della Sala, 2010). This deficit does not appear in healthy older adults (Brockmole et al., 2008) or in individuals who have depression but not dementia (Parra, Abrahams, Logie, & Della Sala, 2010). These binding problems are not due to impairments in memory for individual features. The idea that binding might arise from communication between domain-specific memory and processing systems is also consistent with at least one computational model of working memory, namely interacting cognitive subsystems (e.g., Barnard, 1999), which also suggests that executive functions and focused attention might also be emergent properties. The details of how this integration process might operate are beyond the scope of the present chapter, but the suggestion does offer a plausible account of a wide range of data from diverse sources, and it generates possible hypotheses that could be tested empirically as well as through computational modelling.

Conclusion

In this chapter, I have discussed both early and more contemporary experimental and neuropsychological evidence suggesting that working memory comprises a range of components, each having a specialist function. In so doing, I have argued that spatial working memory can be thought of in terms of recalling an array of locations, or in terms of recalling a sequence of movements to target locations. Evidence from studies of healthy adults and children, and of patients with focal brain damage suggests that these two forms of spatial working memory rely on separable cognitive systems, and both appear to be separable from the part of the cognitive system that retains the visual appearance of a stimulus, which in turn is separable from temporary verbal memory. This chapter explored studies that have argued against these kinds of dissociations, and noted that in experimental studies that do so, there is insufficient consideration of the strategies available to participants that might undermine the assumptions of the experimenter, such as the possibility of using verbal codes to remember nonverbal material. This chapter also noted that individual differences in maximum scores on a range of cognitive tests are likely to be insensitive to the possibility that multiple cognitive systems might contribute to the scores obtained. This suggests that the individual differences approach is ill suited to addressing the debate as to whether working memory, and particularly visuospatial working memory, comprises a domain-general attentional system or a set of diverse, specialist cognitive systems that operate in concert. The chapter closed with a discussion of evidence pointing towards an empirically testable model that includes a range of domain-specific systems for visual, for spatial, and for verbal online processing and temporary storage in online cognition. Functions such as feature binding are attributed to an emergent property of the communication between these domain-specific systems rather than invoking a separate system specifically for undertaking and retaining integrated representations of multiple features of stimuli. The chapter has not addressed the detailed orchestration of this cognitive concert, an issue that is considered elsewhere (Logie & van der Meulen, 2009), and would merit empirical test in future studies. However, it seems clear that healthy human cognition is not entirely limited by general purpose focused attention, and has a range of functions that can operate concurrently to support cognitive performance.

References

Alberoni, M., Baddeley, A., Della Sala, S., Logie, R., & Spinnler, H. (1992). Keeping track of a conversation: Impairments in Alzheimer's disease. *International Journal of Geriatric Psychiatry, 7,* 639–646.

Allen, R., Baddeley, A. D., & Hitch, G. J. (2006). Is the binding of visual features in working memory resource-demanding? *Journal of Experimental Psychology: General, 135,* 298–313.

Allen, R. J., Hitch, G. J., & Baddeley, A. D. (2009). Cross-modal binding and working memory. *Visual Cognition, 17,* 83–102.

Baddeley, A. D. (1966). The capacity for generating imformation by randomization. *Quarterly Journal of Experimental Psychology, 18,* 119–129.

Baddeley, A. D. (2000). The episodic buffer: A new component of working memory? *Trends in Cognitive Sciences, 4,* 417–423.

Baddeley, A., Allen, R., & Vargha-Khadem, F. (2010). Is the hippocampus necessary for visual and verbal binding in working memory? *Neuropsychologia, 48,* 1089–1095.

Baddeley, A. D., & Hitch, G. (1974). Working memory. In G. H. Bower (Ed.), *The psychology of learning and motivation* (Vol. 8, pp. 47–89). New York: Academic Press.

Baddeley, A. D., & Lieberman, K. (1980). Spatial working memory. In R. S. Nickerson (Ed.), *Attention and performance* (Vol. VIII, pp. 521–539). Hillsdale, NJ: Lawrence Erlbaum Associates, Inc.

Baddeley, A. D. & Logie, R. H. (1999). Working memory: The multiple component model. In A. Miyake & P. Shah (Eds.), *Models of working memory* (pp. 28–61). New York: Cambridge University Press.

Baddeley, A., Logie, R., Bressi, S., Della Sala, S., & Spinnler, H. (1986). Senile dementia and working memory. *Quarterly Journal of Experimental Psychology, 38A,* 603–618.

Barnard, P. (1999). Interacting cognitive subsystems. In A. Miyake & P. Shah (Eds.), *Models of working memory* (pp. 298–339). New York: Cambridge University Press.

Barrouillet, P., Bernardin, S., & Camos, V. (2004). Time constraints and resource sharing in adults' working memory spans. *Journal of Experimental Psychology: General, 133,* 83–100.

Beschin, N., Cocchini, G., Della Sala, S., & Logie, R. H. (1997). What the eyes perceive, the brain ignores: A case of pure unilateral representational neglect. *Cortex, 33,* 3–26.

Bisiach, E., & Luzzatti, C. (1978). Unilateral neglect of representational space. *Cortex, 14,* 129–133.

Bozzali, M., Cherubini, A. (2007). Diffusion tensor MRI to investigate dementias: a brief review. *Magnetic Resonance Imaging, 25,* 969–977.

Brandimonte, M. A., Hitch, G. J., & Bishop, D. (1992). Verbal recoding of visual stimuli impairs mental image transformations. *Memory and Cognition, 20,* 449–455.

Broadbent, D. E., & Broadbent, M. H. P. (1981). Recency effects in visual memory. *Quarterly Journal of Experimental Psychology, 33A,* 1–15.

Brockmole, J. R., Parra, M. A., Della Sala, S., & Logie, R. H. (2008). Do binding deficits account for age-related decline in visual working memory? *Psychonomic Bulletin and Review, 15,* 543–547.

Brooks, L. R. (1967). The suppression of visualisation by reading. *Quarterly Journal of Experimental Psychology, 19,* 289–299.

Brooks, L. R. (1968). Spatial and verbal components in the act of recall. *Canadian Journal of Psychology, 22,* 349–368.

Byrne, P., Becker, S., & Burgess, N. (2007). Remembering the past and imagining the future: a neural model of spatial memory and imagery. *Psychological Review, 114,* 340–375.

Caplan, D. & Waters, G. (1999). Working memory and sentence comprehension. *Behavioral and Brain Sciences, 22,* 77–126.

Carlesimo, G., Perri, R., Turriziani, P., Tomaiuolo, F., & Caltagirone, C. (2001). Remembering what but not where: independence of spatial and visual working memory. *Cortex, 36,* 519–534.

Chua, T. C., Wen, W., Slavin, M. J., & Sachdev, P. S. (2008). Diffusion tensor imaging in mild cognitive impairment and Alzheimer's disease: a review. *Current Opinion in Neurology, 21,* 83–92.

Cocchini, G., Logie, R. H., Della Sala, S., MacPherson, S. E., & Baddeley, A. D. (2002). Concurrent performance of two memory tasks: evidence for domain specific working memory systems. *Memory and Cognition, 30,* 1086–1095.

Cornoldi, C., Logie, R. H., Brandimonte, M. A., Kaufmann, K., & Reisberg, D. (1996). *Stretching the imagination: Representation and transformation in mental imagery.* New York: Oxford University Press.

Cowan, N. (2005). *Working memory capacity.* Hove, UK: Psychology Press.

Cowan, N., Elliott, E. M., Scott Saults, J., Morey, C. C., Mattox, S., Hismatullina, A., & Conway, A. R. (2005). On the capacity of attention: Its estimation and its role in working memory and cognitive aptitudes. *Cognitive Psychology, 51,* 42–100.

Daneman, M. & Hannon, B. (2007). What do working memory span tasks like reading span really measure? In N. Osaka, R. H. Logie, & M. D'Esposito (Eds.), *The cognitive neuroscience of working memory* (pp. 21–42). Oxford: Oxford University Press.

Darling, S., Della Sala, S., & Logie, R. H. (2009). Segregation within visuo-spatial working memory: appearance is stored separately from location. *Quarterly Journal of Experimental Psychology, 62,* 417–425.

Darling, S., Della Sala, S., Logie, R. H., & Cantagallo, A. (2006). Neuropsychological evidence for separating components of visuo-spatial working memory. *Journal of Neurology, 253,* 176–180.

Deary, I. J., Whiteman, M. C., Whalley, L. J., Fox, H. C., & Starr, J. M. (2004). The impact of childhood intelligence on later life: Following up the Scottish Mental Surveys of 1932 and 1947. *Journal of Personality and Social Psychology, 86,* 132–147.

Della Sala, S., Darling, S., & Logie, R. H. (2010). Items on the left are better remembered. *Quarterly Journal of Experimental Psychology, 63,* 848–855.

Della Sala, S., Gray, C., Baddeley, A., Allamano, N., & Wilson, L. (1999) Pattern span: A tool for unwelding visuo-spatial memory. *Neuropsychologia, 37,* 1189–1199.

Denis, M., Beschin, N., Logie, R. H., & Della Sala, S. (2002). Visual perception and verbal descriptions as sources for generating mental representations: Evidence from representational neglect. *Cognitive Neuropsychology, 19,* 97–112.

Evans, F. J. (1978). Monitoring attention deployment by random number generation: An index to measure subjective randomness. *Bulletin of the Psychonomic Society, 12,* 35–38.

Farmer, E., Berman, I., & Fletcher, Y. (1986). Evidence for a visuo-spatial scratchpad in working memory. *Quarterly Journal of Experimental Psychology, 38A,* 675–688.

Friedman, N. P., Miyake, A., Young, S. E., DeFries, J. C., Corley, R. P., & Hewitt, J. K. (2008). Individual differences in executive functions are almost entirely genetic in origin. *Journal of Experimental Psychology: General, 137,* 201–225.

Funahashi, S., Takeda, K., & Watanabe, Y. (2004). Neural mechanisms of spatial working memory: Contributions of the dorsolateral prefrontal cortex and the thalamic nucleus. *Cognitive, Affective, and Behavioral Neuroscience, 4,* 409–420.

Gajewski, D. A., & Brockmole, J. R. (2006). Feature bindings endure without attention: Evidence from an explicit recall task. *Psychonomic Bulletin & Review, 13*, 581–587.

Guariglia, C., Padovani, A., Pantano, P., & Pizzamiglio, L. (1993). Unilateral neglect restricted to visual imagery. *Nature, 364,* 235–237.

Hannula, D. E., & Ranganath, C. (2008). Medial temporal lobe activity predicts successful relational memory binding. *Journal of Neuroscience, 28,* 116–124.

Hecker, R., & Mapperson, B. (1997). Dissociation of visual and spatial processing in working memory. *Neuropsychologia, 35,* 599–603.

Helstrup, T., & Logie, R. H. (Eds.) (1999). *Working memory and mental discovery*. Hove, UK: Psychology Press.

Kane, M. J., & Engle, R. W. (2002). The role of prefrontal cortex in working memory capacity, executive attention, and general fluid intelligence: An individual differences perspective. *Psychonomic Bulletin and Review, 9,* 637–671.

Kane, M. J., Hambrick, D. Z., Tuholski, S. W., Wilhelm, O., Payne, T. W., & Engle, R. W. (2004). The generality of working memory capacity: A latent-variable approach to verbal and visuospatial memory span and reasoning. *Journal of Experimental Psychology: General, 133,* 189–217.

Kinsbourne, M. (2006). From unilateral neglect to the brain basis of consciousness. *Cortex, 42,* 869–874.

Klauer, K. C., & Zhao, Z. M. (2004). Double dissociations in visual and spatial short-term memory. *Journal of Experimental Psychology: General,* 133, 355–381.

Logie, R. H. (1986). Visuo-spatial processing in working memory. *Quarterly Journal of Experimental Psychology, 38A*, 229–247.

Logie, R. H. (1995). *Visuo-spatial working memory.* Hove, UK: Psychology Press.

Logie, R. H. (2003). Spatial and visual working memory: A mental workspace. In D. Irwin and B. Ross (Eds.), *Cognitive vision: The psychology of learning and motivation* (Vol. 42, pp. 37–78). New York: Elsevier Science.

Logie, R. H., Beschin, N., Della Sala, S., & Denis, M. (2005). Dissociating mental transformations and visuo-spatial storage in working memory. Evidence from representational neglect. *Memory, 13,* 430–434.

Logie, R. H., Cocchini, G., Della Sala, S., & Baddeley, A. D. (2004). Is there a specific executive capacity for dual task co-ordination? Evidence from Alzheimer's disease. *Neuropsychology, 18,* 504–513.

Logie, R. H., & Della Sala, S. (2005). Disorders of visuo-spatial working memory. In A. Miyake, & P. Shah (Eds.), *Handbook of Visuospatial Thinking* (pp. 81–120). New York: Cambridge University Press.

Logie, R. H., Della Sala, S., Laiacona, M., Chalmers, P., & Wynn, V. (1996). Group aggregates and individual reliability: The case of verbal short-term memory. *Memory and Cognition, 24,* 305–321.

Logie, R. H., Della Sala, S., Wynn, V., & Baddeley, A. D. (2000). Visual similarity effects in immediate verbal serial recall. *Quarterly Journal of Experimental Psychology, 53A,* 626–646.

Logie, R. H., & Pearson, D. G. (1997). The inner eye and the inner scribe of visuo-spatial working memory: Evidence from developmental fractionation. *European Journal of Cognitive Psychology, 9,* 241–257.

Logie, R. H., & van der Meulen, M. (2009). Fragmenting and integrating visuo-spatial working memory. In J. R. Brockmole (Ed.), *Representing the visual world in memory* (pp. 1–32). Hove, UK: Psychology Press.

Logie, R. H., & Vecchi, T. (2006). Motor components and complexity effects in visuo-spatial processes. In T. Vecchi, & G. Bottini (Eds.), *Imagery and spatial cognition: Methods, models and clinical assessment* (pp. 173–184). Amsterdam: John Benjamins Publishers.

Logie, R. H., Zucco, G. M., & Baddeley, A. D. (1990). Interference with visual short-term memory. *Acta Psychologica, 75,* 55–74.

Luck, S. J., & Vogel, E. K. (1997). The capacity of visual working memory for features and conjunctions. *Nature, 390,* 279–281.

MacPherson, S. E., Della Sala, S., Logie, R. H., & Willcock, G. K. (2007). Specific AD impairment in concurrent performance of two memory tasks. *Cortex, 43,* 858–865.

McGeorge, P., Beschin, N., Colnaghi, A., Rusconi, M. L., & Della Sala, S. (2007). A lateralized bias in mental imagery: Evidence for representational pseudoneglect. *Neuroscience Letters, 421,* 259–263.

Milner, B. (1971). Interhemispheric differences in the localization of psychological processes in man. *British Medical Bulletin, 27,* 272–277.

Morey, C. C., & Cowan, N. (2004). When visual and verbal memories compete: Evidence of cross-domain limits in working memory. *Psychonomic Bulletin & Review, 11,* 296–301.

Morey, C. C., & Cowan, N. (2005). When do visual and verbal memories conflict? The importance of working-memory load and retrieval. *Journal of Experimental Psychology: Learning, Memory, and Cognition, 31,* 703–713.

Morris, R. G. (2004). Neurobiological abnormalities in Alzheimer's disease: structural, genetic, and functional correlates of cognitive dysfunction. In R. G. Morris, & J. Becker (Eds.), *Cognitive neuropsychology of Alzheimer's disease* (pp. 299–319). Oxford: Oxford University Press

Olson, I. R., Zhang, J. X., Mitchell, K. J., Johnson, M. K., Bloise, S. M., & Higgins, J. A. (2004). Preserved spatial memory over brief intervals in older adults. *Psychology and Aging, 19,* 310–317.

Paivio, A. (1971). *Imagery and verbal processes*. New York: Holt, Rinehart and Winston.
Paivio, A. (1986). *Mental representations. A dual coding approach*. New York: Oxford University.
Parra, M. A., Abrahams, S., Fabi, K., Logie, R., Luzzi, S., & Della Sala, S. (2009). Short term memory binding deficits in Alzheimer's Disease. *Brain, 132,* 1057–1066.
Parra, M. A., Abrahams, S., Logie, R. H., & Della Sala, S. (2009). Age and binding within-domain features in visual short term memory. *Neuroscience Letters, 449,* 1–5.
Parra, M. A., Abrahams, S., Logie, R. H., & Della Sala, S. (2010). Visual short-term memory binding in Alzheimer's disease and depression. *Journal of Neurology, 257,* 1160–1169.
Parra, M. A., Abrahams, S., Logie, R. H., Méndez, L. G., Lopera, F., & Della Sala, S. (2010). Visual short-term memory binding deficits in Familial Alzheimer's Disease. *Brain, 133,* 2702–2713.
Parra, M. A., Della Sala, S., Logie, R. H., & Abrahams, S. (2010). Selective impairment in visual short-term memory binding. *Cognitive Neuropsychology*, *26*, 583–605.
Phillips, W. A., & Christie, D. F. M. (1977a). Components of visual memory. *Quarterly Journal of Experimental Psychology, 29,* 117–133.
Phillips, W. A., & Christie, D. F. M. (1977b). Interference with visualization. *Quarterly Journal of Experimental Psychology, 29,* 637–650.
Pickering, S. J., Gathercole, S. E., Hall, S., & Lloyd, S. (2001). Development of memory for pattern and path: Further evidence for the fractionation of visual and spatial short-term memory. *Quarterly Journal of Experimental Psychology, 54A,* 397–420.
Piekema, C., Kessels, R. P., Mars, R. B., Petersson, K. M., & Fernandez, G. (2006). The right hippocampus participates in short-term memory maintenance of object-location associations. *NeuroImage, 33,* 374–382.
Quinn, J. G. (1994). Towards a clarification of spatial processing. *Quarterly Journal of Experimental Psychology, 47A,* 465–480.
Quinn, J., & McConnell, J. (1996). Irrelevant pictures in visual working memory. *Quarterly Journal of Experimental Psychology, 49A,* 200–215.
Quinn, J. G., & McConnell, J. (1999). Manipulation of interference in the passive visual store. *European Journal of Cognitive Psychology, 11,* 373–389.
Quinn, J., & McConnell, J. (2006). The interval for interference in conscious visual imagery. *Memory, 14,* 241–252
Quinn, J. G., & Ralston, G. E. (1986). Movement and attention in visual working memory. *The Quarterly Journal of Experimental Psychology, 38A,* 689–703.
Robertson, I. H., & Halligan, P. W. (1999). *Spatial neglect: A clinical handbook for diagnosis and treatment.* Hove, UK: Psychology Press.
Roskos-Ewoldsen, B., Intons-Peterson, M., & Anderson, R. (Eds.). (1993). *Imagery, creativity, and discovery: A cognitive approach* (pp. 39–76). Amsterdam: Elsevier.
Ross, E. D. (1980). Sensory-specific and fractional disorders of recent memory in man. I. Isolated loss of visual recent memory. *Archives of Neurology, 37,* 193–200.
Ruchkin, D. S., Johnson, R., Jr., Grafman, J., Canoune, H., & Ritter, W. (1997). Multiple visuospatial working memory buffers: Evidence from spatiotemporal patterns of brain activity. *Neuropsychologia, 35,* 195–209.
Rudkin, S. J., Pearson, D. G. & Logie., R. H. (2007). Executive processes in visual and spatial working memory tasks. *Quarterly Journal of Experimental Psychology, 60,* 79–100.

Rypma, B., Prabhakaran, V., Desmond, J. E., Glover, G. H., & Gabrieli, J. D. E. (1999). Load-dependent roles of frontal brain regions in the maintenance of working memory. *Neuroimage, 9,* 216–226.

Saito, S., Logie, R. H., Morita, A., & Law, A. (2008). Visual and phonological similarity effects in verbal immediate serial recall: A test with kanji materials. *Journal of Memory and Language, 59,* 1–17.

Salway, A. F. S., & Logie, R. H. (1995). Visuo-spatial working memory, movement control and executive demands. *British Journal of Psychology, 86,* 253–269.

Saults, J. S., & Cowan, N. (2007). A central capacity limit to the simultaneous storage of visual and auditory arrays in working memory. *Journal of Experimental Psychology: General, 136,* 663–684.

Sebastian, M. V., & Menor, J. (2006). Attentional dysfunction of the central executive in AD: Evidence from dual task and perseveration errors. *Cortex, 42,* 1015–1020.

Shah, P., & Miyake, A. (1996). The separability of working memory resources for spatial thinking and language processing: An individual differences approach. *Journal of Experimental Psychology: General, 125,* 4–27.

Shallice, T., & Warrington, E.K. (1970). Independent functioning of verbal memory stores: A neuropsychological study. *Quarterly Journal of Experimental Psychology, 22,* 261–273.

Smith, E. E., & Jonides, J. (1995). Working memory in humans: Neuropsychological evidence. In M. S. Gazzaniga (Ed.), *The cognitive neurosciences* (pp. 1009–1020). Cambridge, MA: MIT Press.

Smith, E. E., & Jonides, J. (1999). Storage and executive processes in the frontal lobes. *Science, 283,* 1657–1661.

Smyth, M. M., & Pendleton, L. R. (1989). Working memory for movements. *Quarterly Journal of Experimental Psychology, 41A,* 235–250.

Smyth, M. M., & Pendleton, L. R. (1990). Space and movement in working memory. *Quarterly Journal of Experimental Psychology, 42A,* 291–304.

Smyth, M. M., & Scholey, K. A. (1994). Characteristics of spatial memory span: Is there an analogy to the word length effect based on movement time? *Quarterly Journal of Experimental Psychology, 47A,* 91–117.

Tresch, M. C., Sinnamon, H. M., & Seamon, J. G. (1993). Double dissociation of spatial and object visual memory: evidence from selective interference in intact human subjects. *Neuropsychologia, 31,* 211–219.

Ungerleider, L. G., & Mishkin, M. (1982). Two cortical visual systems. In D. J. Ingle, M. A. Goodale, & R. J. W. Mansfield (Eds.), *Analysis of visual behavior* (pp. 549–586). Cambridge, MA: MIT Press.

Unsworth, N., Redick, T. S., Heitz, R. P., Broadway, J. M., & Engle, R. W. (2009). Complex working memory span tasks and higher-order cognition: A latent-variable analysis of the relationship between processing and storage. *Memory, 17,* 635–654.

Vallar, G. & Shallice, T. (1990). *Neuropsychological impairments of short-term memory.* Cambridge: Cambridge University Press.

Van der Meulen, M., Logie, R. H., & Della Sala, S. (2009). Selective interference with image retention and generation: Evidence for the workspace model. *Quarterly Journal of Experimental Psychology, 62,* 1568–1580.

Vandierendonck, A., Kemps, E., Fastame, M. C., & Szmalec, A. (2004). Working memory components of the Corsi blocks task. *British Journal of Psychology, 95,* 57–79.

Vergauwe, E., Barrouillet, P., & Camos, V. (2009). Visual and spatial working memory are not that dissociated after all: A time-based resource-sharing account. *Journal of Experimental Psychology-Learning Memory and Cognition, 35,* 1012–1028.

Vergauwe, E., Barrouillet, P., & Camos, V. (2010). Verbal and visuo-spatial working memory: A case for domain-general time-based resource sharing. *Psychological Science, 21,* 384–390.

Warrington, E. K., & Shallice, T. (1972). Neuropsychological evidence of visual storage in short-term memory tasks. *Quarterly Journal of Experimental Psychology, 24,* 30–40.

Wilson, J. T. L., Scott, J. H., & Power, K. G. (1987). Developmental differences in the span of visual memory for pattern. *British Journal of Developmental Psychology, 5,* 249–255.

Wolbers, T., Hegarty, M., Büchel, C., & Loomis, J. M. (2008). Spatial updating: How the brain keeps track of changing object locations during observer motion. *Nature Neuroscience, 11,* 1223–1230.

3 Spatial information in (visual) working memory

Hubert D. Zimmer and Heinrich R. Liesefeld

Introduction

We permanently process and transform many different kinds of mental representations. In some cases the representations are supported by external cues, in others the representations have to be temporarily maintained because the represented entities are no longer present. Usually therefore this mental work has a memory as well as an active transformation component. This is the reason why the term working memory was coined for the mental system(s) that provide these cognitive processes. Accordingly, different research traditions exist. Some people focus on temporary memory (often called short-term memory), which is frequently investigated in change detection tasks (e.g., Luck & Vogel, 1997), whereas others focus on processes (e.g., Oberauer, Süβ, Schulze, Wilhelm, & Wittmann, 2000), and still others focus on the division in structural components that are mainly defined by their specific content (e.g., Baddeley & Hitch, 1974). Specifically in the latter type of models usually a distinction between a verbal and a visual subcomponent can be found. Visual working memory is the component that represents and transforms visually perceived information. Additionally, within visual working memory processing of visual and spatial information is frequently distinguished. However, it is rarely specified what spatial information is and how it is represented.

In this chapter we make an attempt to make up for these shortcomings. We analyse the types of spatial information that are processed in different working memory tasks. We start with the Corsi Blocks Task (CBT), which is probably the most frequently used task in research on visual working memory. In this task participants have to reproduce a sequence of spatial locations. We continue by looking at other types of spatial memory tasks, for example, memory for object locations or patterns. We show that different types of spatial information are processed in these tasks. We will demonstrate that neither the modality of a stimulus (e.g., auditory or visual) alone, nor the task demands (e.g., memory for a location or a sequence of locations) alone, nor specific characteristics of the information (e.g., static versus dynamic) alone determine the way visuospatial information is processed. The type of processing is not solely a consequence of the external stimulus. In contrast, it is the way participants mentally encode spatial information in order to solve the task. We suggest distinguishing between two types of spatial mental representations: egocentric spatial representations and spatial configurations. Egocentric spatial representations encode locations as coordinates relative to the observer. In contrast, spatial configurations encode spatial locations as relations between perceptual entities very similar to (global) shapes. Whether egocentric spatial representations or configurations are used we consider as decisive for the effects that are observed when spatial information is processed. The former should be the used if a process addresses individual locations (e.g., in spatially guided actions); the latter should be used if processing spatial relations between items or object parts suffices. Egocentric processing is assigned to the dorsal stream starting at the occipital and going to the parietal cortex – its core element may be the parietal window (Byrne, Becker, & Burgess, 2007) – and configural processing is assigned to the ventral stream starting at the occipital and going to the lateral-occipital and inferior temporal cortex. We suggest that the distinction between these two types of representations may provide a suitable principle for analysing different spatial working memory tasks and their neural underpinnings.

Spatial information in the multicomponent model of working memory

Baddeley (1986) discussed the visuospatial sketchpad as the visual subcomponent of working memory. It was mainly seen as a spatial device, because visuospatial tracking (Baddeley, Grant, Wight, & Thomson, 1975) as well as auditory tracking (tracking blindfolded a moving sound source) impaired memory (Baddeley & Lieberman, 1980). At that time the Brooks Matrix Task was a widely used working memory task. Participants had to remember an imaginary path through a 4 × 4 matrix that was generated on verbal commands. This path would normally be considered spatial. Following on from this Logie (1989) suggested differentiating the visual from the spatial component, which he later called the visual cache and the inner scribe. The visual cache is the visual working memory component that is 'passive and contains information about static visual patterns' (Logie, 1995, p. 2) including colour, shape, and brightness. A typical visual task is the pattern span in which participants have to memorize a pattern of randomly filled cells in matrices with increasing set size (cf. Della Sala, Gray, Baddeley, Allamano, & Wilson, 1999). The inner scribe is the spatial working memory component that 'retains dynamic information about movement and movement sequences, and is linked with the control of physical actions' (Logie, 1995, p. 2). Movement is used in a broad sense making reference to physical as well as to imagined movement (cf. p. 78). At the neuronal level the visual cache was assigned to the ventral stream ('what'-path) and the inner scribe to the dorsal stream ('where'-path).

Focusing on dynamic information and movement the CBT became the predominant spatial working memory task. In the original CBT the individual is shown nine cubes arranged in an unsystematic fashion affixed to cardboard (cf. Berch, Krikorian, & Huha, 1998, for a review). The experimenter taps a sequence of cubes and the subject is required to reproduce this sequence. Because blocks shall be tapped in the correct sequence, the representation needs to include the ordinal temporal information of which cube followed which one. Increasingly long sequences are tapped until the limit of the subject's performance is reached. The individual limit (the spatial span) typically lies between four and eight (e.g., Smyth & Scholey, 1994). Modern variants of this task present the stimuli on computer screens, cubes are replaced with squares or discs, and different types of arrays and timings are used. This can change the affordances of the task drastically. For example, cubes are usually visible during retention. They therefore provide external spatial cues. Hence, coarse categorical spatial information is sufficient for rehearsal. In contrast, when the array is erased during retention, more precise spatial coordinates are needed to refresh locations. A variant of the CBT is the 'Dot Task' (e.g., Saint-Aubin, Tremblay, & Jalbert, 2007). The procedure and affordances of these tasks are so similar that we treat all of them as versions of the CBT. All these tasks have in common the fact that a sequence of locations has to be reproduced and we therefore subsume both tasks under the heading of remembering spatial sequences. In order to find out how such sequences are remembered, we first analyse memory in CBTs more carefully and then we turn our attention to static spatial information.

Remembering sequences of spatial locations

Eye movements and preparation of eye movements as spatial rehearsal mechanisms

A first plausible candidate for retaining sequential spatial information is eye movements. By eye-tracking it was shown that items overtly rehearsed (i.e., focused in the order consistent with presentation) are better recalled than those not rehearsed (Guérard, Tremblay, & Saint-Aubin, 2009; Tremblay, Saint-Aubin, & Jalbert, 2006b). In contrast to this, Pearson and Sahraie (2003) did not find any evidence for consistent eye movements during a 5 s retention interval. Furthermore, they observed clear above chance memory performance even in the absence of such eye movements as did Guérard et al. (2009) and Tremblay et al. (2006b). Hence, eye movements might be helpful for memory but they cannot be a necessary condition for spatiotemporal short-term memory.

On the other hand, it was shown that concurrent voluntary saccadic eye movements can impair memory in CBTs. It was already observed in the 1980s that spatial memory (the Brooks Task) can be impaired by eye movements (reported in Baddeley, 1986 and later published by Postle, Idzikowski, Della Sala, Logie, & Baddeley, 2006). Similar results were reported for the CBT (e.g., Hale, Myerson, Rhee, Weiss, & Abrams, 1996; Lawrence, Myerson, Oonk, & Abrams, 2001; Pearson & Sahraie, 2003). In Tremblay et al.'s study (2006b), memory performance was better if overt eye movements were allowed. When eye movements were suppressed memory performance was reduced to the level of recall that was observed without overt rehearsal with eye movements, which however, was still high (about .45 for a 7-item list). This suggests that overt eye movements can support memory but that they are not necessary. However, it does not seem to be movement *per se* that impairs memory because reflexive movement of the eyes induced by postrotational nystagmus does not impair memory (as reported in Baddeley, 1986). It is active movement that causes additional memory impairments. Pearson and Sahraie (2003) compared several eye-movement conditions. They observed strongest interference with voluntary eye movements with open eyes (–60 %), followed by pursuit eye movements and voluntary eye movements with closed eyes (–40 %), and they got the lowest interference effects with covert attention shifts and spatial tapping (–20%). The effect of open eyes is not an effect of additional visual input. Watching a moving background with holding eyes still had no effect (Idzikowsky cited in Baddeley, 1986) nor did attending to colours (Pearson & Sahraie, 2003). Hence, intentional overt eye movements seem to influence spatial memory in the CBT by different mechanisms.

There are three reasonable explanations for these interference effects. First, eye movements with open eyes cause an updating of spatial locations and this impairs spatial representations (Golomb, Chun, & Mazer, 2008). Second, voluntary eye movements need cognitive control and this interferes with voluntary rehearsal. Third, a voluntary eye movement makes it necessary to specify the landing position and this may happen within the same spatial representation that is used in the CBT. The spatial information may be represented in the same system (supposedly the superior colliculus, cf. Kastner & Ungerleider, 2000) that is also responsible for programming eye movements. Theeuwes, Olivers, and Chizk (2005) reported evidence for this (see also Postle, Chapter 5, this volume).

Theeuwes and colleagues (2005) monitored participants' saccades between two points. Remembering a location close to the ideal (i.e., straight) trajectory of a saccade caused the eyes to curve away from this location. The authors assumed that in order to avoid a movement to the remembered location instead of to the correct target, this position has to be suppressed during execution of the saccade. Further evidence comes from the memory-guided saccade task that directly relates oculomotor planning to spatial working memory. Subjects (monkeys in most cases) execute a saccade to a position that was presented some time (e.g., 10 s) earlier. Studies employing this task suggest that neural structures involved in the control of eye movements, such as frontal and supplementary eye fields, contribute to memory. For example, Curtis, Rao, and D'Esposito (2004) found frontal eye field (FEF) and intraparietal sulcus (IPS) activity to be positively correlated with the accuracy (measured continually in degrees of visual angle) of the subsequent saccade. It is therefore assumed that the network that controls oculomotor activity also contributes to (spatial) working memory (see Curtis, 2006, for a review). Theeuwes, Belopolsky, and Olivers (2009) summarized the current knowledge on brain structures involved in this network. A preocolumotor attentional map (probably in the IPS) represents the target location, which serves as input to the saccade map (most likely the superior colliculus) where the final programming takes place, and an inhibitory control system (dorsolateral prefrontal cortex and FEF) causes inhibition so that the movement is delayed. If a programme for an eye movement indeed constitutes the memory entry for one specific location, then it is only natural to assume that a sequence of positions is represented by programming a sequence of eye movements (e.g., Logie, 1995; Pearson & Sahraie, 2003;

Tremblay, Saint-Aubin, & Jalbert, 2006b). If eye movements *per se* are not relevant, but instead it is the plan for the movement, this would also explain why overt eye movements are not of major importance in retaining information in CBTs.

However, we want to point to a critical flaw that is often overlooked when spatial memory mechanisms are reduced to the oculomotor system. Humans represent not only spatial information in their field of view but also locations outside of this field, for example, locations behind the observer, and these locations are remembered. As we will discuss in more detail later, auditory spatial information seems to be maintained by the same memory system as visual spatial information (Lehnert & Zimmer, 2008a). Representing information outside the visual field, for example, behind the observer's back, in some motoric way, would impose the need for storing whole sequences of coordinated body, limb, and eye movements. We consider this quite implausible. We therefore do not assume that oculomotor programmes are the general means to represent spatial information in working memory. On the contrary, a commonly used representation of spatial locations also provides input to the oculomotor system – specifying the landing position – and it is this spatial representation that is also used in working memory tasks. During the preparation for voluntary eye movements, additional components get activated or the same components are differently activated in order to control the movement and this additionally influences memory performances.

Covert shifts of spatial attention as rehearsal mechanism

Another mechanism of spatial memory is seen in focusing spatial attention. Several authors (Awh & Jonides, 2001; Awh, Jonides, & Reuter-Lorenz, 1998; Awh, Vogel, & Oh, 2006; Postle, Awh, Jonides, Smith, & D'Esposito, 2004; Smyth & Scholey, 1994) assumed shifts of attention being the rehearsal mechanism in spatial tasks. Awh and colleagues (1998) found that retaining the position of a letter improved the processing of a stimulus that was presented at that location during retention, that maintaining the identity of the letter did not cause memory enhancement, and that orientating attention away from this location impaired memory. This indicates that during retention of locations spatial attention was directed to the position of the letter (cf. Awh, Armstrong, & Moore, 2006, for a review). Further support for this idea can be seen in the interference effects of shifts of spatial attention away from target locations. Lawrence, Myerson, and Abrams (2004) showed that attention shifts towards symbols presented to the left and right of fixation selectively disturbed a spatial sequential but not a verbal sequential task (see also Guérard et al., 2009; Tremblay et al., 2006b). Accordingly, the observed interference effects by eye movements may not be caused by the execution of an active movement but by covarying variables, for example, detailed focusing of spatial attention (see also Quinn, 2008). Indeed, tracking a moving sound source interfered with a spatial Brooks Matrix Task even when the subjects were blindfolded (Baddeley & Lieberman, 1980) and spatial span was disrupted by shifts of attention in the absence of any eye movements (Smyth & Scholey, 1996).

The same mechanism would explain why other types of movements interfere with spatial working memory. A frequently used task is spatial tapping in which the hand has to be moved across a number of spatial positions, for example, across a matrix, around a shape, across keys, etc. In many experiments such a spatial movement impaired spatial working memory (Farmer, Berman, & Fletcher, 1986; Hale, et al., 1996; Lawrence, et al., 2001; Logie & Marchetti, 1991; Morris, 1987; Quinn & Ralston, 1986; Salway & Logie, 1995; Smyth, Pearson, & Pendleton, 1988; Smyth & Pendleton, 1989; Smyth & Waller, 1994; Vandierendonck, Kemps, Fastame, & Szmalec, 2004; Zimmer, Speiser, & Seidler, 2003). When the spatial component was removed and spatial tapping was changed to one-place tapping (repeatedly pushing a button), no interference was observed any more (Hegarty, Mayer, Kriz, & Keehner, 2005; Smyth & Pelky, 1992). Similarly, movement without a pointing component (patterned finger movements or squeezing a tube) did not interfere with spatial span tasks (Smyth, et al., 1988; Smyth & Pendleton, 1989, 1990) although it did impair motor span tasks. This shows that the interference is not caused by the execution itself but by the necessity to process spatial information. Because focusing of attention is a prerequisite for spatially guided motor actions an interference at the level of spatial attention would be a parsimonious explanation of these effects (see Lawrence et al., 2004, for a similar reasoning). However, because spatial movements and also spatial attention have to be directed to specific ('landing') locations, an equally parsimonious explanation would be assuming that interference occurs at the level of spatial selection or spatial processing within a general spatial representation system.

The importance of sequential information for the CBT

For the CBT subjects need to remember a temporal sequence of locations and consequentially not only spatial but also sequential information is essential for correct memory. Some researchers therefore focused on temporal instead of sequential information when analysing performances in the CBT. Jones, Farrand, Stuart, and Morris (1995) found a pattern of serial position errors in a spatial span task with clear primacy and recency effects similar to those found in sequential-verbal tasks (cf. also Meiser & Klauer, 1999; Parmentier, Elford, & Maybery, 2005; Smyth & Scholey, 1996; Tremblay, Parmentier, Guérard, Nicholls, & Jones, 2006a). Parmentier, Andrés, Elford, and Jones (2006) additionally observed that spatiotemporal memory is preferably grouped according to temporal clusters and not spatial ones if either of these features can be used to organize the to-be-remembered sequence (see Parmentier, Chapter 4, this volume). This suggests that besides spatial and order information temporal information (its timing) is (or can be) also memorized in the CBT. An open question however, is whether the temporal aspect originates from the spatial representation underlying the CBT or from the output phase. If the individual items are addressed in a 'rhythmic' manner the output process itself can stamp a temporo-hierarchical structure on purely spatial information.

However, Jones and colleagues provided evidence that sequential information is of more general relevance (Jones et al., 1995). They showed that both verbal and spatial sequential tasks are disrupted by the same spatial and verbal secondary tasks. The important feature of the secondary tasks was their 'changing state' characteristic, i.e., that (in the motor secondary task) not only one movement, but a series of movements and (in the verbal secondary task) not only one letter but a series (e.g., a–g) of letters had to be repeated. They found interference even if participants only passively perceived a changing state sequence. These results indicate that spatial and verbal working memory share one system for representing sequential information (see also Depoorter & Vandierendonck, 2009; Vandierendonck & Szmalec, Chapter 1, this volume). However, Meiser and Klauer (1999) did not find that articulatory suppression causes stronger memory impairments with changing states. They found changing states to increase the disruptive effect of tapping during encoding only. This selective interference effect is suggestive of a contribution from a modality-specific component. The interference reported by Jones et al. (1995) might be traced back to the central executive, which is active during encoding but less so during maintenance of sequential information. Support for this can be seen in a number of studies that demonstrated an interference effect at an abstract level. Klauer and Stegmaier (1997) found interference between spatial span and pitch discrimination, Fisk and Sharp (2003) showed interference by random letter generation, and Vandierendonck et al. (2004) by random interval generation. In some way general purpose control processes seem to be needed in the CBT. The contribution of central executive functions to the CBT is also supported by the observation that performances in this task correlate with performances on a number of executive tests (Thompson et al., 2006).

One process that contributes to this relationship is binding. Information about order is possible only in conjunction with item information. Considering the ordering of something implies that there is something unique about it that has a certain position in time. Each object or event needs a feature in addition to its temporal position to be perceived as an individual, be it a perceptual property or just its position in space (cf. Zimmer et al., 2003). Therefore, the results of Jones et al. (1995), Rudkin, Pearson, and Logie (2007), as well as Depoorter and Vandierendonck (2009) might be caused by the necessity of binding features whenever a spatial sequence has to be retained. That attention is necessary to bind object features has been discussed theoretically (Treisman, 2006) and there is empirical evidence in favour of it (e.g., Elsley & Parmentier, 2009; Fougnie & Marois, 2009; Hyun, Woodman, & Luck, 2009; Saiki & Miyatsuji, 2007; Treisman, 2006). Unfortunately counterevidence has also been reported (e.g., Allen, Baddeley, & Hitch, 2006; Gajewski & Brockmole, 2006; Johnson, Hollingworth, & Luck, 2008). The existence of different types of binding that differ in their dependence on attentive processing is a probable reason for this discrepancy (see Zimmer, 2008; Zimmer & Ecker, 2010 for a discussion). If this is true, attention may not be necessary for the explicit binding of location and item information although it is probably beneficial. Consequentially, interference at the level of central attention might (partially) be caused by an impairment of binding location and object information.

The contribution of visual information to the CBT

In the CBT, items that mark the locations usually do not differ visually. Because participants have to remember only locations, at first view, a spatial span task does not include visual aspects. However, participants can nevertheless build up a representation that is in some sense visual. Participants can represent the configuration that the target locations would depict if presented simultaneously. People are able to integrate complex visual information (a map) from sequentially presented picture fragments (Zimmer, 2004). Accordingly, not only the number of locations but also their configuration (the traced path) influences memory (Kemps, 1999; Smirni, Villardita, & Zappala, 1983). Kemps (2001) found that performance in spatial span is influenced by structuring principles of the path, described by the sequence of positions, like symmetry (around vertical, horizontal, or 45° axes), repetition (part of the path was repeated in translated locations), and continuation (absence of crossings). Parmentier et al. (2005) showed that path length also had an effect, and that the number of intersections in a path and the average angle (the steeper the worse) of its turns (with path length kept constant) influence the performance independently (cf. also Busch, Farrell, Lisdahl-Medina, & Krikorian, 2005). If the paths in spatial span tasks were only coded as a sequence of separate shifts of attention or eye movements – i.e., if exclusively the current position cues the respective following movement – subjects should not even recognize intersections or angles. They should only represent separate trajectories connecting two (temporally) adjacent points. The configuration effects therefore show that positions are not remembered solely in dyads representing only pairs of starting and landing positions.

These effects of visual characteristics of the trajectory on memory performance could be explained by assuming that participants (additionally) built up a representation of the spatial configuration – like a curve connecting the blocks. An additional marker would indicate the start and/or end positions (Parmentier et al., 2005). If no crossings exist and the mapping of the configuration to external spatial locations is unambiguous, a configuration can be sufficient to reproduce the sequence of individual locations. Therefore, even in a typical spatial task like the CBT, visual features (the configuration) can be encoded in addition. However, please note, in order to address individual locations, e.g., during rehearsal or recall, the locations must be specified in egocentric coordinates again.

Multiple resources (can) contribute to performances in the CBT

At this point we can summarize that several components (spatial attention, oculomotor, configural, temporal) are relevant for temporary memory of sequential spatial information. These representations (and also some others such as, for example, conceptual or verbal information, which we did not discuss here) can be used in parallel. It is very likely that different participants behave differently depending on their habits or personal disposition. But even within the same individual, different types of representations may be used dependent on tasks demands and parameters, for example, the available encoding time and number of items. Participants may even strategically use multiple encodings in order to enhance their performances. For example, there may be a tendency to use additional representations if the preferred system is overloaded in trials with higher set sizes or if it is (going to be) disturbed by a secondary task (Dent & Smyth, 2005; Postma & De Haan, 1996).

This possibility has already been considered by other researchers. For example, Rudkin et al. (2007) noted that many (if not all) tasks will require an interaction between several components, even if one is utilized to a greater extent than another. Parmentier et al. (2005) supposed that a dynamic representation of a path is possible beside a static configuration and that the difficulty of the task and/or the kind of stimulus influences which of these types of encoding is used. For example, Bor and colleagues found higher performances for sequences describing structured paths than for those describing unstructured ones and prefrontal activity was higher in the first case (Bor, Duncan, Wiseman, & Owen, 2003). This additional prefrontal activity may be a correlate of recoding the sequential spatial information into a static configuration. This and many of the results cited above reveal that the representation underlying retention in the CBT is not a unitary one. It depends on the type of information that participants are processing. The representation is induced but not determined by the stimulus and the type of task. The task is therefore open to strategic recoding and this possibility is one reason for the reported correlations between performances in Corsi and central executive tasks (Thompson et al., 2006).

What then makes the CBT special and different from a visual task? We assume that the most important difference is the one between information on individual locations and configural information. The former represents spatial locations in the environment relative to the observer. It is therefore egocentric. Each location can directly be addressed by its spatial coordinates. The egocentric representation is used for the purpose of planning actions, i.e., it represents spatial locations as goals for movement (Andersen, Snyder, Bradley, & Xing, 1997), which can be an eye movement, a pointing gesture, or a shift of spatial attention. We assume that this is the locus of the spatial interference effects. In contrast, the spatial information encoded in configural representations abstracts from egocentric coordinates. It represents spatial information as spatial relations between items independent from their actual position relative to the observer. Because spatial information is only implicitly represented in a configuration, it has to be transformed into an egocentric representation, if individual locations have to be processed. We will come back to this distinction in the closing discussion.

Other types of working memory tasks that use spatial information

The CBT is by no means the only task that has been used to investigate spatial working memory. Another classical task looks at memory for the locations of individual objects (e.g., Postma & De Haan, 1996). In this context it was considered that participants make use of two types of information: the information on locations and the information about which object was presented there. This is the already mentioned distinction between 'what' and 'where' information and it also points to the necessity of binding. Accordingly, some researchers tried to identify the neural structures that represent these two types of information. Mecklinger and Pfeifer (1996) analysed event-related potentials during the retention interval; presenting a set of different geometric objects in their object task and a configuration of squares in their spatial task. During maintenance in the object condition a negative slow wave was observed over the prefrontal cortex that increased with set size. In contrast, in the spatial task (detecting a change of location in the layout of identical stimuli) a comparable slow wave was observed over the parietal cortex. With meaningless material again a parietal negativity was found in the spatial task, but now a parietal-occiptal posivity was observed in the object task (Bosch, Mecklinger, & Friederici, 2001). This demonstrates that different neural networks contribute to visual and spatial tasks, and that very likely it is the parietal region that represents spatial information. Importantly, in these studies static spatial information was used. Thus, not only dynamic information is processed within the dorsal stream but also static location information.

If the parietal region represents static spatial information the question arises whether this is confined to visual input. Also sound sources have a location and it is therefore possible that spatial locations in the environment have a common coding in spatial working memory (Lehnert & Zimmer, 2008b). In order to investigate this we presented visual and auditory objects in a spatial working memory task (pictures and natural sounds of objects). We observed identical performances in modality-pure and mixed lists, which demonstrates that additional items in a different modality cause the same memory load as items in the same modality (Lehnert & Zimmer, 2006). A comparable result was observed by Saults and Cowan (2007). In a further study we analysed slow potentials in a spatial working memory task presenting pictures and sounds in modality-pure lists. We observed load effects over occipitoparietal regions during maintenance, and these effects were almost the same for both modalities (Lehnert & Zimmer, 2008a). Similarly, in a functional magnetic resonance imaging (fMRI) study, Arnott, Grady, Hevenor, Graham, and Alain (2005) found that if locations of sounds had to be memorized they observed activations in the parietal cortex similar to those found for visual objects, and Sestieri et al. (2006) observed task-related activity in the right intraparietal sulcus if a cross-modal match of locations was required. These results suggest that parietal neural structures represent environmental locations and provide a spatial working memory independent of the input modality.

Effects of spatial memory were even observed in change detection tasks in which spatial location were irrelevant. Participants had to detect whether or not a specific feature of the stimulus has changed from S1 to S2. Changing the objects' positions prolonged response times even though objects' locations were task irrelevant (Santa, 1977; Zimmer, 1998). Jiang, Olson, and Chun (2000) observed that this is an effect of configuration and not of the absolute position. A change of configuration impaired memory, but if the absolute position was changed only and the configuration was preserved memory performance was not impaired. The authors concluded that spatial relations between objects are represented as a configuration even if spatial information is not relevant. A comparable result had already been reported by Phillips (1974) who observed that shifts of spatial configurations that preserved the relative spatial relations but changed the absolute (egocentric) spatial locations did not impair short-term memory. Also Boduroglu and Shah (2009) observed that participants have a bias classifiying displays with a matching global configuration as 'same' independent of the match of the absolute locations of objects. We recently demonstrated that this effect is not based on a low-level visual image but rather on a global representation of the spatial configuration (Zimmer & Lehnert, 2006).

1. Strong visual interference between S1 and S2 did not reduce the negative effect of changed configurations.
2. The effect even occured without any shared visual features (words were presented during study and pictures during testing, and vice versa).
3. The mismatch effect was graded according to the similarity of the configurations of locations (identical < shrinking/enlargment < rotation < new configuration). Based on these results we suggested that the spatial configuration of objects is represented and stored in (long-term) memory like a shape. However, it is not an abstract verbal description, because the effect of a configuration mismatch occured similarly with easily to-be-named as well as with arbitrary configurations (Zimmer & Lehnert, 2006). We assume that configurations are automatically processed during perception and maintained without the necessity of a continous refresh. At the time of testing this information can be reactivated and the pattern can be completed even if the former pattern of locations is only partially represented in working memory. Direct support for this can be seen in the observation that additional visual input during maintenance did not impair memory for spatial configurations or patterns (Avons & Sestieri, 2005; Zimmer et al., 2003).

Another prominent spatial task is the mental rotation task (Shepard & Metzler, 1971). In this task participants are required to compare two stimuli with each other and to decide whether they depict the same object (figure) irrespective of rotation. The two stimuli have an angular disparity that varies between 0° and ± 180° and in the case of a mismatch one is additionally mirror-reversed along its main axis. The response times are almost a linear function of the angle of rotation (cf. Shepard & Podgorny, 1978). During mental rotation activity in the parietal cortex specifically the IPS was observed (Gauthier, Hayword, Tarr, Anderson, Skudlarski, & Gore, 2002; Harris, Egan, Sonkkila, Tochon-Danguy, Paxinos, & Watson, 2000; Just, Carpenter, Maguire, Diwadkar, & McMains, 2001) and transcranial magnetic stimulation (TMS) of these areas demonstrated that they are functionally relevant for mental rotation (Harris & Miniussi, 2003; Zacks, Gilliam, & Ojemann, 2003). In electrophysiological studies negative slow waves were observed during mental rotation over parietal regions and they increased with the amount of rotation (Heil, Bajric, Rösler, & Hennighausen, 1996; Rösler, Heil, Bajric, Pauls, & Hennighausen, 1995). These data clearly support a contribution of the parietal region to mental rotation even though they do not reveal how a stimulus is rotated.

Finally, tasks that require transformations or comparisons of spatial information also activate parietal regions. In the clock task, for example, two different times are verbally presented to participants. They are asked to decide which of these translates to the larger angle between the hands of analogue clocks. In this task, the IPS was specifically active (see Trojano, Linden, & Formisano, 2004) and it was also shown by repeating TMS that this structure is functionally relevant to the task (Formisano et al., 2002; Sack et al., 2002). Similarly, scanning of mental maps activated the parietal cortex (see Mazard, Tzourio-Mazoyer, & Crivello, 2004, for a review). Even during the construction of mental models in spatial reasoning tasks activation in the superior and inferior parietal cortex has been found (Knauff, Mulack, Kassubek, Salih, & Greenlee, 2002).

Obviously the parietal cortex was found active in many spatial tasks no matter whether the required spatial information was dynamic or static. Hence, this feature cannot be critical for the assignment of a spatial task to the inner scribe (dorsal stream). A recent interference study supports this view (van der Meulen, Logie, & Della Sala, 2009). Spatial tapping, which is considered as a spatial suppressor task, impaired a retention task (remembering case, identity, and order of upper and lower case letters) that was classified as visual in other contexts (Logie, Della Sala, Wynn, & Baddeley, 2000). It therefore is a surprise that a spatial suppressor task impairs this memory. Interestingly in this paper the authors highlight the distinction between image generation and visuospatial working memory instead of potential differences between static and dynamic spatial information within visuospatial working memory. This interpretation is in line with our view on these two types of tasks.

Types of tasks and types of spatial representations in working memory

Obviously, visual input can vary along a continuum from a basically visual condition (e.g., a silhouette of a triangle) to a spatial sequential condition (e.g., a sequence of dots that define the borders of an imaginary triangle when overlaid) (Cornoldi & Vecchi, 2003; see also Cornoldi & Mammarella, Chapter 6, this volume). However, on the one hand, even the triangular silhouette – although a visual shape – provides spatial information, for example, the orientation of the triangle's edge or the locations of its corners in the egocentric space of the observer, on the other hand, configural encoding of a spatial sequence provides visual information. The term 'spatial' therefore has many different aspects. It can refer to spatial relationships between objects or to the observer, it can refer to simultaneously or sequentially presented information, and it is sometimes related to movement and sometimes to static stimuli. Spatial information can furthermore be provided in different frames of reference. It can be encoded in object space, for example, relative to the object's envelope (inside the object's boundary), its principal axis (side-connected), or to other objects and external reference points (landmarks). However, it can also be encoded relative to the observer in an egocentric coordinate system.

Burgess (2008) discussed the fact that spatial information is represented in multiple parallel reference frames. Early visual information should have a retinotopic organization, auditory input a head-centred one, and actions represent the appropriate body-centred coordinates. Higher-order spatial information is considered either as egocentric representation relative to the subject or as allocentric information relative to environmental cues; which is also relevant for working memory. Byrne, Becker, and Burgess (2007) suggested that a 'parietal window' provides a head-centred egocentric spatial representation that is used in short-term memory, but also in mental imagery, planning, and navigation. The parietal window strongly resembles the visual buffer as it was discussed by Kosslyn (1994). Besides the parietal window, the parahippocampus and hippocampus should provide (in their terminology allocentric) spatial information on the environment that is also the basis of long-term memory. The content of the parietal window is generated from a combination of perceptual input and long-term memory. Similarly, we assume that configural information provided by the spatial layout of objects can be reconstructed from representations in long-term memory. Our analysis of types of information used in the CBT can be mapped on the distinction proposed by Byrne and colleagues (2007). Spatial information in the narrower sense is egocentric spatial information processed within the parietal window (in the dorsal stream); in contrast, (allocentric) spatial information represented in patterns and configurations is processed in the ventral stream, together with other types of visual information, such as colour. This implies a distinction between spatial tasks that are assigned to the inner scribe and visual cache instead of a distinction between dynamic and static spatial information.

Both types of spatial information are investigated in visual working memory tasks. A pattern span is distinguished from a spatial span (Corsi). The former is considered as visual, the latter as spatial (Logie, 1995). Support for this distinction is seen in a double dissociation between type of task (Corsi and pattern span) and type of interference (spatial and visual) (Della Sala et al., 1999; see also Logie, Chapter 2, this volume; Hamilton, Chapter 7, this volume). However, stimuli employed in the pattern span and the CBT are often quite similar. In both tasks a pattern of filled matrix cells may be presented and each is defined by its location. The difference between the tasks is their demands. In the CBT, the sequence of used locations has to be reproduced, in the pattern span task it is their configuration. We assume that this difference causes different kinds of spatial encoding. In the CBT individual locations within a configuration have to be selected as target locations for shifts of spatial attention during rehearsal or as landing positions for pointing. The configuration is (usually) not sufficient because due to the need to order information each location has to be individuated. It is therefore necessary to represent each target location in coordinates that can be used by a process that addresses the specific location. For this purpose an egocentric coordinate system is probably needed. In contrast, in the pattern task it is sufficient to process locations like defining a configuration. The spatial relations within a group of filled neighbouring cells provide a local configuration (or shape). These local configurations can again be spatially related to each other forming a hierarchy of spatially arranged patterns. The resulting representation is similar to structural descriptions as discussed in the context of shape perception (Palmer, 1977) or object identification. For example, in the recognition by components theory of object identification it is assumed that spatial relationships between geons (primitive three-dimensional forms) are encoded during identification, for example, a geon is on top of or to the side of another (Biederman, 1987). Consequentially, early visual information processes already provide information on spatial relationships between elements. If patterns are represented in this way they represent spatial information but individual locations are not made explicit in egocentric space. Space is only encoded relative to other units of the percept. We assume that it is this feature that distinguishes the pattern span task from the CBT and not the distinction between static and dynamic information. However, please note that information can be recoded. In the CBT locations can additionally be encoded as configuration, and in the pattern task a location-based scanning strategy can be used as a rehearsal mechanism.

Some general conclusions

What follows from this point of view for designing an adequate model of spatial (visual) working memory? We assume that the distinction between individual spatial locations in an egocentric space and representations of spatial configurations representing spatial relationships between units is central for such a model. We can stay with the terms inner scribe and visual cache, but the difference between these two is not the one between dynamic and static spatial information. We would assign tasks that need representations of individual (egocentric) locations to the inner scribe, and tasks in which configurations are sufficient to the visual cache. Hence, we still distinguish two components, but the relevant feature is different.

However, we prefer speaking of different types of spatial representations instead of stores. We do not assume that an additional device is necessary for the purpose of storage, it can be the same part systems that are used for visual encoding (Zimmer, 2008). Additionally, we do not restrict these representations to visual input but we assume that other modalities also provide input, at least to the egocentric spatial coordinate system. Interference occurs at the level of these representations. The way participants represent a stimulus and the task demands determine which kind of representation is used, in which process, and therefore which effects are observed.

Spatial coordinate tasks are handled by an egocentrically organized system, probably the parietal window. In the parietal window spatial information is explicitly represented. Each individual location can be addressed by its egocentric coordinate, and spatial transformation processes are operating on this representation. Also spatial attention uses this representation. Active rehearsal of the CBT happens in the parietal window and target locations for spatially guided actions are also processed there. That all these tasks use spatial coordinates is very likely the reason for the known interference effects. They occur if processes compete for selection of locations in the coordinate space. The parietal window is probably also the workspace for the generation of detailed visual images (see also Quinn, 2008). This is the reason why imagery main tasks are impaired by spatial secondary tasks.

In contrast, if it is sufficient to process a spatial configuration, the parietal window is not necessarily used. The same is true for perceptual features such as colours. No or less interference is therefore observed if these tasks are combined with 'spatial coordinate' tasks. Spatial configuration is encoded during object and pattern analysis and these patterns are temporarily available in memory – even without active rehearsal. If the pattern was not kept active in memory, it can be reactivated at testing using the to-be-judged pattern as a retrieval cue. Because of its relational quality, information on the configuration can be used to fill in information that is missed. This is the reason why visual input during retention did not impair memory for patterns (Avons & Sestieri, 2005; Zimmer et al., 2003). However, if individual coordinates of items included in a spatial configuration have to be processed, the parietal window must make spatial information on coordinates explicit. This, for example, may be the case when a detailed high-resolution image of visual information is demanded. Correspondingly, now even a visual task can be impaired by so called spatial secondary tasks (van der Meulen et al., 2009).

In other words, the type of spatial information that is demanded by a task (or is habitually processed) is the key concept for understanding spatial working memory. The way of processing – accessing individual coordinates or spatial configuration – determines which type of spatial representation has to be addressed. Because spatial coordinate and configural information is provided by different neural structures – the dorsal and ventral path respectively – these two ways of processing specify the neural network that we expect to find active in a visual working memory task.

References

Allen, R. J., Baddeley, A. D., & Hitch, G. J. (2006). Is the binding of visual features in working memory resource-demanding? *Journal of Experimental Psychology: General, 135,* 298–313.

Andersen, R. A., Snyder, L. H., Bradley, D. C., & Xing, J. (1997). Multimodal representation of space in the posterior parietal cortex and its use in planning movements. *Annual Review of Neuroscience, 20,* 303–330.

Arnott, S. R., Grady, C. L., Hevenor, S. J., Graham, S., & Alain, C. (2005). The functional organization of auditory working memory as revealed by fMRI. *Journal of Cognitive Neuroscience, 17,* 819–831.

Avons, S. E., & Sestieri, C. (2005). Dynamic visual noise: No interference with visual short-term memory or the construction of visual images. *European Journal of Cognitive Psychology, 17,* 405–424.

Awh, E., Armstrong, K. M., & Moore, T. (2006). Visual and oculomotor selection: Links causes and implications for spatial attention. *Trends in Cognitive Sciences, 10,* 124–130.

Awh, E., & Jonides, J. (2001). Overlapping mechanisms of attention and spatial working memory. *Trends in Cognitive Sciences, 5,* 119–126.

Awh, E., Jonides, J., & Reuter-Lorenz, P. A. (1998). Rehearsal in spatial working memory. *Journal of Experimental Psychology: Human Perception and Performance, 24,* 780–790.

Awh, E., Vogel, E. K., & Oh, S.-H. (2006). Interactions between attention and working memory. *Neuroscience, 139,* 201–208.

Baddeley, A. D. (1986). *Working memory*. Oxford: Oxford University.

Baddeley, A. D., Grant, S., Wight, E., & Thomson, N. (1975). Imagery and visual working memory. In P. M. Rabbit & S. Dornic (Eds.), *Attention and performance* (Vol. V, pp. 205–217). London: Academic Press.

Baddeley, A. D., & Hitch, G. (1974). Working memory. In G. A. Bower (Ed.), *Recent advances in learning and motivation* (Vol. 8, pp. 47–90). New York: Academic Press.

Baddeley, A. D., & Lieberman, K. (1980). Spatial working memory. In R. Nickerson (Ed.), *Attention and Performance* (Vol. VIII, pp. 521–539). Hillsdale, NJ: Lawrence Erlbaum Associates, Inc.

Berch, D. B., Krikorian, R., & Huha, E. M. (1998). The Corsi block-tapping task: Methodological and theoretical considerations. *Brain and Cognition, 38,* 317–338.

Biederman, I. (1987). Recognition-by-components: A theory of human image understanding. *Psychological Review, 94,* 115–147.

Boduroglu, A., & Shah, P. (2009). Effects of spatial configurations on visual change detection: An account of bias changes. *Memory and Cognition, 37,* 1120–1131.

Bor, D., Duncan, J., Wiseman, R. J., & Owen, A. M. (2003). Encoding strategies dissociate prefrontal activity from working memory demand. *Neuron, 37,* 361–367.

Bosch, V., Mecklinger, A., & Friederici, A. D. (2001). Slow cortical potentials during retention of object, spatial, and verbal information. *Cognitive Brain Research, 10,* 219–237.

Burgess, N. (2008). Spatial cognition and the brain. *Annals of the New York Academy of Sciences, 1124,* 77–97.

Busch, R. M., Farrell, K., Lisdahl-Medina, K., & Krikorian, R. (2005). Corsi block-tapping task performance as a function of path configuration. *Journal of Clinical and Experimental Neuropsychology, 27,* 127–134.

Byrne, P., Becker, S., & Burgess, N. (2007). Remembering the past and imagining the future: A neural model of spatial memory and imagery. *Psychological Review, 114,* 340–375.

Cornoldi, C., & Vecchi, T. (2003). *Visuo-spatial working memory and individual differences*. Hove, UK: Psychology Press.

Curtis, C. E. (2006). Prefrontal and parietal contributions to spatial working memory. *Neuroscience, 139,* 173–180.

Curtis, C. E., Rao, V. Y., & D'Esposito, M. (2004). Maintenance of spatial and motor codes during oculomotor delayed response tasks. *Journal of Neuroscience, 24,* 3944–3952.

Della Sala, S., Gray, C., Baddeley, A. D., Allamano, N., & Wilson, L. (1999). Pattern span: A tool for unwelding visuo-spatial memory. *Neuropsychologia, 37,* 1189–1199.

Dent, K., & Smyth, M. M. (2005). Verbal coding and the storage of form-position associations in visual-spatial short-term memory. *Acta Psychologica, 120,* 113–140.

Depoorter, A., & Vandierendonck, A. (2009). Evidence for modality-independent order coding in working memory. *The Quarterly Journal of Experimental Psychology, 62,* 531–549.

Elsley, J. V., & Parmentier, F. B. R. (2009). Is verbal-spatial binding in working memory impaired by a concurrent memory load? *Quarterly Journal of Experimental Psychology, 62,* 1696–1705.

Farmer, E. W., Berman, J. V. F., & Fletcher, Y. L. (1986). Evidence for a visuo-spatial scratch-pad in working memory. *Quarterly Journal of Experimental Psychology: A, Human Experimental Psychology, 38A,* 675–688.

Fisk, J. E., & Sharp, C. A. (2003). The role of the executive system in visuo-spatial memory functioning. *Brain and Cognition, 52,* 364–381.

Formisano, E., Linden, D. E., Di Salle, F., Trojano, L., Esposito, F., Sack, A. T., Grossi, D., Zanella, F. E., & Goebel, R. (2002). Tracking the mind's image in the brain I: Time-resolved fMRI during visuospatial mental imagery. *Neuron, 35,* 185–194.

Fougnie, D., & Marois, R. (2009). Attentive tracking disrupts feature binding in visual working memory. *Visual Cognition, 17,* 48–66.

Gajewski, D. A., & Brockmole, J. R. (2006). Feature bindings endure without attention: Evidence from an explicit recall task. *Psychonomic Bulletin & Review, 13,* 581–587.

Gauthier, I., Hayword, W. G., Tarr, M. J., Anderson, A. W., Skudlarski, P., & Gore, J. C. (2002). BOLD activity during mental rotation and viewpoint-dependent object recognition. *Neuron, 34,* 161–171.

Golomb, J. D., Chun, M. M., & Mazer, J. A. (2008). The native coordinate system of spatial attention is retinotopic. *Journal of Neuroscience, 28,* 10654–10662.

Guérard, K., Tremblay, S., & Saint-Aubin, J. (2009). The processing of spatial information in short-term memory: Insights from eye tracking the path length effect. *Acta Psychologica, 132,* 136–144.

Hale, S., Myerson, J., Rhee, S. H., Weiss, C. S., & Abrams, R. A. (1996). Selective interference with the maintenance of location information in working memory. *Neuropsychology, 10,* 228–240.

Harris, I. M., Egan, G. F., Sonkkila, C., Tochon-Danguy, H. J., Paxinos, G., & Watson, J. D. G. (2000). Selective right parietal lobe activation during mental rotation: A parametric PET study. *Brain: A Journal of Neurology, 123,* 65–73.

Harris, I. M., & Miniussi, C. (2003). Parietal lobe contribution to mental rotation demonstrated with rTMS. *Journal of Cognitive Neuroscience, 15,* 315–323.

Hegarty, M., Mayer, S., Kriz, S., & Keehner, M. (2005). The role of gestures in mental animation. *Spatial Cognition and Computation, 5,* 333–356.

Heil, M., Bajric, J., Rösler, F., & Hennighausen, E. (1996). Event-related potentials during mental rotation: Disentangling the contributions of character classification and image transformation. *Journal of Psychophysiology, 10,* 326–335.

Hyun, J. S., Woodman, G. F., & Luck, S. J. (2009). The role of attention in the binding of surface features to locations. *Visual Cognition, 17,* 10–24.

Jiang, Y., Olson, I. R., & Chun, M. M. (2000). Organization of visual short-term memory. *Journal of Experimental Psychology: Learning, Memory, and Cognition, 26,* 683–702.

Johnson, J. S., Hollingworth, A., & Luck, S. J. (2008). The role of attention in the maintenance of feature bindings in visual short-term memory. *Journal of Experimental Psychology: Human Perception and Performance, 34,* 41–55.

Jones, D. M., Farrand, P., Stuart, G., & Morris, N. (1995). Functional equivalence of verbal and spatial information in serial short-term memory. *Journal of Experimental Psychology: Learning, Memory, and Cognition, 21,* 1008–1018.

Just, M. A., Carpenter, P. A., Maguire, M., Diwadkar, V., & McMains, S. (2001). Mental rotation of objects retrieved from memory: A functional MRI study of spatial processing. *Journal of Experimental Psychology: General, 130,* 493–504.

Kastner, S., & Ungerleider, L. G. (2000). Mechanisms of visual attention in the human cortex. *Annual Review of Neuroscience, 23,* 315–341.

Kemps, E. (1999). Effects of complexity on visuo-spatial working memory. *European Journal of Cognitive Psychology, 11,* 335–356.

Kemps, E. (2001). Complexity effects in visuo-spatial working memory: Implications for the role of long-term memory. *Memory, 9,* 13–27.

Klauer, K. C., & Stegmaier, R. (1997). Interference in immediate spatial memory: Shifts of spatial attention or central-executive involvement? *Quarterly Journal of Experimental Psychology: A, Human Experimental Psychology, 50,* 79–99.

Knauff, M., Mulack, T., Kassubek, J., Salih, H. R., & Greenlee, M. W. (2002). Spatial imagery in deductive reasoning: A functional MRI study. *Cognitive Brain Research, 13,* 203–212.

Kosslyn, S. M. (1994). *Image and brain. The resolution of the imagery debate.* Cambridge: MIT Press.

Lawrence, B. M., Myerson, J., & Abrams, R. A. (2004). Interference with spatial working memory: An eye movement is more than a shift of attention. *Psychonomic Bulletin and Review, 11,* 488–494.

Lawrence, B. M., Myerson, J., Oonk, H. M., & Abrams, R. A. (2001). The effects of eye and limb movements on working memory. *Memory, 9,* 433–444.

Lehnert, G., & Zimmer, H. D. (2006). Auditory and visual spatial working memory. *Memory & Cognition, 34,* 1080–1090.

Lehnert, G., & Zimmer, H. D. (2008a). Common coding of auditory and visual spatial information in working memory. *Brain Research, 1230,* 158–167.

Lehnert, G., & Zimmer, H. D. (2008b). Modality and domain specific components in auditory and visual working memory tasks. *Cognitive Processing, 9,* 53–61.

Logie, R. H. (1989). Characteristics of visual short-term memory. *European Journal of Cognitive Psychology, 1,* 275–284.

Logie, R. H. (1995). *Visuo-spatial working memory.* Hove, UK: Lawrence Erlbaum Associates Ltd.

Logie, R. H., Della Sala, S., Wynn, V., & Baddeley, A. D. (2000). Visual similarity effects in immediate verbal serial recall. *Quarterly Journal of Experimental Psychology: A, Human Experimental Psychology, 53A,* 626–646.

Logie, R. H., & Marchetti, C. (1991). Visuo-spatial working memory: Visual, spatial or central executive. In R. H. Logie & M. Denis (Eds.), *Mental images in human cognition* (pp. 105–115). Amsterdam: North Holland.

Luck, S. J., & Vogel, E. K. (1997). The capacity of visual working memory for features and conjunctions. *Nature, 390,* 279–281.

Mazard, A., Tzourio-Mazoyer, N., & Crivello, F. (2004). A PET meta-analysis of object and spatial mental imagery. *European Journal of Cognitive Psychology, 16,* 673–695.

Mecklinger, A., & Pfeifer, E. (1996). Event-related potentials reveal topographical and temporal distinct neuronal activation patterns for spatial and object working memory. *Cognitive Brain Research, 4,* 211–224.

Meiser, T., & Klauer, K. C. (1999). Working memory and changing-state hypothesis. *Journal of Experimental Psychology: Learning, Memory, and Cognition, 25,* 1272–1299.

Morris, N. (1987). Exploring the visuo-spatial scratch pad. *Quarterly Journal of Experimental Psychology: A, Human Experimental Psychology, 39A,* 409–430.

Oberauer, K., Süβ, H. M., Schulze, R., Wilhelm, O., & Wittmann, W. W. (2000). Working memory capacity—facets of a cognitive ability construct. *Personality and Individual Differences, 29,* 1017–1045.

Palmer, S. E. (1977). Hierarchical structure in perceptual representation. *Cognitive Psychology, 9,* 441–474.

Parmentier, F. B. R., Andrés, P., Elford, G., & Jones, D. M. (2006). Organization of visuo-spatial serial memory: Interaction of temporal order with spatial and temporal grouping. *Psychological Research, 70,* 200–217.

Parmentier, F. B. R., Elford, G., & Maybery, M. (2005). Transitional information in spatial serial memory: Path characteristics affect recall performance. *Journal of Experimental Psychology: Learning Memory and Cognition, 31,* 412–427.

Pearson, D. G., & Sahraie, A. (2003). Oculomotor control and the maintenance of spatially and temporally distributed events in visuo-spatial working memory. *Quarterly Journal of Experimental Psychology Section A: Human Experimental Psychology, 56 A,* 1089–1111.

Phillips, W. A. (1974). On the distinction between sensory storage and short-term visual memory. *Perception and Psychophysics, 16,* 283–290.

Postle, B. R., Awh, E., Jonides, J., Smith, E. E., & D'Esposito, M. (2004). The where and how of attention-based rehearsal in spatial working memory. *Cognitive Brain Research, 20,* 194–205.

Postle, B. R., Idzikowski, C., Della Sala, S., Logie, R. H., & Baddeley, A. D. (2006). The selective disruption of spatial working memory by eye movements. *Quarterly Journal of Experimental Psychology: A, Human Experimental Psychology, 59,* 100–120.

Postma, A., & De Haan, E. H. F. (1996). What was where? Memory for object locations. *Quarterly Journal of Experimental Psychology: A, Human Experimental Psychology, 49A,* 178–199.

Quinn, J. G. (2008). Movement and visual coding: The structure of visuo-spatial working memory. *Cognitive Processing, 9,* 35–43.

Quinn, J. G., & Ralston, G. E. (1986). Movement and attention in visual working memory. *Quarterly Journal of Experimental Psychology: A, Human Experimental Psychology, 38A,* 689–703.

Rösler, F., Heil, M., Bajric, J., Pauls, A. C., & Hennighausen, E. (1995). Patterns of cerebral activation while mental images are rotated and changed in size. *Psychophysiology, 32,* 135–149.

Rudkin, S. J., Pearson, D. G., & Logie, R. H. (2007). Executive processes in visual and spatial working memory tasks. *Quarterly Journal of Experimental Psychology: A, Human Experimental Psychology, 60,* 79–100.

Sack, A. T., Sperling, J. M., Prvulovic, D., Formisano, E., Goebel, R., Di Salle, F., Dierks, T., & Linden, D. E. (2002). Tracking the mind's image in the brain II: Transcranial magnetic stimulation reveals parietal asymmetry in visuospatial imagery. *Neuron, 35,* 195–204.

Saiki, J., & Miyatsuji, H. (2007). Feature binding in visual working memory evaluated by type identification paradigm. *Cognition, 102,* 49–83.

Saint-Aubin, J., Tremblay, S., & Jalbert, A. (2007). Eye movements and serial memory for visuo-spatial information: Does time spent fixating contribute to recall? *Experimental Psychology, 54,* 264–272.

Salway, A. F. S., & Logie, R. H. (1995). Visuo-spatial working memory, movement control and executive demands. *British Journal of Psychology, 86,* 253–269.

Santa, J. L. (1977). Spatial transformations of words and pictures. *Journal of Experimental Psychology: Human Learning and Memory, 3,* 418–427.

Saults, J. S., & Cowan, N. (2007). A central capacity limit to the simultaneous storage of visual and auditory arrays in working memory. *Journal of Experimental Psychology: General, 136,* 663–684.

Sestieri, C., Di Matteo, R., Ferretti, A., Del Gratta, C., Caulo, M., Tartaro, A., Olivetti Belardinelli, M., & Romani, G. (2006). 'What' versus 'where' in the audiovisual domain: An fMRI study. *Neuroimage, 33,* 672–680.

Shepard, R. N., & Metzler, J. (1971). Mental rotation of three-dimensional objects. *Science, 171,* 701–703.

Shepard, R. N., & Podgorny, P. (1978). Cognitive processes that resemble perceptual processes. In W. Estes (Ed.), *Handbook of learning and cognitive processes* (pp. 189–237). New York: John Wiley.

Smirni, P., Villardita, G., & Zappala, G. (1983). Influence of different paths on spatial memory performance in the block-tapping test. *Journal of Clinical Neuropsychology, 5,* 355–360.

Smyth, M. M., Pearson, N. A., & Pendleton, L. R. (1988). Movement and working memory: Patterns and positions in space. *Quarterly Journal of Experimental Psychology: A, Human Experimental Psychology, 40A,* 497–514.

Smyth, M. M., & Pelky, P. L. (1992). Short-term retention of spatial information. *British Journal of Psychology, 83,* 359–374.

Smyth, M. M., & Pendleton, L. R. (1989). Working memory for movements. *Quarterly Journal of Experimental Psychology: A, Human Experimental Psychology, 41A,* 235–250.

Smyth, M. M., & Pendleton, L. R. (1990). Space and movement in working memory. *Quarterly Journal of Experimental Psychology: A, Human Experimental Psychology, 42A,* 291–304.

Smyth, M. M., & Scholey, K. A. (1994). Characteristics of spatial memory span: Is there an analogy to the word length effect, based on movement time? *Quarterly Journal of Experimental Psychology: A, Human Experimental Psychology, 47A,* 91–117.

Smyth, M. M., & Scholey, K. A. (1996). Serial order in spatial immediate memory. *Quarterly Journal of Experimental Psychology: A, Human Experimental Psychology, 49A,* 159–177.

Smyth, M. M., & Waller, A. (1994). Movement imagery in rock climbing: Patterns of interference from visual, spatial and kinaesthetic secondary tasks. *Applied Cognitive Psychology, 12,* 145–157.

Theeuwes, J., Belopolsky, A., & Olivers, C. N. L. (2009). Interactions between working memory, attention and eye movements. *Acta Psychologica, 132,* 106–114.

Theeuwes, J., Olivers, C. N. L., & Chizk, C. L. (2005). Remembering a location makes the eyes curve away. *Psychological Science, 16,* 196–199.

Thompson, J. M., Hamilton, C. J., Gray, J. M., Quinn, J. G., Mackin, P., Young, A. H., & Ferrier, N. (2006). Executive and visuospatial sketchpad resources in euthymic bipolar disorder: Implications for visuospatial working memory architecture. *Memory, 14,* 437–451.

Treisman, A. (2006). Object tokens, binding and visual memory. In H. D. Zimmer, A. Mecklinger, & U. Lindenberger (Eds.), *Handbook of binding and memory: Perspectives from cognitive neuroscience* (pp. 315–338). Oxford: Oxford University Press.

Tremblay, S., Parmentier, F. B. R., Guérard, K., Nicholls, A. P., & Jones, D. M. (2006a). A spatial modality effect in serial memory. *Journal of Experimental Psychology: Learning, Memory, and Cognition, 32,* 1208–1215.

Tremblay, S., Saint-Aubin, J., & Jalbert, A. (2006b). Rehearsal in serial memory for visual-spatial information: Evidence from eye movements. *Psychonomic Bulletin and Review, 13,* 452–457.

Trojano, L., Linden, D. E. J., & Formisano, E. (2004). What clocks tell us about the neural correlates of spatial imagery. *European Journal of Cognitive Psychology, 16,* 653–672.

van der Meulen, M., Logie, R. H., & Della Sala, S. (2009). Selective interference with image retention and generation: Evidence for the workspace model. *Quarterly Journal of Experimental Psychology, 62,* 1568–1580.

Vandierendonck, A., Kemps, E., Fastame, M. C., & Szmalec, A. (2004). Working memory components of the Corsi blocks task. *British Journal of Psychology, 95,* 57–79.

Zacks, J. M., Gilliam, F., & Ojemann, J. G. (2003). Selective disturbance of mental rotation by cortical stimulation. *Neuropsychologia, 41,* 1659–1667.

Zimmer, H. D. (1998). Spatial information with pictures and words in visual short-term memory. *Psychological Research, 61,* 277–284.

Zimmer, H. D. (2004). The construction of mental maps based on a fragmentary view of physical maps. *Journal of Educational Psychology, 96,* 603–610.

Zimmer, H. D. (2008). Visual and spatial working memory: From boxes to networks. *Neuroscience and Biobehavioral Reviews, 32,* 1372–1395.

Zimmer, H. D., & Ecker, U. K. H. (2010). Remembering perceptual features unequally bound in object and episodic tokens: Neural mechanisms and their electrophysiological correlates. *Neuroscience & Biobehavioral Reviews, 34,* 1066–1079.

Zimmer, H. D., & Lehnert, G. (2006). The spatial mismatch effect is based on global configuration and not on perceptual records within the visual cache. *Psychological Research, 70,* 1–12.

Zimmer, H. D., Speiser, H. R., & Seidler, B. (2003). Spatio-temporal working-memory and short-term object-location tasks use different memory mechanisms. *Acta Psychologica, 114,* 41–65.

4 Exploring the determinants of memory for spatial sequences

Fabrice B. R. Parmentier

In this chapter, I will briefly review evidence for a modular distinction between verbal and spatial short-term memory systems, as well as evidence highlighting their functional similarities with respect to the processing of order. The concept of transition will be argued to be potentially useful as one spanning beyond modality boundaries. I will then review the evidence indicating that such concepts translate, in the visuospatial domain, as the spatial path formed by successive to-be-remembered locations, as revealed by the impact of path complexity manipulations on order memory.

The modular view on visuospatial short-term memory

The distinction between verbal and spatial representations in short-term memory is widely accepted among cognitive psychologists and clearly articulated within the working memory model (Baddeley, 1986).

The most prominent argument for a distinction between verbal and visuospatial representations emanates from empirical studies crossing verbal and visuospatial primary tasks with verbal and visuospatial secondary tasks and seeking to demonstrate selective interference effects (e.g., Baddeley, Grant, Wight, & Thomson, 1975; Baddeley & Lieberman, 1980; Farmer, Berman, & Fletcher, 1986; Logie, Zucco, & Baddeley, 1990; Morris, 1987). Many studies used variations of the Corsi Blocks Task (CBT) (Corsi, 1972) in which participants encode and recall the order of presentation of spatial locations marked in sequence out of a fixed set of locations (visible throughout encoding, maintenance, and recall). For example, using this method, Smyth, Pearson, and Pendleton (1988) found that the participants' spatial span decreased when they concurrently tapped around a set of four metal plates arranged in a square but not when they performed an articulatory suppression task.

A second line of evidence for the distinction between verbal and nonverbal subsystems comes from neuropsychological data, and particularly from the reports of a brain-damaged patient presenting a deficit in a digit span task and normal performance in the CBT (De Renzi & Nichelli, 1975), while another demonstrated the opposite dissociation (Hanley, Young, & Pearson, 1991). This evidence, cited in almost every paper dedicated to the study of the visuospatial sketch pad (VSSP), remains the only one of its kind, however.

Finally, the use of brain imagery techniques allowed the study of the neurological substrate of the phonological loop and the VSSP. Retention of verbal information typically results in the activation of left frontal cortical regions, whereas the retention of visuospatial information is accompanied by spots of activation in the right frontal region, the right parietal, and the right occipital areas (e.g., Jonides, 1995).

Taken together, the findings reported above seem to support Baddeley's (1986) decomposition of working memory. Although the phonological loop has been the object of intensive research work, the VSSP remains relatively less explored in comparison. According to Logie (1995), the VSSP might be structurally similar to the phonological loop, exhibiting a certain capacity for information and its maintenance through continuous refreshing. In this model, 'the visual store is subject to decay and to interference from new information coming in. The spatial store is seen as a system that can be used to plan movement, but can also be used to rehearse the contents of the visual store' (Logie, 1995, p. 126).

The modular perspective inherent to the working memory model's overall architecture has also been applied to the VSSP, leading several authors to propose a distinction between visual and spatial components. For example, Logie and Marchetti (1991) reported that irrelevant pictures selectively disrupted memory for colours while irrelevant (unseen) arm movements selectively affected memory for a sequence of spatial locations (both secondary tasks being presented during a retention interval). Converging evidence was reported by Tresch, Sinnamon, and Seamon (1993) in a study using tasks tapping memory for locations and shapes. Other demonstrations of selective interference effects (e.g., Della Sala, Gray, Baddeley, Allamano, & Wilson, 1999; Logie, 1995) are found in the literature and certainly constitute one important pillar of the visual-spatial distinction (see also Logie, Chapter 2, this volume). To this type of evidence one may add examples of double dissociations observed in patients with brain trauma (e.g., Farah, Hammond, Levine, & Calvanio, 1998; Luzzatti, Vecchi, Agazzi, Cesa-Bianchi, & Vergani, 1998), as well as findings from imaging studies distinguishing distinct neural pathways for the processing of visual and spatial information (Courtney, Ungerleider, Keil, & Haxby, 1996). Finally, developmental research also suggests that memory for visual and spatial information develops at distinct rates (e.g., Logie & Pearson, 1997). For example, Pickering, Gathercole, Hall, and Lloyd (2001) found a steeper development of memory for the dynamic presentation of a labyrinth path compared with its static presentation across children aged 5, 8, and 10.

While the dominant decomposition of visuospatial short-term memory follows a visual-spatial distinction, alternative views have been proposed. For example, Vecchi and colleagues (e.g., Vecchi & Cornoldi, 1999; Vecchi & Girelli, 1998; see also Cornoldi & Mammarella, Chapter 6, this volume) proposed a passive/active distinction according to which separate memory systems underpin the maintenance of visuospatial information in the format in which it was presented (passive maintenance) and the retention of information resulting from a mental transformation applied to the stimuli presented (active maintenance). Pickering et al. (2001), on the other hand, suggested a distinction between memory for static and dynamic representations (the latter involving a representation of spatial information across time). Overall, these distinctions offer various ways of separating different types of stimuli. Unfortunately, however, they do not offer a description of the processes through which information is being processed.

Beyond the modular horizon: Evidence for common order processes

Studies using order tasks have generated a number of findings pointing out the functional similarity between memory for sequences of verbal and nonverbal stimuli, complementing a purely modular view. For example, Jones, Farrand, Stuart, and Morris (1995) found that tapping, articulatory suppression, and irrelevant speech affect both memory for visuospatial and verbal sequences as long as the irrelevant information involved stimuli changing across time (see also Guérard, Tremblay, & Saint-Aubin, 2009; Tremblay, Macken, & Jones, 2001), leading these authors to argue that verbal and visuospatial serial memory appear to be functionally equivalent when tasks are equated and require the processing of order information (see also Avons, 1998). The fact that tasks sharing a strong order requirement interfere with each other beyond modular boundaries is supported by results reported by Depoorter and Vandierendonck (2009; see also Vandierendonck & Szmalec, Chapter 1, this volume). These authors orthogonally crossed the requirement (order/item) and modality (verbal/spatial) of primary and secondary tasks. While part of their data supported a modality-based interference in line with a pure modular view of working memory, cross-modal interference was found when primary and secondary tasks involved the processing of order. There are in fact a number of studies highlighting functional similarities between verbal and visuospatial (or even auditory-spatial) short-term memory, in some cases reporting effects often thought to be emblematic of verbal short-term memory. These effects are briefly reviewed below.

The shape of the serial curve

One of the first empirical arguments in favour of a modular theory of short-term memory was the finding of distinct serial position curves for verbal and nonverbal stimuli. In contrast to the U-shape curve observed in verbal serial recall tasks, visuospatial stimuli appeared to yield a J-shape curve, that is, a curve displaying recency but no primacy (e.g., Potter & Levy, 1969). Early studies focused on memory for visual information. The best known studies of this type are those of Phillips and Christie (1977a, 1977b) and Broadbent and Broadbent (1981). Their methodology involved presenting participants with sequences of abstract visual stimuli before requiring them to make a recognition decision on a subsequent test stimulus. When plotting recognition performance as a function of the position of the recognition probe in the original sequence, a J-shape curve was obtained (see also Neath, 1993; Walker, Hitch, & Duroe, 1993).

Studies reporting J-shaped curves involved a recognition judgement for the identity of to-be-remembered items, and not the processing of their order, in stark contrast with the requirement of the digit span task (usually used for comparison). In tasks requiring the processing of order information, visuospatial stimuli exhibit primary and recency effects, just as verbal stimuli do. This is the case for example in Smyth and Scholey's (1996) study using a computerized version of the CBT (De Renzi & Nichelli, 1975). The role of order in generating the U-shaped serial position curve is nicely illustrated by the results of their Experiment 3, in which they presented participants with sequences of six spatial locations followed by a probe stimulus for recognition. No effect of serial position was found in the recognition test. However, when participants were required to allocate the recognized items to their serial position, the proportion of items correctly assigned was higher for the first and last items. When reporting serial position curves, studies requiring participants to recall the order of presentation of spatial locations invariably exhibit U-shaped serial position curves, be it in the visual (e.g., Farrand, Parmentier, & Jones, 2001; Jones, Farrand, Stuart, & Morris, 1995), tactile (e.g., Mahrer & Miles, 1999; Nairne & McNabb, 1985), or auditory (Parmentier & Jones, 2000; Parmentier, Maybery, & Jones, 2004; Parmentier, Maybery, Huitson, & Jones, 2008) modalities. It is noteworthy that U-shaped curves are also found when participants are required to encode the identity of stimuli rather than their spatial location, so long as the processing of their order forms a requirement of the task. This is true for visual stimuli such as concrete pictures, abstract pictures, or faces (e.g., Avons, 1998; Manning and Schreier, 1988; Ward, Avons, & Melling, 2005), but also auditory stimuli such as musical notes, environmental sounds, or patterns of frequencies (Frankish, 1996; Greene & Samuel, 1986; McFarland & Cacace, 1992; Rowe & Rowe, 1976; Surprenant, Pitt, & Crowder, 1993).

In sum, verbal and spatial stimuli exhibit functionally similar serial position curves in tasks requiring the processing of order, as argued by several authors (Avons, 1998; Jones et al., 1995; Ward et al., 2005).

Generalization gradients

Apart from the overall shape of the serial position curve, the incidence of particular classes of errors offers interesting insights in the maintenance of order information. Several studies have shown that items incorrectly assigned to a serial position tend to be recalled in a serial position close to its correct position. More specifically, the probability of an item being recalled in the wrong temporal position decreases as the temporal distance between correct and recalled position increases. This observation, first made in verbal studies (e.g., Bjork & Whitten, 1974; Estes, 1972), has since been reported in numerous studies using nonverbal stimuli: visual (e.g., Avons, 1998), visuospatial (Parmentier, Andrés, Elford, & Jones, 2006; Smyth & Scholey, 1996), and auditory (e.g., Parmentier & Jones, 2000). For both verbal and nonverbal stimuli in tasks requiring the recall of order information, a plot of the proportion of errors against the temporal distance between correct and recalled positions exhibits a negatively accelerated exponential curve, reinforcing the idea of the modality-free status of order representations.

Suffix effect

The suffix effect consists of the reduction of the recency part of the serial position curve when the to-be-remembered list is followed by a to-be-ignored item, even when participants fully expect it. Well-established in the verbal literature (e.g., Baddeley & Hull, 1979; Penney, 1985), this phenomenon has long been interpreted to be in favour of the existence of an acoustic verbal store (but see Nicholls & Jones, 2002a, for a perceptual account). Typically, authors have assumed that a verbal suffix gains obligatory access to the phonological store, masking the last to-be-remembered verbal item before it is refreshed and consolidated by rehearsal. However, evidence shows that the suffix effect is not specific to verbal materials, for it is also observed for tactile (Mahrer & Miles, 1999), olfactory (Miles & Jenkins, 2000), visual (Manning & Schreier, 1988), and visuospatial (Parmentier, Tremblay, & Jones, 2004) stimuli.

Effect of temporal grouping

Listing of items organized in groups by the insertion of relatively long pauses between certain items results in the improvement of serial recall accuracy (e.g., Frankish, 1989), primacy and recency effects within the subseries (e.g., Hitch, Burgess, Towse, & Culpin, 1996; Ng & Maybery, 2002), and the reduction of the probability of items migrating to adjacent positions if a migration involves crossing from one subseries to another (e.g., Ng & Maybery, 2002). While this effect is accounted for within models of verbal serial memory (e.g., Burgess & Hitch, 1999), recent findings show that it is also observed for nonverbal stimuli. For example, Parmentier et al. (2004) reported a temporal grouping effect for auditory spatial sequences exhibiting all the characteristics observed elsewhere with verbal stimuli. Similar findings were also reported for visuospatial sequences (Parmentier et al., 2006). Temporal grouping is also a factor thought to underpin the von Restorff effect observed in verbal and spatial serial memory (Guérard, Hughes, & Tremblay, 2006).

Modality effect

Numerous studies show that serial recall of verbal items presented auditorily yields a greater recency effect than the serial recall of visually presented verbal stimuli (e.g., Crowder & Morton, 1969; Frankish, 1996; Penney, 1989). This modality effect is typically considered to reflect the lasting availability of some acoustic or phonological information (e.g., Burgess & Hitch, 1999; Crowder & Morton, 1969). Yet, again, evidence indicates that the effect is observed for stimuli other than verbal ones. Indeed, Greene and Samuel (1986) reported it for musical notes, Rowe and Rowe (1976) for environmental sounds, and more critically, Tremblay, Parmentier, Guérard, Nicholls, and Jones (2006) for spatial locations. Using order reconstruction tasks, Tremblay et al. (2006) systematically compared visual and auditory presentation of verbal and spatial information and found similar modality effects for both types of stimuli.

Interference effects

As mentioned earlier, the finding of selective interference effects, often in studies failing to match tasks in terms of their processing requirements, is challenged by the reporting of cross-modal interference effects by secondary tasks in studies using tasks designed to tap the processing of order (e.g., Guérard et al., 2009; Jones et al., 1995; Tremblay et al., 2001), including evidence of similarities in the nature of errors (Guérard & Tremblay, 2008). The functional similarity between verbal and spatial stimuli extends to another interference effect: the sandwich effect. This effect, predominantly reported in verbal studies, reflects the decrement in serial recall performance when irrelevant stimuli are interpolated among the to-be-remembered items (e.g., Baddeley, Papagno, & Andrade, 1993; Hamilton & Hockey, 1974). Tremblay, Nicholls, Parmentier, and Jones (2005) reported that this effect is also observed in the visuospatial domain, as performance in an order reconstruction task for spatial locations significantly decreased when an irrelevant location (centre of the screen, presented in the same colour as the to-be-remembered locations) was presented in between the to-be-remembered locations. Moreover, the authors demonstrated that, as is the case in verbal memory (Nicholls & Jones, 2002b; Watkins & Sechler, 1989), the sandwich effect was reduced or eliminated when sandwich and to-be-remembered items were made perceptually distinct (in this case by using distinct colours).

The Hebb repetition effect

In an influential study, Hebb (1961) presented participants with 24 lists of nine digits each and measured the impact, on immediate serial recall, of the regular repetition (every three trials) of the same sequence (participants not informed of that manipulation). Performance improved with repetition, compared to that measured in nonrepeating trials. This 'learning through repetition' effect was replicated on many occasions using verbal stimuli (e.g., Bower & Winzenz, 1969; Cumming, Page, & Norris, 2003; Hitch, Fastame, & Flude, 2005). With the recent resurgence of interest in this phenomenon have appeared demonstrations of the amodal nature of this effect (see also Vandierendonck & Szmalec, Chapter 1, this volume). Indeed, the Hebb repetition effect has now been reported for visuospatial locations (Couture & Tremblay, 2006; Gagnon, Bédard, & Turcotte, 2006; Gould & Glencross, 1990; Turcotte, Gagnon, & Poirier, 2005), pictures (Page, Cumming, Norris, Hitch, & McNeil, 2006), and auditory spatial locations (Parmentier et al., 2008). The study by Couture and Tremblay (2006) is especially interesting as it demonstrates that, as is the case with verbal stimuli, the Hebb repetition effect observed with visuospatial locations is not affected by whether or not participants become aware of the repetition. Furthermore, using a within-participants design, these authors showed that the magnitude of learning was identical for verbal and spatial materials.

In conclusion, while much evidence supports the modular distinction between verbal and spatial representations, a number of findings point towards the existence of common mechanisms for the maintenance of order information irrespective of the nature of the stimuli. Recent evidence clearly indicates that data support both modular and unitary views (e.g., Depoorter & Vandierendonck, 2009; Guérard & Tremblay, 2008), so that the relationship between these views should be seen as complementary rather than antagonistic. There is no denying that distinct neural activations can be observed when comparing verbal and, say, spatial stimuli. It is well-established that perceptual areas are, up to a point where cross-modal integration occurs, segregated (see also Postle, Chapter 5, this volume). Thus it is not surprising to obtain patterns of brain activation unique to specific classes of stimuli or behavioural dissociations with certain tasks. The point, however, is that such patterns of activations, if signalling item-based distinctions, fail to capture the nature of common cognitive processes. Consider for example the possibility that the processing of order may occur as the product of neuronal activity. If so, order processing may obey the same rules regardless of where activity occurs in the brain, or indeed what stimuli are being processed.

Is the idea of order processing as the product of neuronal activity far fetched? Perhaps not. Recent advances in neuroscience include the discovery that:

1. neurons firing repeatedly in succession results in their synaptic connection being physically modified, enhancing the excitability of the synapse for periods of hours and even weeks (Bliss & Lømo, 1973; Martinez & Derrick, 1996); and that
2. synaptic efficacy is also enhanced by the temporal coincidence of presynaptic inputs to the same assembly of neurons (Fuster, 1995).

Based on these basic principles, some authors (Jensen, 2006; Jensen & Lisman, 2005; Lisman, 2005) have proposed a computational model able to encode and maintain a sequence of events in a cortical buffer able to drive the hippocampal long-term memory system and consolidate order memory through synaptic changes. In a nutshell, what these studies suggest is that the encoding and maintenance of order can emerge as a function of the way assemblies of neurons interact and connect to other brain areas. These findings, however, have been relatively ignored by psychologists studying order memory. Yet they offer, at least conceptually, potentially crucial insights and are fully compatible with the finding of common functional characteristics of serial memory for different types of mental representations.

If empirical evidence supports the notion of central order mechanisms, it remains to examine how order is extracted and defined in the case of visuospatial stimuli. The next section addresses this issue in relation to the concept of transitional information, presented as a concept general enough to apply to multiple modalities while affording modality-specific definitions.

The role of spatial transitions and their complexity

Anyone familiar with research on verbal serial memory will know that a great deal of theoretical development emerged from the observation that certain characteristics of the to-be-remembered items constrain performance in the verbal serial recall task (such as, for example, the degree of phonological similarity of the items, e.g., Larsen, Baddeley, & Andrade, 2000; or their length, e.g., Hulme, Thomson, Muir, & Lawrence, 1984). Yet, such an approach has not been systematically adopted to study the maintenance of visuospatial sequences. In particular, the role of configural aspects of visuospatial stimuli has received little interest despite findings clearly suggesting their importance (described below). The paucity of studies on the topic may follow in part from the methodological constrains inherent to the CBT, the most commonly used spatial serial memory task in clinical (e.g., Kaplan, Fein, Morris, & Delis, 1991) as well as experimental settings (e.g., Smyth & Scholey, 1994a, 1994b). Over the years, numerous variations of the CBT have been reported, including computerized ones (e.g., Davis, Bajszar, & Squire, 1993), rendering comparisons across studies somewhat complicated (Berch, Krikorian, & Huha, 1998). Because the CBT involves a fixed set of locations, it offers little control over the spatial characteristics of the sequences presented. In fact, the actual sequences have rarely been considered as an important issue and little research addressed it despite the finding that spatial span varies with the set of sequences used (Smirni, Villardita, & Zappalà, 1983). Smirni et al. compared spatial span in eight sets of sequences, four drawn from the digit span task of the Wechsler Intelligence Scale for Children and the Wechsler Adult Intelligence Scale, and four new sets. They found that spatial span varied with the sets. Unfortunately, the authors fell short of exploring the underlying origin of this variation. This issue was highlighted by Berch et al. (1998) in a comprehensive review of the literature on the CBT, in part based on their interpretation of Smirni et al.'s results: '58% of subjects who failed on shorter paths subsequently succeeded on longer paths. However, after statistically controlling for differential path difficulty (as measured by mean performances), only 6% of subjects succeeded on trials with longer paths after having failed a trial with a shorter path' (Berch et al., 1998, p. 326).

The effect of path complexity

Few studies sought to manipulate the spatial characteristics of the to-be-remembered locations in Corsi-like tasks, such as the arrangement of the set of locations or the path defined by the to-be-remembered sequences among those locations. Perhaps the earliest relevant study is that of Smyth and Scholey (1994a), who were looking for a potential visuospatial equivalent to the word length effect (e.g., Hulme et al., 1984) by manipulating the time taken by participants to move between spatial locations. This was achieved by altering the size and distance between locations (while maintaining the relative configuration of locations intact). Their data revealed that even in participants showing strong differences in movement times between the different spatial arrangements, spatial span was not affected by the distance between locations, leading the authors to conclude that the rehearsal mechanism(s) supporting the maintenance of spatial sequences is not correlated with the overt movement time between locations. It is worth noting however that by varying the scale of a unique spatial configuration, the density of locations varied across experimental conditions. As the authors pointed out themselves in their Experiment 3 (in which each target location was accompanied by two spatially close distracters), the close proximity of distracter locations most probably made the relative encoding of the locations more difficult. It is therefore possible that a potential positive effect of reducing distances between locations may have been cancelled out by a relatively more difficult encoding of locations. Thus one cannot categorically reject a possible effect of path length in Smyth and Scholey's (1994a) study.

Kemps (1999) too varied the arrangement of the blocks in a Corsi-like task but with the clear objective of examining the impact of stimulus complexity on memory for sequences of spatial locations. In her study, the complexity of the set of locations was manipulated in two ways: by varying the number of locations in the set, and by varying their configuration. Regarding the latter, Kemps' results showed that for a fixed number of nine locations, spatial span was best when these were arranged along a 3 × 3 matrix and decreased as the arrangement's redundancy was reduced (the worst performance was observed when no two locations shared the same horizontal or vertical alignment). Using a similar manipulation, Bor, Duncan, Wiseman, and Owen (2003) found no such effect, however. With respect to the number of locations in the set, Kemps found that spatial span decreased as that number increased, a finding easily explained by assuming a greater encoding difficulty when locations are confusable and numerous spatial distracters are present. Interestingly, this effect was cancelled when certain subsets of locations only were relevant for the task and participants were aware of them.

Another way to manipulate the complexity of visuospatial sequences is to vary the characteristics of the *path* formed by successive locations. This is especially interesting because it touches upon a concept spanning outside the area of spatial serial memory, namely that of transitions, and because there is good evidence that locations presented sequentially are encoded relative to each other (Avons, 2007). This concept, because it essentially refers to some probabilistic relationship between stimuli without assumptions as to their nature, may potentially provide a good theoretical starting point to model serial memory across modalities. Transitions have been somewhat neglected in the study of verbal serial memory, as past studies have typically centred on effects pertaining to local item information (e.g., lexical status, Hulme, Roodenrys, Brown, & Mercer, 1995; word frequency, e.g., Lewandowsky & Farrell, 2000; concreteness, Neath, 1997; age of acquisition, Dewhurst, Hitch, & Barry, 1998) or factors characterizing whole sequences (e.g., phonological similarity, Larsen et al., 2000). There is, however, evidence that serial memory for verbal stimuli is influenced by the participant's knowledge about stimuli regularities. For example, recall performance for letter strings is superior when strings contain high-frequency letter transitions compared with low-frequency transitions (Miller & Selfridge, 1951; Kantowitz, Ornstein, & Schwartz, 1972). The idea that transitional probabilities condition order memory also underlies a study by Stuart and Hulme (2000) in which participants were pre-exposed to pairs of words drawn from two arbitrary sets. The authors reported that sequences made of cooccurring words were substantially better recalled than mixed-set sequences, a finding not attributable to familiarization effects. Furthermore, Botvinick and Bylsma (2005) provide a neat demonstration of the role of sequence regularities by training participants to learn transitions based on an artificial grammar. They reported that:

1 participants' performance in a serial recall task increased with the predictability of the sequence based on the learnt transitions; and that
2 the errors they produced consisted of forming sequences matching the learnt grammar better than that presented (regularization errors).

It should also be noted that a network model of serial memory underpinned by transitions and associations (Botvinick & Plaut, 2006) appears able to reproduce landmark aspects of serial memory (e.g., primary and recency effects, generalization gradients) and fit a pattern of data (Baddeley, 1968) typically viewed as a strong argument against associative models of serial memory. Furthermore, in the domain of articulatory transitions, Murray and Jones (2002) found that increasing the difficulty to co-articulate words in a to-be-remembered sequence reduced verbal memory span. Finally, one could also argue that the Hebb repetition (e.g., Hebb, 1961) effect, observed for both verbal and spatial stimuli (e.g., Couture & Tremblay, 2006), may reflect the building of associative probabilities between items.

If general enough to span across modalities, the concept of transition requires a specific definition in each modality. In the spatial domain, this concept can arguably be defined with respect to the complexity of the path formed by successive to-be-remembered locations. This complexity was varied in different ways in a few studies. The first study to adopt a systematic approach to this issue was that of Kemps (2001), measuring spatial span in a Corsi-like task and comparing performance for structured and unstructured sequences. Structured sequences were built using at least one of the following principles: symmetry (the spatial path was symmetrical about the horizontal, vertical, and/or the 45° axis of the matrix display), repetition (a part of the path was repeated in translated locations), and continuation (the path contained no crossings). Unstructured sequences, on the other hand, did not involve any of these principles. The results revealed a superior serial recall performance for structured sequences, an effect that was not altered when participants undertook concurrent tapping (i.e., the repeated tapping of the participant's finger around four metal plates positioned in a square pattern, a task commonly used to suppress spatial memory, e.g., Farmer et al., 1986). The lack of interference from the tapping task led Kemps to conclude, by elimination, that structured sequences benefited from long-term memory influences (such as the concept of symmetry; see also Pieroni, Rossi-Arnaud, & Baddeley, Chapter 8, this volume). Kemps' (2001) data echo Smirni et al.'s (1983) findings that not all sequences are equally remembered in order and suggest that characteristics of the path formed by successive locations may be an important mediator of serial memory performance.

Further evidence of the impact of path complexity of visuospatial serial memory comes from a functional magnetic resonance imaging study by Bor et al. (2003), who compared serial recall performance for structured and unstructured sequences, using a definition slightly different from that of Kemps (2001). In Bor et al.'s study, structure was imposed by ensuring that each to-be-remembered location was on the same horizontal, vertical, or diagonal as the preceding to-be-remembered location (leading to more symmetrical and shape-like paths). Recall performance was enhanced in the structured condition and brain activation data suggested that this condition encourages the strategic chunking of locations. Additional evidence can also be found in Schumman-Hengsteler, Strobl, and Zoelch's (2004) description of a series of unpublished studies in which they manipulated the complexity of the path formed by spatial sequences in the CBT by varying both the spatial length formed by path segments and whether or not the path formed crossings. The authors reported that, in one study in which path length and crossings were combined to form simple and complex sequences, recall performance was negatively affected by complexity in 5- to 10-year-old children as well as in adults. In a separate study in which path length, crossings, and whether or not the path travelled over unused locations were crossed orthogonally, independent effects of the first two factors were observed in 10-year-old children and adults (but not in 6-year-old children).

In a systematic examination of the effect of path complexity on visuospatial serial memory, Parmentier, Elford, and Maybery (2005) reported the results of four experiments assessing the impact of path crossing, path length, directional change, and path angles (see below). The Dots Task (Jones et al., 1995) was used, in which a fixed number of quasi-randomly generated locations (different in every trial) are presented sequentially (one location visible at a time). At recall, all the locations are re-presented simultaneously and participants are required to mark them in their order of presentation. A major advantage of using this task to study path complexity effects, compared with the CBT, is the possibility to constrain the choice of locations in order to impose very strictly controlled spatial characteristics. The results of Parmentier et al.'s (2005) Experiment 1 showed that serial recall performance decreased significantly as the number of path crossings (zero, three, or six) contained in the spatial sequences increased. However, a more detailed analysis of the path forming these sequences highlighted the fact that the generation of paths containing crossings tends, in a limited two-dimensional space, to result in longer path segments, so that path crossing and path length tend to correlate. Experiment 2 showed that an effect of path crossing remained when path length was controlled for, however. Converging with unpublished data described by Schumann-Hengsteler et al. (2004), Experiment 3 demonstrated independent effects of these two factors in an orthogonal manipulation. Parmentier et al. then re-examined performance across all the sequences used in their Experiments 1–3 and ran regression analyses to examine the proportion of variance independently explained by path crossing, path length, as well as two new factors: the number of directional changes and the mean path angle. A path 'turning' in the same direction throughout the sequence (e.g., always to the right after reaching a new to-be-remembered location) would contain no directional change. Hence the directional changes aimed to measure the randomness of 'turns'. The analysis confirmed the negative impact of path crossing and path length and revealed an additional effect of angles such that sequences with smaller mean angles (i.e., sequences in which the path tends to 'come back on itself' rather than 'follow through' locations) were significantly less well recalled in order than sequences with larger mean angles. Directional changes did not affect performance. Experiment 4 confirmed the effect of angle using sequences in which path length and the number of crossings were fixed.

The locus of path complexity effects

Path complexity effects are especially interesting because factors such as path crossing and path length relate to aspects of the stimuli that are not visible *per se* to participants. In a computerized CBT or in the Dots Task, participants are presented with a sequence of discrete spatial locations, not a dynamic path. Hence the finding that aspects of the path mediate serial recall memory performance, mixed with the long hypothesized rehearsal mechanism for visuospatial stimuli, leads naturally to the following question: Could path complexity effects reflect a maintenance mechanism consisting of the repeated mental reproduction of the path formed by a sequence? For Schumman-Hengsteler et al. (2004), the link between these effects and rehearsal seemed so obvious that this question took the form of a prediction and the authors went as far as suggesting a vehicle for such effects: 'We assume that visuospatial rehearsal is used to encode and maintain spatiotemporal information by means of repeated activation of the imagined path connecting successive locations using eye movements' (Schumman-Hengsteler et al., 2004, p. 114). Various vehicles for rehearsal have been proposed in the past, such as eye movements, spatial attention shifts, and motor processes (Awh et al., 1999; Lawrence, Myerson, & Abrams, 2004; Pearson & Sahraie, 2003; Smyth et al., 1988; Zimmer, Speiser, & Seidler, 2003). However, a study by Tremblay, Saint-Aubin, and Jalbert (2006), using the Dots Task, provided clear evidence that eye movements do play a key role in the maintenance of visuospatial sequences. Indeed, these authors found that spontaneous eye movements recorded during a 10 s retention interval mediated, to an extent, serial recall performance and that imposing irrelevant eye movements reduced performance to a level comparable with that observed in the absence of eye movement-based rehearsal. Guérard et al. (2009) further reported that the path length effect observed in the Dots Task is abolished when eye movements are suppressed during encoding or retention, suggesting that the effect may relate to the use of eye movements to rehearse the to-be-remembered spatial sequence. Certain aspects of eye movements were affected by path length but not by ocular suppression, making the results somewhat difficult to interpret. A short path elicited longer fixations of the dots during presentation and yielded more successive fixations on consecutive to-be-remembered locations during a retention interval. Together, these findings suggest that path length may affect the quality of the encoding of the sequence of spatial locations, determining the nature of the information to be maintained, which appears to benefit from eye movements as a vehicle for rehearsal. Thus in conclusion, one may argue that eye movements may underpin, at least in part, the rehearsal of to-be-remembered spatial locations, but that the path-length effect might originate in the encoding of the stimuli rather than their active maintenance. One possible explanation of the suppression of the path-length effect by ocular suppression is that ocular suppression, combined with the encoding/rehearsal of the to-be-remembered locations, may have contributed to the forming of very long paths combining relevant and irrelevant locations, and possibly contributed to a distortion of memory for the relevant locations. Thus, while interfering with the participants' eye movements impacts negatively on order memory performance, it is not clear that such effect identifies rehearsal as the locus of the path-length effect.

A similar conclusion follows from a study by Parmentier and Andrés (2006) aiming to determine the locus of the effect of path crossing. In one experiment, the amount of rehearsal was manipulated by comparing immediate and delayed order reconstruction. The rationale was that if the path-crossing effect reflected processes at play during rehearsal, increasing the number of rehearsal cycles should amplify this effect. Despite a sizable main effect of the retention interval, the effect of path crossing remained unaffected, however. In a second experiment, rehearsal was impeded by imposing a changing-state tapping task (known to disrupt the maintenance of visuospatial sequences; e.g., Della Sala et al., 1999; Jones et al., 1995). Here again, despite a relatively large impact of the secondary task, the path-crossing effect remained unaffected. Taken together, these data suggest that the path-crossing effect does not result from the active rehearsal of the to-be-remembered locations, leading to the conclusion that these 'results are in line with the encoding hypothesis according to which the effect of crossing occurs prior to the involvement of rehearsal processes. Once the damage caused by crossing is done (at that early stage of processing), rehearsal can only recycle an already impoverished representation of the sequence' (Parmentier & Andrés, 2006, p. 1872).

Overall, the finding of path-complexity effects, coupled with the suggestion that such effects do not reflect memory maintenance processes *per se*, should encourage researchers to exert caution when interpreting performance in visuospatial serial tasks. For example, an abnormally low spatial span score measured in a patient using the CBT should not be assumed to necessarily reflect a memory deficit for the simple reason that the span procedure confounds sequence length and path complexity. Indeed, as the number of blocks presented in sequence increases, the spatial length of the path formed by those blocks will increase, as will the number of crossings (exponentially). Very few studies publish both the arrangement of blocks as well as the sequences they used. Yet, examining one of the very few to do so (Kessels, van Zandvoort, Postma, Kappelle, & de Haan, 2000), it can be demonstrated that the number of crossings increased sharply as the number of blocks per sequence increases. This means that a patient may potentially present with a low score in the CBT due to a difficulty dealing with a change in complexity across sequences, and not necessarily because of some limitation of memory capacity.

Concluding comment

In this chapter, I reviewed evidence suggesting that while a number of studies reported dissociations between verbal and nonverbal short-term memory, others showed that memory for order exhibits a number of functional characteristics spanning across stimulus modalities. The processing of visuospatial sequences appears to involve two types of mechanisms. Some are modality specific, such as the encoding and maintenance of item information, preserving perceptual aspects of stimuli. Mechanisms underpinning the maintenance of information and using specific rehearsal vehicle (e.g., inner speech for verbal material, eye movements for visuospatial stimuli) can also be distinguished across domains. The concept of transitional information, because it refers to abstract concepts such as probabilities, association, and prediction, is general enough to span across modalities, however. In the case of visuospatial sequences, this concept translates as the spatial path formed by successive spatial locations, as suggested by recent evidence showing that recall performance is mediated by the complexity of this path. While path crossing, path length, and angular variations have been identified as factors contributing to the complexity of spatial sequences, the locus of their effect has been the object of little work. Based on the evidence available so far, encoding (rather than rehearsal) processes seem most sensitive to these factors. Finally, the finding of path-complexity effects in visuospatial serial memory tasks should encourage researchers to consider carefully the spatial characteristics of their stimuli when designing experiments and interpreting results.

References

Avons, S. E. (1998). Serial report and item recognition of novel visual patterns. *British Journal of Psychology, 89,* 285–308.

Avons, S. E. (2007). Spatial span under translation: A study of reference frames. *Memory & Cognition, 35,* 402–417.

Awh, E., Jonides, J., Smith, E. E., Buxton, R. B., Frank, L. R., Love, T., Wong, E. C., & Gmeindl, L. (1999). Rehearsal in spatial working memory: Evidence from neuroimaging. *Psychological Science, 10,* 433–437.

Baddeley, A. D. (1968). How does acoustic similarity influence short-term memory? *Quarterly Journal of Experimental Psychology, 20,* 249–264.

Baddeley, A. D. (1986). *Working memory*. Oxford: Oxford University Press.

Baddeley, A. D., Grant, S., Wight, E., & Thomson, N. (1975). Imagery and visual working memory. In P. M. A. Rabbitt and S. Dornic (Eds.), *Attention and Performance* (Vol. V, pp. 295–317). London: Academic Press.

Baddeley, A. D., & Hull, A. (1979). Prefix and suffix effects: Do they have a common basis? *Journal of Verbal Learning and Verbal Behavior, 18,* 129–140.

Baddeley, A. D., & Lieberman, K. (1980). Spatial working memory. In R. S. Nickerson (Ed.), *Attention and Performance* (Vol. VIII, pp. 521–539). Hillside, N.J.: Lawrence Erlbaum Associates, Inc.

Baddeley, A. D., Papagno, & Andrade, J. (1993). The sandwich effect: The role of attentional factors in serial recall. *Journal of Experimental Psychology: Learning, Memory and Cognition, 19,* 862–870.

Berch, D. B., Krikorian, R., & Huha, E. M. (1998). The Corsi-Tapping Task: Methodological and theoretical considerations. *Brain & Cognition, 38,* 317–338.

Bjork, R.A., & Whitten, W,B. (1974). Recency-sensitive retrieval processes in long-term free recall. *Cognitive Psychology, 6,* 173–189.

Bliss, T. V. P., & Lømo, T. (1973). Long-lasting potentiation of synaptic transmission in the dentrate area of the anesthetized rabbit following stimulation of the perforant path. *Journal of Physiology, 232,* 331–356.

Bor, D., Duncan, J., Wiseman, R. J., & Owen, A. M. (2003). Encoding strategies dissociate prefrontal activity from working memory demand. *Neuron, 37,* 361–367.

Botvinick, M. M., Byslma, L. M. (2005). Regularization in short-term for serial order. *Journal of Experimental Psychology: Learning, Memory & Cognition, 31,* 351–358.

Botvinick, M. M., & Plaut, D. C. (2006). Short-term memory for serial order: A recurrent neural network model. *Journal of Experimental Psychology: Learning, Memory & Cognition, 113,* 201–233.

Bower, G. H., & Winzenz, D. (1969). Group structure, coding, and memory for digits series. *Journal of Experimental Psychology Monograph Supplement, 80,* 1–17.

Broadbent, D. E., & Broadbent, M. H. P. (1981). Recency effects in visual memory. *Quarterly Journal of Experimental Psychology, 33,* 1–15.

Burgess, N., & Hitch, G. J. (1999). Memory for serial order: A network model of the phonological loop and its timing. *Psychological Review, 106,* 551–581.

Corsi, P. M. (1972). Human memory and the medial temporal region of the brain. *Dissertation Abstracts International, 34 (02),* 891B (University Microfilms No. AAI05–77717).

Courtney, S. M., Ungerleider, L. G., Keil, K., & Haxby, J. V. (1996). Object and spatial visual working memory activate separate neural systems in human cortex. *Cerebral Cortex, 6,* 39–49.

Couture, M., & Tremblay, S. (2006). Exploring the characteristics of the visuo-spatial Hebb repetition effect. *Memory & Cognition, 34,* 1720–1729.

Crowder, R. G. & Morton, J. (1969). Precategorical acoustical storage (PAS). *Perception & Psychophysics, 5,* 365–373.

Cumming, N., Page, M., & Norris, D. (2003). Testing a positional model of the Hebb effect. *Memory, 11,* 43–63.

Davis, H. P., Bajszar, Jr. G., & Squire, L. R. (1993). *Colorado neuropsychological tests.* Colorado Springs, Co: Colorado Neuropsychological Tests.

De Renzi, E., & Nichelli, P. (1975). Verbal and nonverbal short term memory impairment following hemispheric damage. *Cortex, 11,* 341–353.

Della Sala, S., Gray, C., Baddeley, A., Allamano, N., & Wilson, N. (1999). Pattern span: a tool for unwelding visuo-spatial memory. *Neuropsychologia, 37,* 1189–1199.

Depoorter, A., & Vandierendonck, A. (2009). Evidence for modality-independent order coding in working memory. *Quarterly Journal of Experimental Psychology, 32,* 531–549.

Dewhurst, S., Hitch, G. J., & Barry, C. (1998). Separate effects of word frequency and age of acquisition in recognition and recall. *Journal of Experimental Psychology: Learning, Memory & Cognition, 24,* 184–298.

Estes, W. K. (1972). An associative basis for coding and organization in memory. In A. W. Melton & E. Martin (Eds.), *Coding processes in human memory* (pp. 161–190). Washington, DC: Winston.

Farah, M. J., Hammond, K. M., Levine, D. N., & Calvanio, R. (1988). Visual and spatial mental imagery: Dissociable systems of representation. *Cognitive Psychology, 20,* 439–462.

Farmer, E. W., Berman, J. V. F., & Fletcher, Y. L. (1986). Evidence for a visuo-spatial scratch-pad in working memory. *Quarterly Journal of Experimental Psychology, 38,* 675–688.

Farrand, P., Parmentier, F. B. R., & Jones, D. M. (2001). Temporal-spatial memory: Retrieval of spatial information does not reduce recency. *Acta Psychologica, 106,* 285–301.

Frankish, C. F. (1989). Perceptual organisation and precategorical acoustic storage. *Journal of Experimental Psychology: Learning, Memory and Cognition, 15,* 469–479.

Frankish, C. (1996). Auditory short-term memory and the perception of speech. In S. E. Gathercole (Ed.), *Models of short-term memory* (pp. 179–207). Hove, UK: Psychology Press.

Fuster, J. M. (1995). *Memory in the cerebral cortex: An empirical approach to neural networks in the human and nonhuman primate.* Cambridge, MA: MIT Press.

Gagnon, S., Bédard, M. J., & Turcotte, J. (2006). The effect of old age on supra-span learning of visuo-spatial sequences under incidental and intentional encoding instructions. *Brain & Cognition, 59,* 225–235.

Gould, J. H., & Glencross, D. J. (1990). Do children with a specific reading disability have a general serial-ordering problem? *Neuropsychologia, 28,* 271–278.

Greene, R. L., & Samuel, A. G. (1986). Recency and suffix effects in serial recall of musical stimuli. *Journal of Experimental Psychology: Learning, Memory, & Cognition, 12,* 517–524.

Guérard, K., Hughes, R. W., & Tremblay, S. (2006). An isolation effect in serial memory for spatial information. *Quarterly Journal of Experimental Psychology, 61,* 752–762.

Guérard, K., & Tremblay, S. (2008). Revisiting evidence for modularity and functional equivalence across verbal and spatial domains in memory. *Journal of Experimental Psychology: Learning, Memory & Cognition, 34,* 556–569.

Guérard, K., Tremblay, S., & Saint-Aubin, J. (2009). The processing of spatial information in short-term memory: Insights from eye tracking the path length effect. *Acta Psychologica, 132,* 136–144.

Hamilton, P., & Hockey, R. (1974). Active selection of items to be remembered: The role of timing. *Cognitive Psychology, 6,* 61–83.

Hanley, J. R., Young, A. W., & Pearson, N. A. (1991). Impairment of the visuo-spatial sketch-pad. *Quarterly Journal of Experimental Psychology, 43,* 101–125.

Hebb, D. O. (1961). Distinctive features of learning in the higher animal. In J. F. Delafresnaye (Ed.), *Brain mechanisms and learning* (pp. 37–51). London: Oxford University Press.

Hitch, G. J., Burgess, N., Towse, J. N., & Culpin, V. (1996). Temporal grouping in immediate recall: A working memory analysis. *Quarterly Journal of Experimental Psychology, 49,* 116–139.

Hitch, G. J., Fastame, M. C., & Flude, B. (2005). How is the serial order of a verbal sequence coded? Some comparisons between models. *Memory, 3–4,* 247–258.

Hulme, C., Roodenrys, S., Brown, G., & Mercer, R. (1995). The role of long-term memory mechanisms in memory span. *British Journal of Psychology, 86,* 527–536.

Hulme, C., Thomson, N., Muir, C., & Lawrence, A. (1984). Speech rate and the development of short-term memory span. *Journal of Memory & Language, 30,* 685–701.

Jensen, O. (2006). Maintenance of multiple working memory items by temporal segmentation. *Neuroscience, 139,* 237–249.

Jensen, O., & Lisman, J. E. (2005). Hippocampal sequence-encoding driven by a cortical multi-item working memory buffer. *Trends in Neurosciences, 28,* 67–72.

Jones, D. M., Farrand, P., Stuart, G., & Morris, N. (1995). Functional equivalence of verbal and spatial information in serial short-term memory. *Journal of Experimental Psychology: Learning, Memory, & Cognition, 21,* 1008–1018.

Jonides, J. (1995). Working memory and thinking. In E. E. Smith, & D. N. Osherson (Eds.), D. N. Osherson (General Ed.), *Thinking (Vol. 3). An invitation to cognitive science* (2nd ed., pp. 215–265). Cambridge: MIT Press.

Kantowitz, B. H., Ornstein, P. A., & Schwartz, M. (1972). Encoding and immediate serial recall of consonant strings. *Journal of Experimental Psychology, 93,* 105–110.

Kaplan, E., Fein, D., Morris, R., & Delis, D. C. (1991). *WAIS-R as a neuropsychological instrument.* New York: The Psychological Corporation.

Kemps, E. (1999). Effects of complexity on visuo-spatial working memory. *European Journal of Cognitive Psychology, 11,* 335–356.

Kemps, E. (2001). Complexity effects in visuo-spatial working memory: Implications for the role of long-term memory. *Memory, 9,* 13–27.

Kessels, R. P. C., van Zandvoort, K. J. E., Postma, A., Kappelle, L. J., & de Haan, E. H. F. (2000). The Corsi block-tapping task: Standardization and normative data. *Applied Neuropsychology, 7,* 252–258.

Larsen, J. D., Baddeley, A. D., & Andrade, J. (2000). Phonological similarity and the irrelevant speech effect: Implications for models of short-term verbal memory. *Memory, 8,* 145–157.

Lawrence, B. M., Myerson, J., & Abrams, R. A. (2004). Interference with spatial working memory: An eye movement is more than a shift of attention. *Psychomonic Bulletin & Review, 11,* 488–494.

Lewandowsky, S., & Farrell, S. (2000). A redintegration account of the effects of speech rate, lexicality, and word frequency in immediate serial recall. *Psychological Research, 63,* 163–173.

Lisman, J. (2005). The Theta/Gamma discrete phase code occurring during the hippocampal phase precession may be a more general brain coding scheme. *Hippocampus, 15,* 913–922.

Logie, R. H. (1995). *Visuo-spatial working memory.* Hove, UK: Lawrence Erlbaum Associates Ltd.

Logie, R. H., & Marchetti, C. (1991). Visuo-spatial working memory: Visual, spatial or central executive? In R. H. Logie & M. Denis (Eds.), *Mental images in human cognition* (pp. 105–115). Amsterdam: North Holland Press.

Logie, R. H., & Pearson, D. G. (1997). The inner eye and the inner scribe of visuo-spatial working memory: Evidence from developmental fractionation. *European Journal of Cognitive Psychology, 9,* 241–257.

Logie, R. H., Zucco, G. M., & Baddeley, A. D. (1990). Interference with visual short-term memory. *Acta Psychologica, 75,* 55–74.

Luzzatti, C., Vecchi, T., Agazzi, D., Cesa-Bianchi, M., & Vergani, C. (1998). A neurological dissociation between preserved visual and impaired spatial processing in mental imagery. *Cortex, 34,* 461–469.

Mahrer, P., & Miles, C. (1999). Memorial and strategic determinants of tactile recency. *Journal of Experimental Psychology: Learning, Memory, & Cognition, 25,* 630–643.

Manning, S. K., & Schreier, H. (1988). Recency and suffix effects in pictures as a function of recall method. *American Journal of Psychology, 101,* 97–109.

Martinez, J. L., & Derrick, B. E. (1996). Long-term potentiation and learning. *Annual Review of Psychology, 47,* 173–203.

McFarland, D. J., & Cacace, A. T. (1992). Aspects of short-term acoustic recognition memory: Modality and serial position effects. *Audiology, 31,* 342–352.

Miles, C., & Jenkins, R. (2000). Recency and suffix effects with immediate recall of olfactory stimuli. *Memory, 8,* 195–206.

Miller, G. A., & Selfridge, J. A. (1951). Verbal context and the recall of meaningful material. *American Journal of Psychology, 63,* 176–185.

Morris, N. (1987). Exploring the visuo-spatial scratch pad. *Quarterly Journal of Experimental Psychology: Human Experimental Psychology, 39,* 409–430.

Murray, A., & Jones, D. M. (2002). Articulatory complexity at item boundaries in serial recall: The case of Welsh and English digit span. *Journal of Experimental Psychology: Learning, Memory & Cognition, 28,* 594–598.

Nairne, J. S., & McNabb, W. L. (1985). More modality effects in the absence of sound. *Journal of Experimental Psychology: Learning, Memory, and Cognition, 11,* 596–604.

Neath, I. (1993). Distinctiveness and serial position effects in recognition. *Memory & Cognition, 21,* 689–698.

Neath, I. (1997). Modality, concreteness, and set-size effects in a free reconstruction of order task. *Memory & Cognition, 25,* 256–263.

Ng, H. L. H., & Maybery, M. T. (2002). Temporal grouping effects in short-term memory: An evaluation of time-dependent models. *Quarterly Journal of Experimental Psychology, 55A,* 391–424.

Nicholls, A. P., & Jones, D. M. (2002a). Capturing the suffix: Cognitive streaming in immediate serial recall. *Journal of Experimental Psychology: Learning, Memory & Cognition, 28,* 12–28.

Nicholls, A. P. & Jones, D. M. (2002b). The sandwich effect reassessed: Effects of streaming, distraction, and modality. *Memory & Cognition, 30,* 81–88.

Page, M. P. A., Cumming, N., Norris, D., Hitch, G. J., & McNeil, A. M. (2006). Repetition learning in the immediate serial recall of visual and auditory materials. *Journal of Experimental Psychology: Learning, Memory & Cognition, 32,* 716–733.

Parmentier, F. B. R., & Andrés, P. (2006). The impact of path crossing on visuo-spatial serial memory: Encoding or rehearsal effect? *Quarterly Journal of Experimental Psychology, 59,* 1867–1874.

Parmentier, F. B. R., Andrés, P., Elford, G., & Jones, D. M. (2006). Hierarchical organisation in visuo-spatial serial memory: Interaction of temporal order with spatial and temporal grouping. *Psychological Research, 70,* 200–217.

Parmentier, F. B. R., Elford, G., & Maybery, M. T. (2005). Transitional information in spatial serial memory: Path characteristics affect recall performance. *Journal of Experimental Psychology: Learning, Memory, & Cognition, 31,* 412–427.

Parmentier, F. B. R., & Jones, D. M. (2000). Functional characteristics of auditory temporal-spatial memory: Evidence from serial order errors. *Journal of Experimental Psychology: Learning, Memory, & Cognition, 26,* 222–238.

Parmentier, F. B. R., Maybery, M. T., Huitson, M., & Jones, D. M. (2008). The perceptual determinants of repetition learning in auditory space. *Journal of Memory & Language, 58,* 978–997.

Parmentier, F. B. R., Maybery, M., & Jones, D. M. (2004). Temporal grouping in auditory spatial serial memory. *Psychonomic Bulletin & Review, 11,* 501–507.

Parmentier, F. B. R., Tremblay, S., & Jones, D. M. (2004). Exploring the suffix effect in serial visuo-spatial short-term memory. *Psychonomic Bulletin & Review, 11,* 289–295.

Pearson, D. G., & Sahraie, A. (2003). Oculomotor control and maintenance of spatially and temporally distributed events in visuo-spatial working memory. *Quarterly Journal of Experimental Psychology, 56A,* 1089–1111.

Penney, C. G. (1985). Elimination of the suffix effect on preterminal list items with unpredictable list length: Evidence for a dual model of suffix effects. *Journal of Experimental Psychology: Learning, Memory, & Cognition, 11,* 229–247.

Penney, C. G. (1989). Modality effects and the structure of short-term verbal memory. *Memory & Cognition, 17,* 398–422.

Phillips, W. A., & Christie, D. F. (1977a). Components of visual memory. *Quarterly Journal of Experimental Psychology, 29,* 117–133.

Phillips, W. A., & Christie, D. F. (1977b). Interference with visualization. *Quarterly Journal of Experimental Psychology, 29,* 637–650.

Pickering, S. J., Gathercole, S. E., Hall, M., & Lloyd, S. A. (2001). Development of memory for pattern and path: Further evidence for the fractionation of visuo-spatial memory. *Quarterly Journal of Experimental Psychology, 54,* 397–420.

Potter, M. C., & Levy, E. I. (1969). Recognition memory for a rapid sequence of pictures. *Journal of Experimental Psychology, 81,* 10–15.

Rowe, E. J., & Rowe, W. G. (1976). Stimulus suffix effects with speech and nonspeech sounds. *Memory & Cognition, 4,* 128–131.

Schumann-Hengsteler, R., Strobl, M., & Zoelch, C. (2004). Temporal memory for locations: On the coding of spatiotemporal information in children and adults. In G. L. Allen (Ed.), *Human spatial memory*. Mahwah, NJ: Lawrence Erlbaum Associates, Inc.

Smirni, P., Villardita, C., & Zappalà, G. (1983). Influence of different paths on spatial memory performance in the block-tapping test. *Journal of Clinical Neuropsychology, 5,* 355–359.

Smyth, M. M., Pearson, N. A., & Pendleton, L. R. (1988). Movement and working memory: Patterns and positions in space. *Quarterly Journal of Experimental Psychology, 40A,* 497–514.

Smyth, M. M., & Scholey, K. A. (1994a). Characteristics of spatial memory span: Is there an analogy to the word length effect based on movement time? *Quarterly Journal of Experimental Psychology, 47A*, 91–117.

Smyth, M. M., & Scholey, K. A. (1994b). Interference in immediate spatial memory. *Memory & Cognition, 22,* 1–13.

Smyth, M. M., & Scholey, K. A. (1996). Serial order in spatial immediate memory. *Quarterly Journal of Experimental Psychology, 49A*, 159–177.

Stuart, G., & Hulme, C. (2000). The effects of word co-occurrence on short-term memory: Associative links in long-term memory affects short-term memory performance. *Journal of Experimental Psychology: Learning, Memory & Cognition, 26,* 796–802.

Surprenant, A. M., Pitt, M. A., & Crowder, R. G. (1993). Auditory recency in immediate memory. *Quarterly Journal of Experimental Psychology, 46A,* 193–223.

Tremblay, S., Macken, W. J., & Jones, D. M. (2001). The impact of broadband noise on serial memory: Changes in band-pass frequency increase disruption. *Memory, 9,* 323–331.

Tremblay, S., Nicholls, A., Parmentier, F. B. R., & Jones, D. M. (2005). Visual distraction and visuo-spatial memory: A sandwich effect. *Memory, 13,* 357–363.

Tremblay, S., Parmentier, F. B. R., Guérard, K., Nicholls, A. P., & Jones, D. M. (2006). Is spatial special? The modality effect in the serial recall of spatial material. *Journal of Experimental Psychology: Learning, Memory & Cognition, 32,* 1208–1215.

Tremblay, S., Saint-Aubin, J., & Jalbert, A. (2006). Rehearsal in serial memory from visual-spatial information: Evidence from eye movements. *Psychonomic Bulletin & Review, 13,* 452–457.

Tresch, M. C., Sinnamon, H. M., & Seamon, J. G. (1993). Double dissociation of spatial and object visual memory: Evidence from selective interference in intact human subjects. *Neuropsychologia, 31,* 211–219.

Turcotte, J., Gagnon, S., & Poirier, M. (2005). The effect of old age on the learning of supraspan sequences. *Psychology and Aging, 20,* 251–260.

Vecchi, T., & Cornoldi, C. (1999). Passive and active manipulation in visuo-spatial working memory: Further evidence from the study of age differences. *European Journal of Cognitive Psychology, 11,* 391–406.

Vecchi, T., & Girelli, L. (1998). Gender differences in visuo-spatial processing: The importance of distinguishing between passive storage and active manipulation. *Acta Psychologica, 99,* 1–16.

Walker, P., Hitch, G. J., & Duroe, S. (1993). The effect of visual similarity on short-term memory for spatial location: Implications for the capacity of visual short-term memory. *Acta Psychologica, 83,* 203–224.

Ward, G., Avons, S. E., & Melling, L. (2005). Serial position curves in short-term memory: Functional equivalence across modalities. *Memory, 13,* 308–17.

Watkins, M. J., & Sechler, E. S. (1989). Adapting to an irrelevant item in an immediate recall task. *Memory & Cognition, 17,* 682–692.

Zimmer, H. D., Speiser, H. R., & Seidler, B. (2003). Spatio-temporal working-memory and short-term object-location tasks use different memory mechanisms. *Acta Psychologica, 114,* 41–65.

5 What underlies the ability to guide action with spatial information that is no longer present in the environment?

Bradley R. Postle

In early evolutionary history, as organisms developed the ability to move through and act on their environment, and to use perception to guide these actions, advantage was surely conferred on those that could, when appropriate, delay their actions relative to the perceived events that prompted them. For example, in some instances the optimal response to perceiving a source of food may not be to instantaneously pounce, but, rather, to withhold that action until the prey re-emerges from the hole into which it has disappeared. Thus, the ability to control actions, including the ability to guide actions with information no longer accessible to sensory receptors, likely evolved as a core function of perception–action systems. This perspective highlights the fact that such terms as *attention*, *response inhibition*, and the topic of this volume, *working memory*, are constructs that have been developed by scientists trying to reverse engineer a highly evolved neurocognitive system. Although unquestionably useful for the categorization and description of certain types of behaviour and/or neurophysiology, they need not correspond to discrete systems that can be meaningfully understood in isolation from the larger system within which they are observed. Rather, they may be better construed as properties or functions of an integrated perception–action system. The focus of this chapter will be on the short-term retention of spatial information that temporally bridges the offset of the sensory stimulus and the onset of the action that is guided by that sensory information. This is typically operationalized experimentally by studying the delay period of tests of delayed recognition and delayed response.

A perception–action framework

A framework that situates spatial working memory in a perception–action perspective holds that incoming visual information that captures attention, whether endogenously or exogenously, automatically, concurrently, activates several brain systems: parietal and frontal systems involved in the control of attention, the eye movement control system in the superior colliculus, and frontal systems that implement inhibitory control (Theeuwes, Belopolsky, & Olivers, 2009). An anatomical substrate for the putative simultaneous engagement of what we will refer to as the *perception–action network* exists in the form of extensive bidirectional connections between striate and extrastriate visual regions and the parietal cortex and between these occipital regions and the superior colliculus (e.g., Schiller, 1986), between superior colliculus and parietal cortex (e.g., Pare & Wurtz, 1997) and superior colliculus and the frontal eye fields (FEF, e.g., Sommer & Wurtz, 2000), and between frontal and parietal cortex (e.g., Selemon & Goldman-Rakic, 1988). The simultaneous, reverberatory activation (or inhibition) of the representation of one or more retinotopically encoded locations at multiple stations of this network produces a state that, depending on behavioural contingencies, can produce an eye movement, covert attention to a location (or an object at a location), or the short-term retention of spatial information, with the relative balance of excitation and inhibition at each level of the system determining which of these behaviours is expressed. The utility of this framework for understanding the short-term retention of spatial information will underpin much of this review.

The frontal eye fields as a source of attentional control

Visual attention is generally assumed to reflect the top–down prioritization of the perceptual processing of one (or more) region(s) of the visual field over others (Posner, 1980). One computational account holds the deployment of attention to emerge from recurrent interactions between posterior perceptual systems and neurons in the FEF (Hamker, 2005). In brief, attentional bias in perceptual regions arises from the interaction of feedforward spatial information encoded in the receptive fields of feature-selective neurons (e.g., in area V4), and the resultant activation of neurons in the FEF. The build-up of activity in the FEF generates spatially selective feedback to visual areas – the attentional bias that has been observed in many electrophysiological studies of visual cognition (e.g., Chelazzi, Miller, Duncan, & Desimone, 1993, 2001; Luck, Chelazzi, Hillyard, & Desimone, 1997; Treue, 1999). Consistent with this theoretical account are the neurophysiological findings that subthreshold stimulation to a region of the FEF with a known motor field produces a covert shift of spatial attention to the very same region of space represented by the motor field (Moore & Fallah, 2001, 2004), and that this microstimulation can also enhance stimulus-specific responses in V4 neurons (Moore & Armstrong, 2003). One perspective on these computational and neurophysiological data (although not universally endorsed, see Awh, Armstrong, & Moore, 2006, for discussion) is that they are consistent with the idea that spatial attention corresponds to the preparation to initiate an action, the 'premotor theory of attention' (Rizzolatti, Riggio, Dascola, & Umiltà, 1987). For the perception–action framework introduced at the beginning of this chapter, they provide explicit computational and neurophysiological demonstrations of the simultaneous and interactive recruitment of attention and of an eye movement plan as a consequence of the perception of a behaviourally relevant stimulus.

Attention and working memory

Turning now to the short-term retention of a location in space, one potent idea has been that of attention-based rehearsal, which holds that the short-term retention of spatial information is accomplished via the covert allocation of spatial attention to one or more to-be-remembered locations (Awh, Jonides, & Reuter-Lorenz, 1998; Awh & Jonides, 2001). Behavioural evidence for this idea comes from the fact that the processing of stimuli presented at a location being held in memory shows the same benefits as those produced when attention is covertly allocated to that location, and that memory suffers when attention is pulled away during the delay period (Awh et al., 1998; Awh & Jonides, 2001). Relevant physiological evidence includes the fact that the short-term retention of spatial information biases event-related potentials (ERP, computed from the electroencephalogram (EEG), Awh, Anllo-Vento, & Hillyard, 2000) and functional magnetic resonance imaging (fMRI) signals (Awh et al., 1999; Postle, Awh, Jonides, Smith, & D'Esposito, 2004) in the same manner as does the covert allocation of spatial attention in tasks that make no overt demands on memory. This is illustrated in Figure 5.1 (see plates), in which an attention-like bias is evident in delay-period activity across the entire cortical manifold of the posterior dorsal stream, the regions responsible for spatial perception and cognition. Inspection of this figure indicates that the magnitude of the putative attentional bias declines monotonically along the caudal to rostral axis, a phenomenon that may reflect the transition along this axis from cortical *sites* to cortical *sources* of attentional control. The superior parietal cortex and FEF have been identified as key sources of the endogenous control of attention in humans (e.g., Corbetta & Shulman, 2002; Yantis & Serences, 2003), and cortical sources of control might be expected to show less topographic variation as a function of the location of attentional focus than the sites experiencing its effects (Ruff et al., 2006).

The concept of attention-based rehearsal can be tied directly to the perception-action framework by considering a recent study in which monkeys were trained to perform an attentional cuing task while activity was recorded from neurons in the FEF (Armstrong, Chang, & Moore, 2009). Each trial began with a lever press, which triggered a visual cue to attend covertly to one of six locations at which oriented-grating stimuli would be presented. After a subsequent delay, an array of stimuli was flashed twice, and the animal signalled the detection of an orientation change in one of the stimuli by releasing the lever (or the absence of change by continuing to depress the lever). Critically, no eye movements were required, and breaks of central fixation were discarded from analyses. Recordings were made in FEF neurons whose movement fields encompassed the location of one of the stimuli. By reference to this group's earlier work (Moore & Fallah, 2001, 2004), this is equivalent to saying that the 'attention field' of the FEF neuron encompassed the location of one of the stimuli. The results indicated that cuing the location represented by an FEF neuron yielded sustained elevated activity across the cue-to-target delay, during the first flash, across the inter-flash interval, and during the second flash. That this can be characterized as an *attentional* effect follows from the fact that behaviourally, change-detection performance benefited from valid spatial cuing in the way that one would expect. That it can also be characterized as a *mnemonic* effect follows from the fact that the strength of the location-specific sustained activity, in the absence of visual stimulation, was predictive of performance on the task. By definition, then, the response fields of these neurons were shown to function as 'memory fields' during portions of the trial when they represented regions of space in the absence of visual stimulation and in the absence of an overt motor plan. An overall conclusion from this experiment, then, which is consistent with a larger body of research not reviewed here (e.g., Sommer & Wurtz, 2001), is that whether these cells support a motoric, an attentional, or a mnemonic function depends entirely on the behavioural and environmental circumstances of the moment. The same point has recently been demonstrated via a pattern classification-based decoding of fMRI data from the FEF of humans performing tasks of eye movements versus visual attention versus spatial working memory (Riggall, Ikkai, Srimal, & Curtis, 2008). From this, one can conclude that the categorical distinctions implied by these labels are not honoured by the nervous system.

Oculomotor control and working memory

Of course, the neurons of the FEF that were the focus of the previous paragraph do not operate in isolation of the perception–action network in which they are located. Just one example of this is the fact that selective cooling of populations of neurons that show spatially tuned, sustained delay-period activity has comparably deleterious effects on delay-task performance whether the targeted tissue is in caudal prefrontal cortex or in posterior parietal cortex (Chafee & Goldman-Rakic, 2000). Indeed, similar response properties of neurons in these two regions (e.g., Chafee & Goldman-Rakic, 1998), together with largely overlapping patterns of connectivity (Selemon & Goldman-Rakic, 1988), makes it difficult to identify relative specialization of function of these two regions. Another region in the perception–action network whose function is less equivocal is the superior colliculus, the subcortical structure that constitutes the sole anatomical route to the muscles that control the position and movement of the eyes. The inferior layers of the superior colliculus are organized in a retinotopic saccade map that encodes current eye position and the location(s) of planned eye movements. As already summarized, the superior colliculus is anatomically and functionally connected with several cortical regions involved in visual perception, attention, working memory, and eye-movement control (Sommer & Wurtz, 2001). A series of clever experiments by Theeuwes and colleagues has taken advantage of our understanding of this structure and its role in eye-movement control to demonstrate that 'working memory is the same as programming an eye-movement' (2009, p. 110). For example, they have shown that remembering a location in space has the same deviating effect on eye-movement trajectories as does the presence of a visual stimulus in that location (Theeuwes, Olivers, & Chizk, 2005; see also Zimmer & Liesefeld, Chapter 3, this volume). Because this phenomenon has been linked to competitive interactions between represented locations in the superior colliculus (Sparks & Hartwich-Young, 1989; Munoz & Istvan, 1998), the implication is that the remembered location is represented in the superior colliculus as a suppressed saccade (i.e., as localized inhibition in the saccade map, Aizawa & Wurtz, 1998).

Theeuwes et al. (2009) hypothesize that a cortical control signal, perhaps from the FEF, inhibits a reflexive saccade to the remembered location, a hypothesis that is consistent with the difficulty that patients with FEF damage have in inhibiting reflexive eye movements (Pierrot-Deseilligny, Rivaud, Gaymard, & Agid, 1991). The same mechanism of an 'inhibitory tag', which is likely represented in parallel at several levels of the perception–action network, can account for the phenomenon of inhibition of return (Godijn & Theeuwes, 2002) and in inhibition of return-like phenomena observed during the short-term retention of spatial information (Belopolsky & Theeuwes, 2009). More generally, the dynamic interplay between the putatively visual, attentional, executive, and motoric elements of the perception–action network can also account for the benefits of responding to stimuli appearing at memorized locations (Awh et al., 1998), for the biasing of remembered locations in the direction of attention-capturing distractors (Van der Stigchel, Merten, Meeter, & Theeuwes, 2007), and for interactions between working memory and visual search (Soto, Heinke, Humphreys, & Blanco, 2005; Olivers, Meijer, & Theeuwes, 2006; Soto, Humphreys, & Rothstein, 2007).

This overview of the role of the perception–action network in many attentional, mnemonic, and motoric behaviours also accounts for the extensive literature on interactions between spatial working memory and several motor effector systems: Working memory for locations is selectively disrupted by concurrent finger tapping (Farmer, Berman, & Fletcher, 1986; Salway & Logie, 1995; Smyth, Pearson, & Pendleton, 1988), pointing (Hale, Myerson, Rhee, Weiss, & Abrams, 1996), eye movements (Baddeley, 1986; Hale et al., 1996; Lawrence, Myerson, Oonk, & Abrams, 2001; Pearson & Sahraie, 2003; Postle, Idzikowski, Della Sala, Logie, & Baddeley, 2006b), and arm movements (Baddeley & Lieberman, 1980; Lawrence et al., 2001; Logie & Marchetti, 1991; Quinn & Ralston, 1986). For example, Postle and Hamidi (2007) had subjects perform delayed recognition of either the identity or location of geometric shapes, and observed a selective pattern of disruption produced by nonvisual secondary tasks performed in the dark – passive listening to nouns or endogenous generation of saccades, respectively. Event-related fMRI of this task indicated that the interference-specific effect corresponded to a relative increase of activity localized to regions associated with the secondary task in question: left hemisphere perisylvian cortex in the case of passive-listening distraction, and frontal oculomotor regions (the FEF and supplementary eye fields) in the case of saccadic distraction. Within these regions the neural interference effects were specific to voxels that showed delay-period activity on unfilled memory trials, and they predicted individual differences in the magnitude of the behavioural interference effect (Figure 5.2, see plate).

The dynamics of the perception–action network

To this point this chapter has considered the brain systems that support the short-term retention of spatial information. We now turn to another level of analysis – task-related neural oscillations measured with EEG – to further explore the mechanistic bases of spatial working memory and related constructs. That is, what are the neural dynamics within the perception–action network that govern the balance between excitation and inhibition that was invoked earlier, and that implement the functions of attentional prioritization, motor preparation, and inhibition that can support the short-term retention of spatial information?

Alpha-band oscillations and visuospatial cognition

The first-ever published report of human EEG data described the phenomenon of oscillations recorded by posterior electrodes, centred on a frequency of 10 Hz, whose magnitude increased when the eyes were closed and decreased when the eyes were opened (Berger, 1929). Replications and extensions of this finding have led to the widely accepted view that posterior alpha-band oscillations correspond to an 'idling' state of brain, with higher-frequency oscillations predominating (i.e., in the beta and gamma bands) when the same networks are engaged in, for example, active visual processing. More recently, important roles for alpha-band oscillations have been established in visual attention and stimulus detection. In one highly cited study by Worden, Foxe, Wang, and Simpson (2000), for example, EEG data collected from subjects performing a Posner (1980)-style cued-attention task indicated that the onset of the attentional cue triggered an increase in the power of alpha-band oscillations in the hemisphere ipsilateral to that cue. That is, the shifting of spatial attention to one visual field prompted an increase in the magnitude of alpha-band oscillations in the other, unattended, visual field. Subsequent work has confirmed and extended this finding, demonstrating both decreases in alpha-band power at attended locations and increases at unattended locations. In one recent account, for example, alpha-band oscillations serve to prioritize internally directed processing (e.g., mental imagery) by gating the sensory processing of stimuli in the environment (Cooper, Croft, Dominey, Burgess, & Gruzelier, 2003). In another, shifts of attention are associated with transient decreases in alpha-band power over the selected region, whereas the sustained maintenance of attention to that area is associated with a later-developing and sustained increase in alpha-band power over unattended regions (Rihs, Michel, & Thut, 2009).

The functional significance of these shifts in posterior alpha-band power is seen in their association with cortical excitability and visual performance. Spontaneous fluctuations in occipital alpha-band power predict cortical excitability, as indexed by the perception of transcranial magnetic stimulation (TMS)-induced visual phosphenes (Romei et al., 2008). They also predict successful detection of at-threshold visual stimuli, with lower power associated with superior detection performance (e.g., Hanslmayr, Aslan, Staudigl, Klimesch, Hermann, & Bauml, 2007; Mathewson, Gratton, Fabiani, Beck, & Ro, 2009; van Dijk, Schoffelen, Oostenveld, & Jensen, 2008). Further, visual performance is also sensitive to the instantaneous phase angle (i.e., position in the cycle) of the spontaneous posterior alpha-band oscillation at the time of stimulus presentation (e.g., Busch, Dubois, & VanRullen, 2009; Mathewson et al., 2009). A related finding is that application of transcranial alternating current to visual cortex evokes phosphenes in a frequency-dependent manner, with maximal effects centred on 10 Hz when delivered in darkness, and shifting to higher frequencies, but still encompassing the alpha-band, when delivered in light (Kanai, Chaleb, Antal, Walsh, & Paulus, 2008). From these, and additional, findings, Thut and Miniussi (2009) induce that 'local α-amplitude carries information about the momentary (excitability) state of neurons within the dorsal processing stream' (p. 185).

Alpha-band oscillations and control

Alpha-band oscillations have also been ascribed an important role in the control of cortical processing. Although high-frequency oscillations are associated with information processing in local cortical modules (e.g., Uhlhaas et al., 2009), lower-frequency oscillations, including in the alpha band, have been proposed as a means of implementing top–down control, including the coordination of processing between anatomically distal modules (e.g., von Stein, Chiang, & Koenig, 2000; Palva, Palva, & Kaila, 2005). One reason for this is that the physics of wave propagation make lower-frequency oscillators better suited to influence larger areas of tissue (Buzsaki, 2006). A mechanism by which this control might be accomplished is by the synchronization of local higher frequency oscillations to a more 'global' alpha-band oscillation (i.e., cross-frequency phase synchrony, Palva & Palva, 2007). Numerous studies, in several species, have demonstrated the behavioural relevance of such large-scale synchrony, with between-region oscillatory synchronization associated with, for example, attention, working memory, and conscious sensory perception (for reviews, see Palva & Palva, 2007; Uhlhaas et al., 2009). The fine-grained physiological basis for this type of top–down control has been demonstrated by simultaneous multicellular recordings made from multiple brain areas. These studies indicate that alpha-band oscillations in infragranular layers of higher-level cortical areas (i.e., deep layers that send feedback projections to upstream cortical areas) act as pacemakers that control the dynamics of alpha-band oscillations in the lower-level areas that receive these feedback projections. (For example, alpha-band oscillations in infragranular layers of parietal cortex govern expectancy-related alpha-band oscillations in primary visual cortex of the cat (von Stein et al., 2000), and laminar differences in alpha-band dynamics between interotemporal cortex versus occipital areas V4 and V2 suggests a substrate whereby the former might control the attentional states of the latter two (Bollimunta, Chen, Schroeder, & Ding, 2008).)

Brain stimulation as a tool to study the role of alpha-band oscillations in visuospatial cognition

The previous section suggests a strategy for developing *a priori* tests of the functional contribution of neuronal oscillations in different frequency bands. We have already reviewed how one study has used transcranial alternating current stimulation to map out the frequency tuning of visual cortex, and analogous approaches have also been applied to the motor system (Pogosyan, Gaynor, Eusebio, & Brown, 2009). In a study targeting visuospatial cognition, Klimesch, Sauseng, and Gerloff (2003) have used repetitive TMS (rTMS) to build on earlier EEG findings that subjects with high pre-trial alpha-band power tended to show greater task-related drops in alpha-band power (a phenomenon known as 'event-related desynchronization'), and tended to be better performers on a wide variety of tasks (Neubauer, Freudenthaler, & Pfurtscheller, 1995; Klimesch, 1999). Importantly, this phenomenon was specific to the upper alpha band, the 2-Hz of the EEG immediately above each subject's individual resting alpha frequency (this frequency varies considerably among healthy individuals (Doppelmayr, Klimesch, Pachinger, & Ripper, 1998)). For this experiment they reasoned that they might improve performance on a mental rotation task by exogenously increasing the pre-trial power of oscillations in the upper alpha band with a conditioning train of rTMS delivered immediately prior to the visual presentation of stimuli. Consistent with their predictions, they found that a train of 24 pulses of TMS, delivered to frontal or to parietal cortex at a rate of IAF + 1 Hz (to target the upper alpha band), produced improved accuracy. The control conditions of 24-pulse trains delivered at IAF – 3 Hz (i.e., the lower alpha band) and at 20 Hz, in contrast, had no significant effects on performance. A second experiment indicated that, for both frontal and parietal cortex, rTMS delivered at IAF + 1 Hz was associated with a greater task-related event-related desynchronization than was sham stimulation of the same areas (Klimesch et al., 2003). Although they did not record the EEG during the delivery of rTMS, the authors speculated that the IAF + 1 result was produced by an rTMS-induced increase in pre-trial power in the upper alpha band. (Another study, although not involving spatial processing, has demonstrated highly specific effects (midline parietal but not left dorsolateral prefrontal; delay period but not probe period; 5 Hz but not 1 Hz or 20 Hz) of rTMS on the short-term retention of letters (Luber, Kinnunen, Rakitin, Ellsasser, Stern, & Lisanby, 2007).)

The role of neuronal oscillations in the short-term retention of location information

Early in this chapter it was suggested that the dynamic state of processing at different levels of the perception–action network will determine whether the behaviour to which it gives rise will be attentional, motoric, or mnemonic. Subsequent sections established the importance of alpha-band oscillations in determining these dynamic states, and the immediately preceding section introduced a methodological approach for carrying out *a priori* tests of the functional relevance of oscillations. Here these threads come together in a set of studies establishing that alpha-band oscillations also play an important role in the short-term retention of spatial information. In the initial study we applied 10 Hz rTMS to the intraparietal sulcus (IPS), the superior parietal lobule (SPL), the FEF, and the dorsolateral prefrontal cortex ((dl)PFC) during the delay period of a spatial delayed-recognition task (Hamidi, Tononi, & Postle, 2008). This frequency of rTMS, which corresponds to the alpha band of the EEG, had previously been effective at disrupting other targeted cognitive processes (e.g., Feredoes, Tononi, & Postle, 2007; Postle et al., 2006a), and the results of this study, too, revealed a selective effect of delay-period rTMS of IPS, SPL, and FEF relative to dlPFC and a control area in the primary somatosensory cortex of the postcentral gyrus (PoCG). The direction of this effect, however, was the opposite of what we had predicted: rTMS of IPS, SPL, and FEF produced a selective *decrease* in reaction time, and no reliable effects on accuracy; that is, it produced improved performance (Hamidi et al., 2008). Although such behavioural facilitation effects are not without precedent (e.g., Luber et al., 2007; Walsh & Pascual-Leone, 2003), we felt it important to follow up with a replication study in which we concurrently recorded the EEG, so as to get a better understanding of how rTMS had produced these effects.

The rTMS/EEG study, like an earlier fMRI study (Postle & Hamidi, 2007), required the short-term retention of either the locations or the identities of four serially presented shapes. On half the trials, unpredictably, a train of 10 Hz rTMS was delivered during the 3 s of the delay period, either to the SPL or the PoCG control area. On $rTMS_{absent}$ trials, the delay period of both location and identity trials was characterized by sustained elevated power in the upper alpha band of the EEG (~10–13 Hz). The rTMS produced nonspecific effects that were commonly observed when it was delivered to PoCG and/or during identity trials. In contrast, specific to location memory trials when rTMS was delivered to SPL, the magnitude and direction of the effect of rTMS on delay-period alpha-band power predicted the magnitude and direction of the effect of rTMS on behaviour. Specifically, the two were negatively correlated, such that rTMS-related increases in alpha-band power were accompanied by decreases in accuracy, and decreases in alpha-band power were accompanied by increases in accuracy (Fig. 5.3 (see plate), Hamidi, Slagter, Tononi, & Postle, 2009).

An additional result from this study, which also fits with the computational considerations spelled out earlier in this chapter, is that rTMS of SPL also influenced alpha:gamma phase synchrony in a task-specific manner, such that rTMS-related increases of 1:4 phase synchrony (i.e., 10 Hz:40 Hz) predicted improved performance on location trials and impaired performance on identity trials. (This effect was independent of the relationship between delay-period alpha-band power and performance.)

An important point to make about all of the results from the Hamidi et al. (2009) study is that they can not be discounted as somehow 'atypical' or not representative of how the brain normally functions because they may have resulted from imposing on the brain an exogenous oscillatory regime that is not typical of its normal functioning. Rather, they clearly reflect a biasing of the endogenous pattern of task-related oscillations. Indeed, a head-to-head comparison of these rTMS data with EEG data in which 10 Hz visual flicker was delivered during the delay period clearly illustrates that the latter produces much stronger entrainment of posterior neural systems than does the former (Johnson, Hamidi, & Postle, 2010). Thus the results from this study indicate that, as is the case for visuospatial perception and attention, oscillations in the alpha band have a functional role for the short-term retention of spatial information.[1]

Towards a unified account of visuospatial cognition

In the first half of this chapter we have seen how the dynamic interplay of elements in the perception–action network gives rise to such nominally varied behaviours as visual attention, oculomotor control, and the short-term retention of spatial information. The second half of the chapter suggests *how* this dynamic interplay may be controlled: It may be that alpha-band oscillatory dynamics, and their interactions with other frequency bands, control the tuning and output of the perception–action network. Although there is a solid theoretical basis for this model (Palva & Palva, 2007), its critical evaluation will require that several outstanding questions be addressed. Many of these questions either require, or lend themselves to, the combined rTMS–EEG method.

- Will the pattern of individual differences of the effects of 10 Hz rTMS on delayed-recognition (Hamidi et al., 2009) generalize to non-memory tasks, such as tests of the endogenous and exogenous control of attention, of oculomotor control, and of visual target detection (e.g., will someone whose spatial working memory performance improves with 10 Hz rTMS to the SPL also show improvements on these other tasks)?
- What factors account for the individual differences in the effect of 10 Hz rTMS on alpha-band power and on behaviour (Hamidi et al., 2009)?
- Once these factors are understood, will varying them systematically as parameters in an rTMS study lead to predictable improvement and impairment of performance within individual subjects?
- How do the effects of rTMS differ as a function of whether it is delivered prior to or during a task? (Note that this is of interest, because whereas Klimesch et al. (2003) assumed that pre-trial rTMS entrained cortical oscillations to the stimulation frequency, our data suggest that delay-period rTMS does not entrain the EEG to its driving frequency, but, rather, modulates the gain of components of the endogenous, behaviourally related EEG (Johnson et al., 2010).)

Addressing these questions will constitute modest steps towards answering the ambitious question that has been the focus of this chapter: How does spatial working memory work?

1 Note that oscillatory dynamics in other frequency bands have also been implicated in working memory function, as well as in other domains of cognition (e.g., Siegel, Warden, & Miller, 2009; Jensen, Kaiser, & Lachaux, 2007). Because these do not relate directly to spatial working memory, however, they will not be considered in this chapter.

References

Aizawa, H., & Wurtz, R. H. (1998). Reversible inactivation of monkey superior colliculus. I. Curvature of saccadic trajectory. *Journal of Neurophysiology, 79,* 2082–2096.

Armstrong, K. M., Chang, M. H., & Moore, T. (2009). Selection and maintenance of spatial information by frontal eye field neurons. *The Journal of Neuroscience, 29,* 15621–15629.

Awh, E., Anllo-Vento, L., & Hillyard, S. A. (2000). The role of spatial selective attention in working memory for locations: evidence from event-related potentials. *Journal of Cognitive Neuroscience, 12,* 840–847.

Awh, E., Armstrong, K. M., & Moore, T. (2006). Visual and oculomotor selection: links, causes and implications for spatial attention. *Trends in Cognitive Sciences, 10,* 124–130.

Awh, E., & Jonides, J. (2001). Overlapping mechanisms of attention and spatial working memory. *Trends in Cognitive Sciences, 5,* 119–126.

Awh, E., Jonides, J., & Reuter-Lorenz, P. A. (1998). Rehearsal in spatial working memory. *Journal of Experimental Psychology: Human Perception & Performance, 24,* 780–790.

Awh, E., Jonides, J., Smith, E. E., Buxton, R. B., Frank, L. R., Love, T., Wong, E. C., & Gmeindl, L. (1999). Rehearsal in spatial working memory: evidence from neuroimaging. *Psychological Science, 10,* 433–437.

Baddeley, A. D. (1986). *Working memory.* Oxford: Oxford University Press.

Baddeley, A. D., & Lieberman, K. (1980). Spatial working memory. In R. S. Nickerson (Ed.), *Attention and performance* (Vol. VIII, pp. 521–539) Hillsdale, NJ: Lawrence Erlbaum, Inc.

Belopolsky, A., & Theeuwes, J. (2009). Inhibition of saccadic eye movements to locations in spatial working memory. *Attention, Perception & Psychophysics, 71,* 620–631.

Berger, H. (1929). Uber das elekroenkephalogramm des menschen. *Archiv fur Psychiatrie und Nervenkrankheiten, 87,* 527–570.

Bollimunta, A., Chen, Y., Schroeder, C. E., & Ding, M. (2008). Neuronal mechanisms of cortical alpha oscillations in awake-behaving macaques. *The Journal of Neuroscience, 28,* 9976–9988.

Busch, N. A., Dubois, J., & VanRullen, R. (2009). The phase of ongoing EEG oscillations predicts visual perception. *The Journal of Neuroscience, 29,* 7869–7876.

Buzsaki, G. (2006). *Rhythms of the brain.* New York: Oxford University Press.

Chafee, M. V., & Goldman-Rakic, P. S. (1998). Matching patterns of activity in primate prefrontal area 8a and parietal area 7ip neurons during a spatial working memory task. *Journal of Neurophysiology, 79,* 2919–2940.

Chafee, M. V., & Goldman-Rakic, P. S. (2000). Inactivation of parietal and prefrontal cortex reveals interdependence of neural activity during memory-guided saccades. *Journal of Neurophysiology, 83,* 1550–1566.

Chelazzi, L., Miller, E. K., Duncan, J., & Desimone, R. (1993). A neural basis for visual search in inferior temporal cortex. *Nature, 363,* 345–347.

Chelazzi, L., Miller, E. K., Duncan, J., & Desimone, R. (2001). Responses of neurons in macaque area V4 during memory-guided visual search. *Cerebral Cortex, 11,* 761–772.

Cooper, N. R., Croft, R. J., Dominey, S. J. J., Burgess, A. P., & Gruzelier, J. H. (2003). Paradox lost? Exploring the role of alpha oscillations during externally vs. internally directed attention and the implications for idling and inhibition hypotheses. *International Journal of Psychophysiology, 47,* 65–74.

Corbetta, M., & Shulman, G. L. (2002). Control of goal-directed and stimulus-driven attention in the brain. *Nature Reviews Neuroscience, 3,* 215–229.

Doppelmayr, M., Klimesch, W., Pachinger, T., & Ripper, B. (1998). Individual differences in brain dynamics, important implications for the calculation of event-related band power. *Biological Cybernetics, 79,* 49–57.

Farmer, E. W., Berman, J. V. F., & Fletcher, Y. L. (1986). Evidence for a visuo-spatial scratch-pad in working memory. *Quarterly Journal of Experimental Psychology, 38A,* 675–688.

Feredoes, E., Tononi, G., & Postle, B. R. (2007). The neural bases of the short-term storage of verbal information are anatomically variable across individuals. The *Journal of Neuroscience, 27,* 11003–11008.

Godijn, R., & Theeuwes, J. (2002). The relationship between inhibition of return and saccade trajectory deviations. *Journal of Experimental Psychology: Human Perception and Performance, 30,* 538–554.

Hale, S., Myerson, J., Rhee, S. H., Weiss, C. S., & Abrams, R. A. (1996). Selective interference with the maintenance of location information in working memory. *Neuropsychology, 10,* 228–240.

Hamidi, M., Slagter, H. A., Tononi, G., & Postle, B. R. (2009). Repetitive transcranial magnetic stimulation affects behavior by biasing endogenous cortical oscillations. *Frontiers in Integrative Neuroscience, 3,* 14.

Hamidi, M., Tononi, G., & Postle, B. R. (2008). Evaluating frontal and parietal contributions to spatial working memory with repetitive transcranial magnetic stimulation *Brain Research, 1230,* 202–210.

Hamker, F. H. (2005). The reentry hypothesis: The putative interaction of the frontal eye field, ventrolateral prefrontal cortex, & areas V4, IT for attention and eye movement. *Cerebral Cortex, 15,* 431–447.

Hanslmayr, S., Aslan, A., Staudigl, T., Klimesch, W., Hermann, C. S., & Bauml, K. H. (2007). Prestimulus oscillations predict visual perception performance between and within subjects. *NeuroImage, 37,* 1465–1473.

Jensen, O., Kaiser, J., & Lachaux, J.-P. (2007). Human gamma-frequency oscillations associated with attention and memory. *Trends in Neurosciences, 30,* 317–324.

Johnson, J. S., Hamidi, M., & Postle, B. R. (2010). Using EEG to explore how rTMS produces its effects on behavior. *Brain Topography, 22,* 281–293.

Kanai, R., Chaleb, L., Antal, A., Walsh, V., & Paulus, W. (2008) Frequency-dependent electrical stimulation of the visual cortex. *Current Biology, 18,* 1839–1843.

Klimesch, W. (1999). EEG alpha and theta oscillations reflect cognitive and memory performance: a review and analysis. *Brain Research Reviews, 29,* 169–195.

Klimesch, W., Sauseng, P., & Gerloff, C. (2003). Enhancing cognitive performance with repetitive transcranial magnetic stimulation at human individual alpha frequency. *European Journal of Neuroscience, 17,* 1129–1133.

Lawrence, B. M., Myerson, J., Oonk, H. M., & Abrams, R. A. (2001). The effects of eye and limb movements on working memory. *Memory, 9,* 433–444.

Logie, R. H., & Marchetti, C. (1991). Visuo-spatial working memory: visual, spatial or central executive? In R. H. Logie, & M. Denis (Eds.), *Mental images in human cognition* (pp. 105–115) Amsterdam: Elsevier.

Luber, B., Kinnunen, L. H., Rakitin, B. C., Ellsasser, R., Stern, Y., & Lisanby, S. H. (2007). Facilitation of performance in a working memory task with rTMS stimulation of the precuneus: Frequency- and time-dependent effects. *Brain Research, 1128,* 120–129.

Luck, S. J., Chelazzi, L., Hillyard, S. A., & Desimone, R. (1997). Neural mechanisms of spatial selective attention in V1, V2, and V4 of macaque visual cortex. *Journal of Neurophysiology, 77,* 24–42.

Mathewson, K. E., Gratton, G., Fabiani, M., Beck, D. M., & Ro, T. (2009). To see or not to see: Prestimulus alpha phase predicts visual awareness. *The Journal of Neuroscience, 29,* 2725–2732.

Moore, T., & Armstrong, K. M. (2003). Selective gating of visual signals by microstimulation of frontal cortex. *Nature, 421,* 370–373.

Moore, T., & Fallah, M. (2001). Control of eye movements and spatial attention. *Proceedings of the National Academy of Science (USA), 30,* 1273–1276.

Moore, T., & Fallah, M. (2004). Microstimulation of the frontal eye field and its effects on covert attention. *Journal of Neurophysiology, 91,* 152–162.

Munoz, D. P., & Istvan, P. J. (1998). Lateral inhibitory interactions in the intermediate layers of the monkey superior colliculus. *Journal of Neurophysiology, 79,* 1193–1209.

Neubauer, A., Freudenthaler, H. H., & Pfurtscheller, G. (1995). Intelligence and spatiotemporal patterns of event-related desynchronization (ERD). *Intelligence, 20,* 249–266.

Olivers, C. N. L., Meijer, F., & Theeuwes, J. (2006). Feature-based memory-driven attentional capture: Visual working memory content affects visual attention. *Journal of Experimental Psychology: Human Perception and Performance, 32,* 1243–1265.

Palva, S., & Palva, J. M. (2007). New vistas for alpha-frequency band oscillations. *Trends in Neurosciences, 30,* 150–158.

Palva, J. M., Palva, S., & Kaila, K. (2005). Phase synchrony among neuronal oscillations in the human cortex. *The Journal of Neuroscience, 25,* 3962–3972.

Pare, M., & Wurtz, R. H. (1997). Monkey posterior parietal cortex neurons antidromically activated from superior colliculus. *Journal of Neurophysiology, 78,* 3493–3497.

Pearson, D. G., & Sahraie, A. (2003). Oculomotor control and the maintenance of spatially and temporally distributed events in visuo-spatial working memory. *Quarterly Journal of Experimental Psychology, 56A,* 1089–1111.

Pierrot-Deseilligny, C., Rivaud, S., Gaymard, B., & Agid, Y. (1991). Cortical control of reflexive visually-guided saccades. *Brain, 114,* 1473–1485.

Pogosyan, A., Gaynor, L.D., Eusebio, A., & Brown, P. (2009). Boosting cortical activity at beta-band frequencies slows movement in humans. *Current Biology, 19,* 1637–1641.

Posner, M. I. (1980). Orienting of attention. *Quarterly Journal of Experimental Psychology, 32,* 3–25.

Postle, B. R., Awh, E., Jonides, J., Smith, E. E., & D'Esposito, M. (2004). The where and how of attention-based rehearsal in spatial working memory. *Cognitive Brain Research, 20,* 194–205.

Postle, B. R., Ferrarelli F., Hamidi, M., Feredoes, E., Massimini, M., Peterson, M. J., Alexander, A., & Tononi, G. (2006a). Repetitive transcranial magnetic stimulation dissociates working memory manipulation from retention functions in prefrontal, but not posterior parietal, cortex. *Journal of Cognitive Neuroscience, 18,* 1712–1722.

Postle, B. R., & Hamidi, M. (2007). Nonvisual codes and nonvisual brain areas support visual working memory. *Cerebral Cortex, 17,* 2134–2142.

Postle, B. R., Idzikowski, C., Della Salla, S., Logie, R. H., & Baddeley, A. D. (2006b). The selective disruption of spatial working memory by eye movements. *Quarterly Journal of Experimental Psychology, 59,* 100–120.

Quinn, J. G., & Ralston, G. E. (1986). Movement and attention in visual working memory. *Quarterly Journal of Experimental Psychology, 38A,* 689–703.

Riggall, A. C., Ikkai, A., Srimal, R., & Curtis, C. E. (2008). *Predicting the direction of spatial attention, working memory, and motor intentions using multivoxel pattern classification.* Paper presented at the Annual Meeting of the Society for Neuroscience Washington, DC.

Rihs, T. A., Michel, C. M., & Thut, G. (2009). A bias for posterior alpha-band power suppression versus enhancement during shifting versus maintenance of spatial attention. *NeuroImage, 44,* 190–199.

Rizzolatti, G., Riggio, L., Dascola, I., & Umiltà, C. (1987). Reorienting attention across the horizontal and vertical meridian: evidence in favor of premotor theory of attention. *Neuropsychologia, 25,* 31–40.

Romei, V., Brodbeck, V., Michel, C., Amedi, A., Pascual-Leone, A., & Thut, G. (2008). Spontaneous fluctuations in posterior alpha-band EEG activity reflect variability in excitability of human visual areas. *Cerebral Cortex, 18,* 2010–2018.

Ruff, C. C., Blankenburg, F., Bjoertomt, O., Bestmann, S., Freeman, E., Haynes, J. D., Rees, G., Josephs, O., Deichmann, R., & Driver, J. (2006). Concurrent TMS-fMRI and psychophysics reveal frontal influences on human retinotopic visual cortex *Current Biology, 16,* 1497–1488.

Salway, A. F. S., & Logie, R. H. (1995). Visuospatial working memory, movement control and executive demands. *British Journal of Psychology, 86,* 253–269.

Schiller, P. H. (1986). The central visual system. *Vision Research, 26,* 1351–1386.

Siegel, M., Warden, M., & Miller, E. K. (2009). Phase-dependent neuronal coding of objects in short-term memory. *Proceedings of the National Academy of Sciences (USA), 106,* 21341–21346.

Selemon, R. D., & Goldman-Rakic, P. S. (1988). Common cortical and subcortical targets of the dorsolateral prefrontal and posterior parietal cortices in the rhesus monkey: Evidence for a distributed neural network serving spatially guided behavior. *Journal of Neuroscience, 8,* 4049–4068.

Smyth, M. M., Pearson, N. A., & Pendleton, L. R. (1988). Movement and working memory: patterns and positions in space. *Quarterly Journal of Experimental Psychology, 40A,* 497–514.

Sommer, M. A., & Wurtz, R. H. (2000). Composition and topographic organization of signals sent from the frontal eye field to the superior colliculus. *Journal of Neurophysiology, 83,* 1979–2001.

Sommer, M. A., & Wurtz, R. H. (2001). Frontal eye field sends delay activity related to movement, memory, and vision to the superior colliculus. *Journal of Neurophysiology, 85,* 1673–1685.

Soto, D., Heinke, D., Humphreys, G. W., & Blanco, M. J. (2005). Early, involuntary top-down guidance of attention from working memory. *Journal of Experimental Psychology: Human Perception and Performance, 31,* 248–261.

Soto, D., Humphreys, G. W., & Rothstein, P. (2007). Dissociating the neural mechanisms of memory-based guidance of visual selection. *Proceedings of the National Academy of Science (USA), 104,* 17186–17191.

Sparks, D. L., & Hartwich-Young, R. (1989). The deeper layers of the superior colliculus. *Reviews of Oculomotor Research, 3,* 213–255.

Theeuwes, J., Belopolsky, A. & Olivers, C. N. L. (2009). Interactions between working memory, attention and eye movements. *Acta Psychologica, 132,* 106–114.

Theeuwes, J., Olivers, C. N. L., & Chizk, C. L. (2005). Remembering a location makes the eyes curve away. *Psychological Science, 16,* 196–199.

Thut, G., & Miniussi, C. (2009). New insights into rhythmic brain activity from TMS-EEG studies. *Trends in Cognitive Sciences, 13,* 182–189.

Treue, S. (1999). Neural correlates of attention in primate visual cortex. *Trends in Neurosciences, 24,* 295–3000.

A.

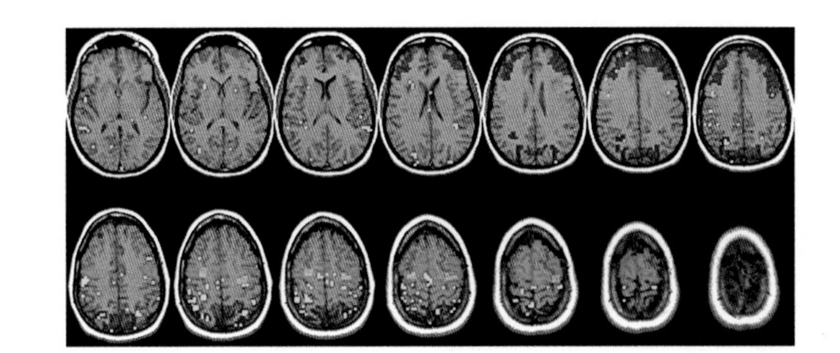

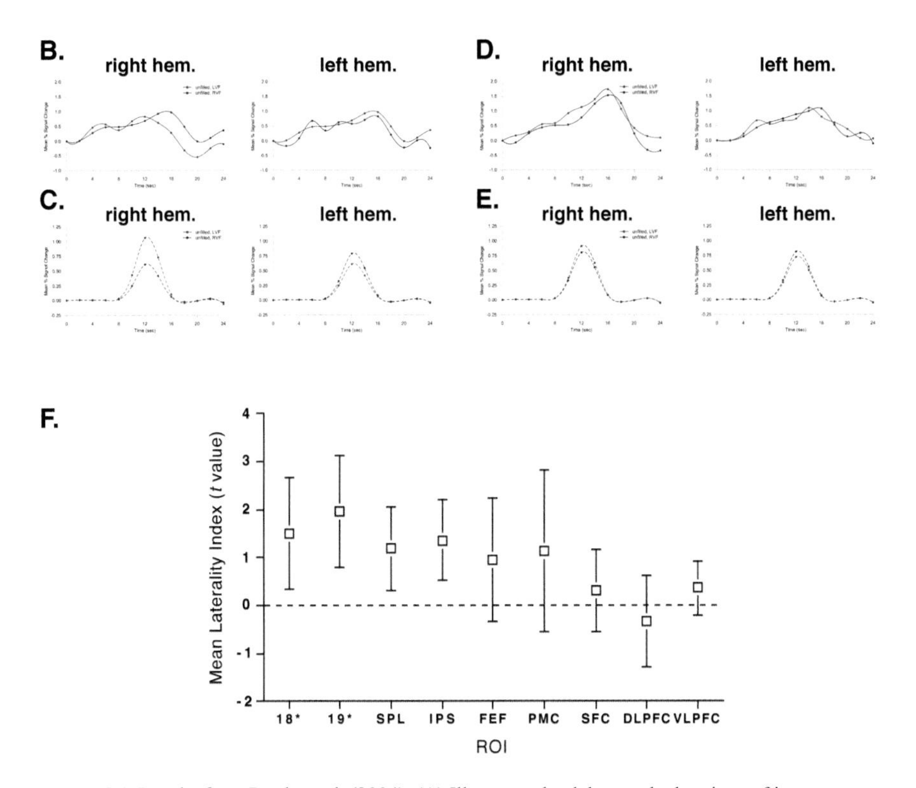

Figure 5.1 Results from Postle et al. (2004). **(A)** Illustrates the delay-evoked regions of interest (ROIs) in a representative participant. Structural ROIs are identified by translucent colours – superior parietal lobule (SPL; dark blue), intraparietal sulcus (IPS; red), premotor cortex (PMC; green), frontal eye fields (FEF; yellow), superior frontal cortex (SFC; orange), dorsolateral prefrontal cortex (DLPFC; fuchsia), ventrolaterial prefrontal cortex (VLPFC; light blue) and are overlaid by delay responsive voxels, which appear yellow and orange. **(B)** Illustrates that, at the group level (mean and 95% confidence interval), the laterality of delay-period activity was significantly biased in favour of the hemisphere contralateral to the remembered location (quantified by a laterality index that was significantly different from 0) in extrastriate Brodmann areas (BA) 18 and 19, and in IPS and SPL, but not in any of the frontal cortical ROIs. These results suggest that attention-based rehearsal is supported by the type of 'baseline shift' that is often observed in studies of sustained attention. **(C)** Illustrates trial-averaged functional magnetic resonance imaging (fMRI) data from unfilled trials for the two hemispheres of the SPL delay-evoked ROI of the participant illustrated in **(A)**. **(D)** Illustrates quantitatively the delay effects (delay-epoch covariates scaled by their parameter estimates) estimated by the generalized linear model (GLM) from the data illustrated in **(C)**. **(E)** Illustrates trial-averaged fMRI data from unfilled trials for the two hemispheres of the IPS delay-evoked ROI of this same participant. **(F)** Illustrates quantitatively the delay effects (delay-epoch covariates scaled by their parameter estimates) estimated by the GLM from the data illustrated in **(E)**. Reprinted from: *Cognitive Brain Research, 20,* Postle, B. R., E. Awh, J. Jonides, E. E. Smith, & M. D'Esposito, The where and how of attention-based rehearsal in spatial working memory, 194–205, 2004, with permission from Elsevier.

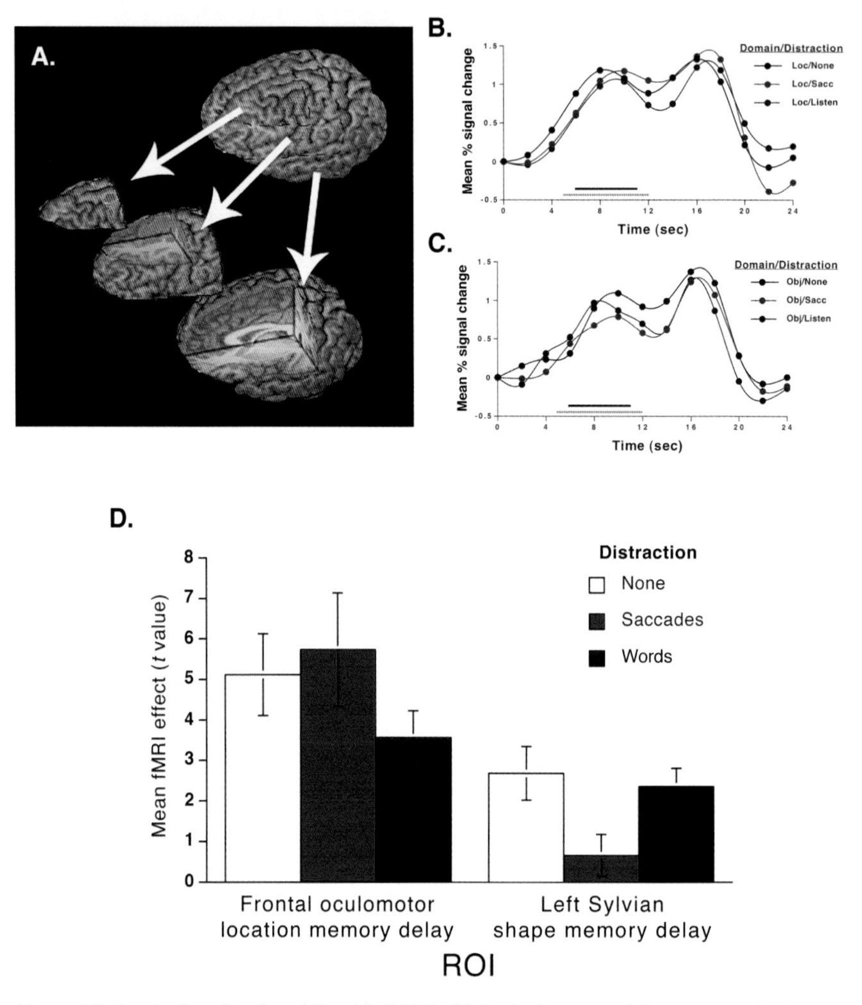

Figure 5.2 Results from Postle and Hamidi (2007). **(A)** Loci of memory-delay responses in the *no distraction* conditions for location (orange) and object (blue) memoranda, in a single subject (#9). The top-left cutout features activity in the frontal eye fields and the supplementary eye fields; the bottom-right cutout in the left Sylvian fissure. **(B)** Trial averaged time series from the location memory-delay voxels in **(A)**. Grey line along horizontal axis indicates duration of delay period; black line indicates duration of secondary-task period. **(C)** Trial averaged time series from the object memory-delay voxels in **(A)**. **(D)** Group data from frontal oculomotor location memory-delay and left Sylvian shape memory-delay regions of interest (ROIs), illustrating a region by secondary-task interaction. This neural double dissociation mirrors the behavioural effects, and illustrates that interference-specific neural effects are anatomically specific. Reproduced from Postle, B. R. & Hamidi, M., Nonvisual codes and nonvisual brain areas support visual working memory, *Cerebral Cortex*, 2007, *17(9)*, 2134–2142, by permission of Oxford University Press.

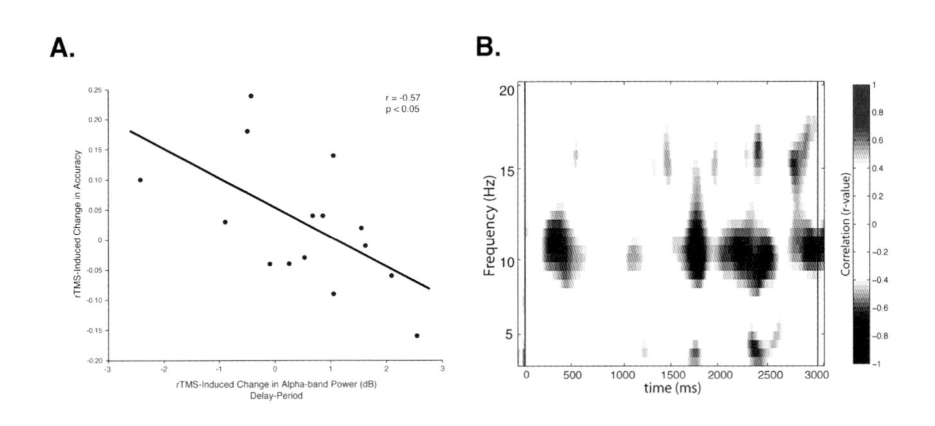

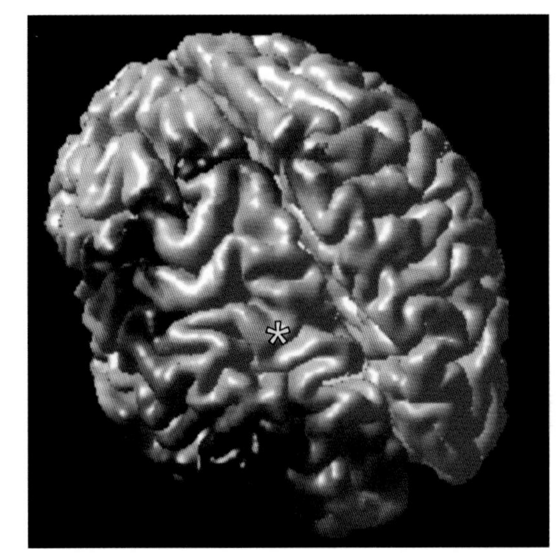

Figure 5.3 Results from Hamidi et al. (2009). **(A)** Plot showing individual differences in the effect of repetitive transcranial magnetic stimulation (rTMS) of superior parietal lobule (SPL) on delay-period alpha-band power and performance. **(B)** Time-frequency plot of r values during the 3 s of the delay period, thresholded to show the time points during which delay period activity correlated significantly with behaviour. In this plot the beginning of the delay period is labelled '0' ms and the end of the delay period '3000' ms. **(C)** Source localization of the regions carrying the correlation illustrated in **(A)** and **(B)**. These included a large region of cortex extending from the left inferior parietal lobule, along the intraparietal sulcus (Brodmann area (BA) 39) to the left extrastriate cortex (BA 18), a region covering the left precentral sulcus (BA 6) and superior frontal gyrus, which included the putative frontal eye fields, as well as a region in the right medial temporal lobe corresponding to the hippocampus (not shown). The yellow asterisk indicates the region of SPL targeted with rTMS. Original figure from Hamidi, M., H. A. Slagter, G. Tononi, and B. R. Postle (2009). Repetitive transcranial magnetic stimulation affects behaviour by biasing endogenous cortical oscillations. *Frontiers in Integrative Neuroscience, 3,* 14. Reprinted with permission.

Uhlhaas, P. J., Pipa, G., Lima, B., Melloni, L., Neuenschwander, S., Nikolic, D., & Singer, W. (2009). Neural synchrony in cortical networks: history, concept and current status. *Frontiers in Integrative Neuroscience, 3,* 17.

Van der Stigchel, S., Merten, H., Meeter, M., & Theeuwes, J. (2007). The effects of a task-irrelevant visual event on spatial working memory. *Psychonomic Bulletin & Review, 14,* 1066–1071.

van Dijk, H., Schoffelen, J. M., Oostenveld, R., & Jensen, O. (2008). Prestimulus oscillatory activity in the alpha band predicts visual discrimination ability. *The Journal of Neuroscience, 28,* 1861–1823.

von Stein, A., Chiang, C., & Koenig, P. (2000). Top-down processing mediated by interareal synchonization. *Proceedings of the National Academy of Science (USA), 97,* 14748–14753.

Walsh, V., & Pascual-Leone, A. (2003). *Transcranial magnetic stimulation: A neurochronometrics of mind.* Cambridge, MIT Press.

Worden, M. S., Foxe, J. J., Wang, N., & Simpson, G. V. (2000). Anticipatory biasing of visuospatial attention indexed by retinotopically specific alpha-band electroencephalography increases over occipital cortex. *Journal of Neuroscience, 20,* RC 63.

Yantis, S., & Serences, J. T. (2003). Cortical mechanisms of space-based and object-based attentional control. *Current Opinion in Neurobiology, 13,* 187–193.

6 The organization of visuospatial working memory

Evidence from the study of developmental disorders

Cesare Cornoldi and Irene C. Mammarella

Visuospatial abilities and their relation to visuospatial working memory

Visuospatial ability is not a unitary process, but instead can be broken down into various distinct types. The differentiation and classification of these types has been influenced by the findings from various instruments chosen to examine visuospatial ability.

Factor-analytic studies of visuospatial ability tasks point to the existence of distinct spatial abilities. For example, some authors (Hegarty & Waller, 2004; McGee, 1979) have distinguished between main aspects, i.e., visualization and orientation. Visualization refers to the ability to mentally rotate and manipulate objects, while orientation refers to the ability to retain spatial orientation with respect to oneself. Linn and Peterson (1985) and Voyer, Voyer, and Bryden (1995) distinguished three categories of spatial ability based on the various different processes required to solve problems representing each ability. These categories were:

1 spatial perception (ability to determine spatial relationships with respect to one's own orientation);
2 mental rotation (ability to mentally rotate a two- or three-dimensional figure rapidly and accurately); and
3 spatial visualization (ability to manipulate spatially presented information in complex ways).

Examples of tests are: for (1) the water level test (Inhelder & Piaget, 1958); for (2) the Mental Rotation Test (Vandenberg & Kruse, 1978); and for (3) the Differential Aptitude Test spatial relations subtest. Carpenter and Just (1986) distinguished only two categories of spatial ability:

1 spatial orientation (ability to identify spatial configurations from a different perspective);
2 spatial manipulation (ability to mentally restructure a two- or three-dimensional object).

Cornoldi and Vecchi (2003, p. 16) instead presented a broader classification, distinguishing between 10 different groups of visuospatial abilities, which included visuospatial working memory. Finally, Bunton and Fogarty (2003) examined the relationship between visual imagery and spatial abilities using a confirmatory factor analysis. Their findings supported the notion that the abilities targeted by the tasks referred to above can be classified along a continuum. The self-report imagery questionnaires are located on the left-hand side of the continuum, while experimental tasks examining spatial-imagery and visuospatial memory can be located at the centre. On the right of the continuum they placed the creative imagery tasks of Finke, Pinker, and Farah (1989), and – at the far end – spatial intelligence tests (primary mental abilities; Thurstone & Thurstone, 1965 and Raven's Advanced Progressive Matrices; Raven, 1965). The main thrust of Bunton and Fogarty (2003) has therefore been to offer a description of the relationships between visual imagery, visuospatial memory, and spatial abilities, also showing their proximity.

In summary, psychometrical research has clearly shown that visuospatial ability is not a homogeneous concept, but consists of subcomponents that are quite distinct, albeit closely related. Nevertheless, despite all the attempts at a suitable classification of the spatial subfactors, the correct operationalization of these factors and their relationships remain unclear. For example, there is evidence to suggest that there is indeed a relationship between working memory capacity and visuospatial ability (Just & Carpenter, 1985). Solving a mental rotation or spatial visualization task requires the ability to maintain an active representation of all the parts and their interrelations, while simultaneously rotating and manipulating the image mentally. This elaboration, involving both storage (holding the constituent parts in memory) and the concurrent processing of spatial representations (the rotation component), fits closely with current conceptions of working memory (Miyake & Shah, 1999). Studies of visuospatial abilities and visuospatial working memory individual differences consequently overlap to some extent.

The individual differences approach in the study of working memory

The individual differences approach – investigating the role of individual differences such as cognitive abilities and personality in human behaviour – can be useful in explaining human differences and finding critical psychological variables which, making individuals different, appear to be central for psychological functioning.

Knowledge of working memory has benefited greatly from studies involving both the consideration of variability within typical populations, and the examination of specific impairments in clinical populations and individual cases (Cornoldi & Vecchi, 2003). One development in the field has concerned the attentional control of irrelevant information. For example, Engle and colleagues have repeatedly explored the role of individual differences in working memory capacity on verbal fluency under various secondary load conditions (Rosen & Engle, 1997), the relationship between working memory capacity and attentional control (Kane,

Bleckley, Conway, & Engle, 2001), individual differences in switching the focus of attention in working memory, and so on (see Unsworth & Engle, 2007 for a review). In general, this work showed that individual differences in working memory, as measured by complex span tasks in which to-be-remembered items are interspersed with some form of distracting activity, arise from differences in attentional control affecting the ability to maintain and retrieve information from memory. In particular, in situations where new and novel information needs to be maintained to generate the correct response, low-working memory capacity individuals are more likely than their working memory counterparts to have their attention distracted and thus lose access to the task goal.

However, to date, experiments have mostly been conducted within the verbal domain (Unsworth & Engle, 2006) rather than the visuospatial (Mammarella & Cornoldi, 2005a; Cornoldi & Mammarella, 2006). In a recent study, Lecerf and Roulin (2009) showed that low-visuospatial working memory participants had deficits in distractor inhibition and that their memory representations were more degraded. Specifically, high-visuospatial working memory participants performed better than low-visuospatial working memory participants, while these latter demonstrated more intrusions of irrelevant information than their high-span counterparts. Thus, low-span participants were less able to suppress items that had to be forgotten. Moreover, inhibitory control was negatively correlated to visuospatial working memory capacity. Similarly, Cornoldi, Bassani, Berto, and Mammarella (2007) demonstrated that elderly individuals performed less well than younger individuals and that errors in visuospatial working memory tasks depend, at least partially, on difficulties in avoiding already activated information.

As mentioned, the individual differences approach has been applied to the study of working memory, enabling analysis of various populations (i.e., elderly, low spatial abilities, low-working memory span individuals, learning disabled children, etc.), at the same time broadening knowledge on the architecture of working memory components (but see also Logie, Chapter 2, this volume). Indeed, the study of individual differences has been critical to the differentiation of cognitive abilities, including working memory components.

In the field of memory, the original Baddeley and Hitch (1974) model with its evolution (Baddeley, 2000) represented an innovative approach to the study of how the temporary memory system functions, and still today remains a relevant theoretical framework. According to this model, working memory is composed of two subsidiary domain-specific components, namely a phonological loop and a visuospatial sketchpad, which are supervised by an amodal unit, the central executive. The phonological loop temporarily stores and manipulates verbalizable items, while the visuospatial sketchpad is responsible for the maintenance and processing of visual (e.g., colour, shape, texture) and spatial (e.g., position of an object in space) information, as well as mental imagery activities. Instead, the central executive component is involved in the regulatory control of the tasks carried out by the two slave systems. Moreover, it serves to focus or switch attention and recover mental representations from long-term memory (Baddeley & Logie, 1999).

Organization of the working memory components within the continuity model

Over the last 20 years, alternative approaches to working memory have been developed that emphasize the articulated architecture of the system and its limits in the amount of information that can be stored and processed. It was on this basis that Cornoldi and Vecchi (2003) put forward a formulation of the working memory model giving a new account of the organization of working memory proposed by the classical Baddeley (1986) model. According to this novel concept, 'working memory system and its subsystems can be viewed as representatives of well-characterised groups of processes along continuous dimensions rather than as discrete entities' (Cornoldi & Vecchi, 2003, p. 50). Working memory functions are not rigidly separated, but instead thought of as being linked in a continuous fashion along horizontal and vertical dimensions. In other words, the continuity model is characterized by two fundamental dimensions based on continuum relations: the horizontal continuum, related to the various types of material involved (e.g., verbal, visual, spatial, haptic); and the vertical continuum, related to the types of process, requiring some degree of active elaboration and manipulation of information (see Figure 6.1). Each process is thus defined on the basis of two dimensions (vertical and horizontal), while distance between positions represents the degree of independence between tasks. An assumption of this type leads to the argument that working memory tasks are defined in terms of their position along both continua. At a lower level of the vertical continuum, expressing the degree of controlled activity involved, there are passive memory tasks, or *simple span tasks*, usually based on rote rehearsal of items (e.g., forward digit span) that are strictly related to the nature of the stimuli to be retained. In contrast, active memory tasks, or *complex span tasks* (Engle, Kane, & Tuholski, 1999), require both maintenance and concurrent processing of information, such as order change (e.g., backwards digit span) or selection and inhibition of irrelevant or no-longer-relevant information (e.g., listening span task). According to Cornoldi

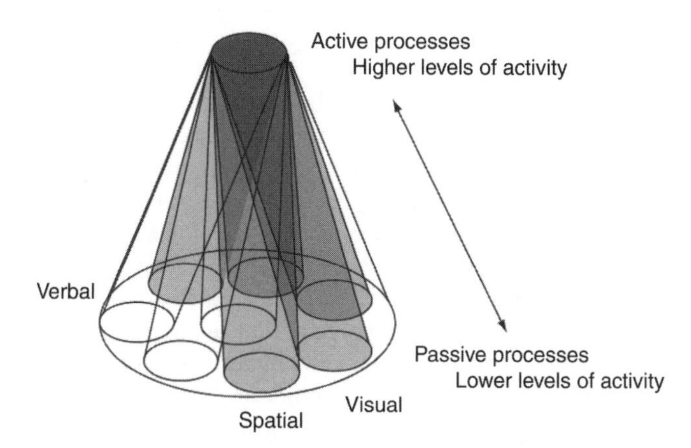

Figure 6.1 The continuity model proposed by Cornoldi and Vecchi (2003).

and Vecchi (2003), complex span tasks may vary in the degree of controlled activity involved and maintain domain-specific characteristics, despite the higher involvement of control processes than that for simple span tasks; thus, for example, it is possible to distinguish between verbal and spatial active tasks.

Although working memory tasks can vary in degree of controlled activity involved and thus occupy different positions on the vertical continuum, they can broadly be located between passive tasks (lowest down in the continuum) and active tasks (highest up). As examples, passive verbal memory tasks include the forward digit span (see also Engle et al., 1999). Passive spatial tasks include the forward Corsi Blocks Test (CBT; Milner, 1971), in which participants have to remember and reproduce the sequence in the same order as that given by the experimenter; another is the Visual Pattern Test (VPT; Della Sala, Gray, Baddeley, & Wilson, 1997) where participants have to memorize patterns of filled cells in matrices of varying sizes, and then fill in cells on a blank matrix to reproduce the original pattern.

An example of an active verbal task is the Reading Span Task (RST) proposed by Daneman and Carpenter (1980). In the commonest version of this task, participants have to read a growing series of sentences (from two to six), deciding whether they are true, and recalling the last word of each sentence. To do so participants have to perform two tasks almost simultaneously, i.e., processing the meaning of each sentence to decide whether it is true or false, and maintaining the last word of each sentence. To be successful in the memory tasks, it has been shown that participants have to be able to keep the last word active while handling interfering information (i.e., the words within sentences) – see for example De Beni, Palladino, Pazzaglia, & Cornoldi, (1998). One active spatial task mirroring the reading span is the selective Visuospatial Working Memory Task (Cornoldi, Marzocchi, Belotti, Caroli, De Meo, & Braga, 2001b; Mammarella & Cornoldi, 2005a; Cornoldi & Mammarella, 2006), involving a series of matrices of increasing length, with one or more coloured cells. For each matrix, three or more sequential locations are presented and participants have to recall only the last. As a secondary task, participants have to press a key when a location corresponds to a coloured cell. Another active spatial task is the active version (Mammarella, Pazzaglia, & Cornoldi, 2008) of the VPT (Della Sala et al., 1997). The task requires memorization of the filled cells on a matrix and, in contrast with the passive version it requires an active transformation of the memory representation with reproduction on a blank matrix of the original pattern by filling in the corresponding cells one row below the positions of the original.

The continuous approach allows distinction of the efficiency of passive maintenance and active working memory processes in each domain (i.e., verbal versus visual or spatial). Within this framework it is possible to predict memory weaknesses and strengths of specific atypically developing categories of individuals (e.g., learning disabled children, individuals with genetic syndromes), as well as the individual differences related to normal cognitive functioning (e.g., age differences and gender-related effects). Evidence of the distinction between active and passive processes comes from studies on individual differences in working memory due to gender (Vecchi & Girelli, 1998) and age (Vecchi & Cornoldi, 1999; Richardson & Vecchi, 2002) and from studies on particular categories of subjects, such as nonverbal learning disabled children (Cornoldi, Dalla Vecchia, & Tressoldi, 1995; Cornoldi, Rigoni, Tressoldi, & Vio, 1999), blind people (Vecchi, Monticelli, & Cornoldi, 1995; Vecchi, 1998), individuals with intellectual disability (Lanfranchi, Cornoldi, & Vianello, 2004; Lanfranchi, Cornoldi, Drigo, & Vianello, 2009), and children with attention deficit hyperactivity disorder (ADHD) (Cornoldi et al., 2001b).

The case of developmental populations with cognitive disabilities is illuminating here (e.g., Cornoldi, Carretti, & De Beni, 2001a; Swanson & Siegel, 2001); in particular, subgroups can be found that apparently have difficulties associated with both a specific modality and a particular degree of control. For instance, in the linguistic domain, it can be predicted that highly intelligent children with specific verbal learning disabilities in low-level skills (e.g., dyslexic) would fail mainly in low-control tasks (*simple span tasks*). In contrast, children with reading comprehension and/or word problem-solving difficulties may have problems at higher levels of control (e.g., intermediate level, where selection and inhibition of specific verbal information is required: *active* or *complex span tasks*). Instead, children with intellectual disability may fail at an even higher level of control, associated with executive function tasks (*high attentional controlled tasks*; for a discussion see Cornoldi et al., 2001a). Children with ADHD seem to represent a particular case, presenting problems in active working memory tasks, independent of modality but dependent on the specific inhibitory request implied by the task (Cornoldi et al., 2001b; Re, De Franchis, & Cornoldi, 2010).

Organization of the visuospatial components of working memory within the continuity model

Visuospatial working memory has been widely explored in recent years, but to date there is no consensus on how it is organized. According to the Logie (1995) model, visuospatial working memory consists of a visual store, known as the *visual cache*, and a rehearsal mechanism, known as the *inner scribe*. The visual cache provides a temporary store for visual information (i.e., colour and shape), while the inner scribe handles information about movement sequences and provides a mechanism through which visual information can be rehearsed in working memory. Consistent with this distinction is a large body of evidence showing a dissociation between visual and spatial memory, very often using the paradigm of selective interference, based on the assumption that two tasks tapping the same cognitive function cannot be executed concurrently without a fall in performance (see Logie, Chapter 2, this volume). Outcomes from studies using selective interference have often been interpreted as supporting the distinction between visual and spatial working memory components (Della Sala, Gray, Baddeley, Allamano, & Wilson, 1999; Klauer & Zhao, 2004; Quinn & McConnell, 1996). For example, Logie and Marchetti (1991) found that one visual and one spatial interference task, involving the presentation of irrelevant pictures and unseen arm movements, respectively, caused a fall in performance of just the primary tasks of the same nature. This split between the visual and spatial working memory components is also corroborated by neuropsychological evidence from patients showing a selective deficit in the performance of either visual or spatial working memory tasks (Carlesimo, Perri, Turriziani, Tomaiuolo, & Caltagirone, 2001; Farah, Hammond, Levine, & Calvanio, 1988; Luzzatti, Vecchi, Agazzi, Cesa-Bianchi & Vergani, 1998).

In addition, there is considerable developmental data in support of a distinction between a visual and a spatial component. In a study by Logie and Pearson (1997), children aged 5–6, 8–9, and 11–12 years were administered the CBT (Milner, 1971), and an adapted version of the VPT (Della Sala et al., 1997). Results showed that performance in both tasks increased with age. However, the performance developed much more rapidly on the VPT than on the CBT. Hamilton and colleagues (Hamilton, Coates, & Heffernan, 2003) also addressed this area, employing tests to assess visual memory (memorizing a series of locations presented simultaneously) and spatial memory (remembering a repeated sequence of spots), and found that visual measures developed faster than spatial ones, concluding that the two kinds of task tapped different cognitive functions (see also Hamilton, Chapter 7, this volume).

Experimental results from use of Corsi- and VPT-type tasks (the two commonest visuospatial working memory tasks to date) to measure the visual and spatial working memory subcomponents (Pickering, 2001) could be interpreted within Logie's (1995) model postulating a distinction between visual and spatial subcomponents of visuospatial working memory, with the VPT presented as a test tapping the visual component, and the CBT associated with the spatial component. However, the differences between the CBT and VPT can be considered from other perspectives. For example, it has been argued that they also differ in terms of how the memory content is presented (Gathercole & Pickering, 2000; Pickering, Gathercole, Hall, & Lloyd, 2001; Pickering, Gathercole, & Peaker, 1998), i.e., static (as in the VPT) as opposed to dynamic (as in the CBT). To seek support for this latter view, Pickering et al. (2001) compared the developmental pattern of two visuospatial working memory tasks – one matrix task similar to the VPT and one task requiring memorization of a pathway within a maze – both presented in static and dynamic format. Although the two formats of each test were based on identical material, they resulted in different developmental patterns: performance in the static format was higher and, importantly, increased more steeply with age. According to Pickering and colleagues, mere distinction between visual and spatial processes cannot explain these results.

Following the reasoning of Pickering and coworkers a tasks analysis could help clarify how visuospatial working memory is organized. The main problem associated with the definition of the VPT as a visual test is that the core features of visual content (shape, texture, colour, etc.) are absent. In fact, in the VPT, matrices composed of partially filled cells are shown to participants, who have to memorize and then reproduce them in the empty matrices provided. In this task, the locations of each filled cell in the learning matrix need to be correctly encoded and retrieved to allow reproduction of the correct pattern in the empty test matrix. It is therefore the locations (and the spatial relationships between different locations) rather than the visual characteristics that are crucial. While it is true that in some matrices a subject can see a visual pattern (such as an L-shape created by the filled cells), this does not mean that this strategy can be used in all cases. Furthermore, the strategy a subject actually employs should not be confused with the basic process involved in performing the task: following similar reasoning, a single person's visualizing the numbers during maintenance in the digit span test would indicate that the task is visual. In contrast, locations in the CBT are presented sequentially and thus the presentation order of locations is paramount.

Lecerf and de Ribaupierre (2005) have distinguished three visuospatial working memory components rather than two. These comprise an extra-figural encoding responsible for anchoring objects with respect to an external frame of reference; and an intra-figural encoding based on the relations each item presents within a pattern, broken down further into pattern encoding (leading to a global visual image), and path encoding (leading to sequential-spatial positions). Similarly, Pazzaglia and Cornoldi (1999; Mammarella et al., 2008) have proposed the following breakdown of visuospatial working memory under the continuity model: visual working memory tasks, requiring memorization of shapes and colours, and two kinds of spatial task, both requiring memorization of patterns of spatial locations but differing in presentation format and type of spatial processes involved: simultaneous in one case (as in the VPT), sequential in the other (as in the CBT). Evidence collected with various groups of children supported the distinction between visual and spatial-simultaneous processes (Mammarella, Cornoldi, & Donadello, 2003) and between spatial-simultaneous and spatial-sequential processes (Mammarella, Cornoldi, Pazzaglia, Toso, Grimoldi, & Vio, 2006).

Testing a group of 162 children attending third- and fourth-grade, Mammarella et al. (2008) compared different theoretical accounts of visuospatial working memory, and used structural equation modelling to find the best theoretical factor model fitting the data. They compared models involving:

1. two simple storage systems (verbal versus spatial) and one complex span system (representing the classical Baddeley model);
2. two visuospatial working memory components and one verbal component (visual versus spatial – or static versus dynamic – versus verbal) without distinction between storage and processing measures;
3. four components corresponding to the distinction between complex span tasks and simple verbal, visual, and spatial tasks; and
4. three different visuospatial working memory components (visual versus spatial-simultaneous versus spatial-sequential), one verbal component, and one active component (representing the continuity model).

They found that the distinction between three visuospatial components suggested by Cornoldi and Vecchi (2003) provides the best fit of the data

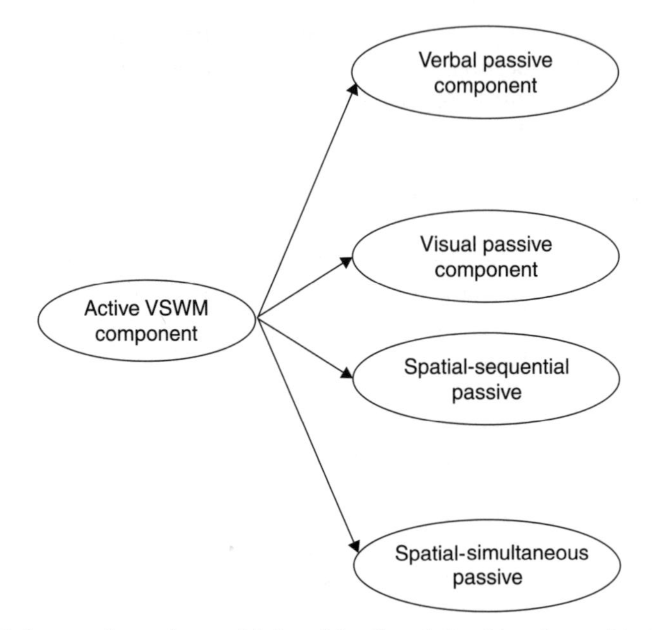

Figure 6.2 Structural equation model describing the relationships observed in typically developing children between different components of visuospatial working memory (VSWM) as predicted by the continuity model (see Mammarella et al., 2008).

(see Figure 6.2). Structural equation modelling showed that visuospatial working memory tasks can be distinguished on the basis of not only their content and presentation format, but also the degree of active control. In fact, in the continuity model (Cornoldi & Vecchi, 2003) active measures partially maintain a distinction based on domain-specific aspects, contrary to Baddeley's original model (1986) in which executive processes are completely independent of presentation format.

Further research reveals that the organization of working memory is complex. For example, Bayliss, Jarrold, Gunn, and Baddeley (2003) examined the extent to which maintenance and processing functions could predict performance in complex span tasks, and found that complex span performance depended not only on maintenance and processing, but also on their coordination. These data support a multiple-component view, distinguishing between complex (i.e., active) and simple storage (i.e., passive) processes within working memory. In a similar vein, Miyake, Friedman, Rettinger, Shah, and Hegarty (2001) examined the relationship between simple storage and complex span tasks in visuospatial format and executive functions, finding them to be equally strongly related to executive functions, in contrast with verbal tasks. Similar results were obtained by Alloway, Gathercole, and Pickering (2006) in 4- to 11-year-olds. Alloway and colleagues also demonstrated that the link between simple visuospatial storage tasks and complex processing tasks was stronger in younger children.

Visuospatial working memory and genetic syndromes within the continuity model

The effect of genetic syndromes on cognitive abilities has been widely investigated in recent years. The continuity working memory model proposed by Cornoldi and Vecchi (2003) can account for the strengths and weaknesses of working memory abilities found in many genetic syndromes.

The horizontal continuum is of particular interest since it may also explain the different types of memory performance associated with the various genotypes. As mentioned, an important series of studies compared Down syndrome and Williams syndrome individuals; the results suggested that individuals with Down syndrome have greater difficulty with tasks involving verbal working memory, whereas those with Williams syndrome have greater difficulty with visuospatial working memory tasks (e.g., Jarrold, Baddeley, & Hewes, 1999). However, more light still needs to be shed on the nature of visuospatial deficits in Down syndrome. A study by Laws (2002) found that individuals with Down syndrome performed significantly better in the CBT (spatial working memory) than typically developing children matched for receptive vocabulary, while the performances of the two groups were not significantly different in a memory for colour task (visual working memory). In a recent study (Lanfranchi, Carretti, Spanò, & Cornoldi, 2009), individuals with Downs were compared with typically developing children matched for verbal mental age. Participants were presented with a battery of spatial-sequential and spatial-simultaneous working memory tasks. The study's main finding is the dissociation between tasks measuring spatial-sequential and those measuring spatial-simultaneous working memory, the former being relatively preserved in Down syndrome, the latter relatively impaired.

Other findings from studies of children with spina bifida offered further support to the distinction between visual, spatial-sequential, and spatial-simultaneous working memory components. It is well-documented that spina bifida children are characterized by a verbal IQ usually higher than their performance IQ (Fletcher et al., 1992). Moreover, dysfunctions in academic skills are quite varied and complex: individuals with spina bifida may show good reading skills but poor text comprehension, spatial difficulties (McComas, Dulberg, & Latter, 1997), visual perception impairments (Denis, Rogers, & Barnes, 2001), and poor mathematical skills (Rourke & Conway, 1997). In a study by Mammarella et al. (2003), children with spina bifida and typically developing children were presented with three tasks: spatial-sequential (i.e., CBT), spatial-simultaneous (i.e., VPT), and visual (i.e., a task, the 'House Visual Span', where participants have to recognize the houses previously presented from a set of house drawings). Children with spina bifida specifically failed on the visual task but not in the VPT, supporting the hypothesis that visual and spatial-simultaneous tasks do not involve the same processes.

The vertical continuum within the continuity model (Cornoldi & Vecchi, 2003) has also been tested. It was postulated (Cornoldi et al., 2001a) that highly intelligent children with specific learning disabilities would show particular failure in low-control tasks; children with reading comprehension and/or problem-solving difficulties (e.g., Passolunghi, Cornoldi, & De Liberto, 1999) would have problems at the intermediate level of control, where selection and inhibition of specific information is required; and children with intellectual disability would fail at the highest levels of control (see also Vicari, Carlesimo, & Caltagirone, 1995). In particular, the predicted relationship between deficit in highly controlled working memory processes and intellectual deficit in people with intellectual disability was consistent with theorists who were attempting to associate intelligence and working memory (e.g., Engle, Tuholski, Laughlin, & Conway, 1999; Miyake et al., 2001). Lanfranchi et al. (2004) explored the role of control processes in verbal and visuospatial working memory performance of individuals with Down syndrome. For verbal working memory, the Down syndrome group showed poorer performance regardless of the involvement of control, with increased impairment associated with increase in degree of active control required. In contrast, considering visuospatial working memory, the results demonstrated that individuals with Down syndrome are poorer in highly controlled visuospatial working memory, whereas in low-control tasks they can be as good as typically developing children with the same mental age. Lanfranchi et al. (2004) concluded that a core deficit in individuals with intellectual disability could reside in a controlled working memory deficit.

Finally, a recent study by Carretti, Belacchi, and Cornoldi (2010) tested participants with intellectual disability, examining whether they differed from typically developing children on tasks involving high active control. Participants were presented with verbal tasks requiring different degrees of active control: forward word span (low control), backward word span (medium-low control), selective word span (medium-high control), and updating word span (high control). Comparison between the group of intellectually disabled individuals and a group of children of similar general capacity showed that, although subjects were matched on fluid intelligence performance, specific differences were found on working memory measures. In particular, updating word span discriminated between groups well, and as effectively as the selective word span. These results confirmed that the intellectual disability group is characterized by poorer control processes in working memory. In a further study, Lanfranchi et al. (2009) analysed the case of individuals with fragile X syndrome. A particular neurocognitive profile has been postulated for this syndrome (Warren & Ashley, 1995), reported as varying somewhat between males and females. For males it shows relative strengths in language, simultaneous information processing, and face and emotion recognition (Turk & Cornish, 1998). In contrast, females with fragile X syndrome show a relative weakness in visuospatial cognition (Cornish, Munir, & Cross, 1999; Freund & Reiss, 1991), and in sequential information processing and reproduction of items in serial or temporal order (Wilding, Cornish, & Munir, 2002). As regards the working memory components there is contradictory evidence over whether fragile X syndrome is associated with a selective deficit in visuo-spatial working memory as opposed to verbal working memory. Moreover, in several studies, deficits at higher levels of attention control/executive functioning are shown to affect boys, adult males, girls, and women with fragile X syndrome (Scerif, Cornish, Wilding, Driver, & Karmiloff-Smith, 2004; Cornish, Munir, & Cross, 2001; Kirk, Mazzocco, & Kover, 2005; Mazzocco, Hagerman, & Pennington, 1992). In order to disentangle whether the deficits of individuals with fragile X syndrome are due to the material implied in working memory tasks (i.e., verbal versus visuospatial) or the attentional control (i.e., passive versus active), Lanfranchi and colleagues (2009) compared a group of boys with and without fragile X syndrome in two batteries of four verbal and four visuospatial working memory tasks requiring different levels of control. Subjects with fragile X syndrome showed performance equal to controls in working memory tasks requiring low and medium-low control, but significant impairment in cases requiring higher control. This working memory deficit in high-control tasks supports the hypothesis of attentional control as a critical variable distinguishing working memory functions and explaining intellectual differences.

Visuospatial working memory and nonverbal (visuospatial) learning disabilities within the continuity model

Children with learning disabilities usually show average or above average intelligence even when performance is poor on scholastic achievement tasks. One large subgroup includes individuals with deficits in linguistic abilities. However, there is a separate subgroup of children with learning disabilities who present a neuropsychological profile characterized by poorer nonverbal than verbal abilities. This disorder has been variously named as nonverbal learning disability (NLD) (Rourke, 1995), developmental right-hemisphere syndrome (Gross-Tsur, Shalev, Manor, & Amil, 1995; Nichelli & Venneri, 1995), or visuospatial learning disability (Mammarella & Cornoldi, 2005a, 2005b). One of the most adopted identifying features of NLD is a significantly higher score in verbal IQ than performance IQ on formal measures of intelligence (Cornoldi, Venneri, Marconato, Molin, & Montinari, 2003; Johnson, 1987; Weintraub & Mesulam, 1983). This finding is a direct result of the expected discrepancy in these children between verbal, language-based cognitive abilities and nonverbal, visuospatial cognitive abilities. Of course, verbal-performance IQ score discrepancies alone are never diagnostic in the absence of other supporting evidence.

According to Rourke (1995; see also Rourke, Ahmad, Collins, Hayman-Abello, Hayman-Abello, & Warriner, 2002) the NLD syndrome is characterized by significant primary deficits in some dimensions of tactile perception, visual perception, complex psychomotor skills, and in dealing with novel circumstances. These primary deficits lead to secondary deficits in tactile and visual attention and to tertiary deficits in visual memory, concept-formation, problem-solving, and hypothesis-testing skills. Finally, there are significant impairments in language prosody, content, and pragmatics. Children with NLD can also have difficulties in a number of aspects of academic learning, especially in drawing, science (Pelleiter, Ahmad, & Rourke, 2001), and arithmetic (Mammarella, Lucangeli, & Cornoldi, 2010; Rourke, 1993; Venneri, Cornoldi, & Garuti, 2003), and also in informal learning during spontaneous play and other social situations. Children with this disorder are also viewed as having substantially increased risk for internalized forms of psychopathology, which seem to result from low competence in comprehending nonverbal communicative signals in social and emotional contexts.

A critical factor underlying the difficulties encountered by children with NLD seems to be related to visuospatial working memory deficits (Cornoldi et al., 1995; Cornoldi et al., 1999; Cornoldi & Vecchi, 2003). These deficits might explain why NLD children fail in a range of activities (mathematics, drawing, spatial orientation, etc.) assumed to involve visuospatial working memory.

There is clearly still a need to find a coherent framework that can incorporate these findings. One approach is through the continuity model of Cornoldi and Vecchi (2003): it is of interest therefore to consider research on NLD and visuospatial working memory in the context of both vertical and horizontal continua of this working memory model. Referring to the vertical continuum, Cornoldi et al. (1999) investigated passive memory and the generation and manipulation of mental images that – according to the continuity model – involve active visuospatial working memory components. Children were asked to recall the locations of three, four, and five filled positions on a 5 × 5 matrix and to use interactive mental images to recall paired-word associates: NLD children were found to fail in these tasks. A more specific analysis of two NLD cases (Cornoldi, Rigoni, Venneri, & Vecchi, 2000) offered evidence in favour of the dissociation between active and passive visuospatial working memory. The study described two individual cases diagnosed with NLD. E.N., a 9-year-old boy, showed difficulties in passive tasks such as the CBT and the VPT, whereas C.I., a 13-year-old girl, had difficulties only on active tasks requiring manipulation of spatial relations or carrying out image subtraction. In a further study by Mammarella and Cornoldi (2005b), NLD children were presented with a visuospatial working memory test that shared some features with the span tests of Daneman and Carpenter (1980), in that only the last part of the material presented had to be remembered. An important finding of this research was that failure in visuospatial working memory appears to be typically associated with specific patterns of errors, in particular an increase in errors due to the processing of irrelevant information, thus involving a malfunctioning of the high level of attentional control.

For the horizontal continuum, research has offered some support for a distinction between visual, spatial-sequential, and spatial-simultaneous processes. In general, there is evidence to suggest that children with NLD are usually poorer in spatial tasks than in visual tasks. For example, Cornoldi et al. (2003) found that a group of NLD children were particularly poor in the spatial CBT, with an estimated effect size approximately twice that found for two visual working memory tasks. Mammarella and Cornoldi (2005b) also showed that the backward Corsi task may be a purer measure of the spatial difficulty of NLD children than the forward Corsi task. This result is coherent with other research by Cornoldi and Mammarella (2008) who tested low versus high spatial ability in young adults, finding a difference between groups in overall Corsi task performance. In particular, performance for the two recall directions (i.e., forward versus backward) was almost identical for the high-ability group, while the low-spatial ability group was impaired in the backward recall direction.

Mammarella et al. (2010) also found that NLD children performed significantly worse in spatial tasks (both sequential and simultaneous) than in visual tasks. This demonstrates that a visuospatial working memory deficit can also be found in NLD children in passive tasks – typically less powerful than active tasks in discriminating between groups, but more specific in distinguishing between different visuospatial working memory components (Cornoldi et al., 1995; Cornoldi & Vecchi, 2003) and in predicting specific learning domain difficulties (Bull, Espy, & Wiebe, 2008). Furthermore, spatial components seem further distinguishable in NLD children, since a double dissociation has been observed. Mammarella et al. (2006) tested three children diagnosed as suffering from a developmental form of NLD: two were characterized by problems on spatial-simultaneous processes, the third by a spatial-sequential process impairment. These results show the importance of considering spatial-sequential and spatial-simultaneous processes, and active and passive processes, in identifying different subtypes of NLD in children. The findings are also important in the design of targeted training programmes based on specific difficulties: three different studies by Mammarella and co-authors have shown the efficacy of training stimulating the various components of visuospatial working memory, namely the visual (Caviola, Toso, & Mammarella, in press); the spatial-sequential (Caviola, Mammarella, Cornoldi, & Lucangeli, 2009); and the spatial-simultaneous (Mammarella, Coltri, Lucangeli, & Cornoldi, 2009).

Overall, the identified contrast between active and passive and the distinctions between visual, spatial-sequential, and spatial-simultaneous processes allow better understanding of how the visuospatial working memory system is organized. Analysis of visuospatial working memory in children with NLD may therefore cast light on the nature of their difficulties and also facilitate exploration of the functioning of visuospatial working memory in individuals with specific nonverbal difficulties.

Conclusions

This chapter has examined the organization of visuospatial working memory according to an individual differences approach; this has also been useful in lending support to the continuity model of Cornoldi and Vecchi (2003). The organization of this model, taking into account not only task material and presentation format (i.e., visual versus spatial-sequential, versus spatial-simultaneous) but also level of attentional control required for the task, offers a useful theoretical framework for explaining working memory patterns of performance found when considering individual differences. In particular, individual and group differences have been considered in both typical and atypical developmental populations, including genetic syndromes such as Down syndrome, spina bifida, and fragile X syndrome and the case of children with NLD. The range of working memory profiles presented in these individuals have been described and interpreted according to the continuity model. Research has been presented that demonstrates the usefulness of both the vertical dimension (distinguishing between active and passive tasks) and the horizontal dimension (distinguishing between visual, spatial-simultaneous, and spatial-sequential tasks) in the study of cognitive strengths and weaknesses of children with different characteristics.

References

Alloway, T. P., Gathercole, S. E., & Pickering, S. J. (2006). Verbal and visuospatial short-term and working memory in children: Are they separable? *Child Development, 77,* 1698–1716.

Baddeley, A. (1986). *Working memory.* Oxford: Oxford University Press.

Baddeley, A. D. (2000). The episodic buffer: A new component of working memory? *Trends in Cognitive Sciences, 4,* 417–422.

Baddeley, A. D. & Hitch, G. (1974). Working Memory. In G. A. Bower, (Ed.), *Recent advances in learning and motivation* (Vol. 8, pp. 47–90). New York: Academic Press.

Baddeley, A. D., & Logie, R. H. (1999). Working memory: The Multiple-component Model. In A. Miyake and P. Shah (Eds.), *Models of working memory: Mechanisms of active maintenance and executive control* (pp. 28–61). Cambridge: University Press.

Bayliss, D. M., Jarrold, C., Gunn, D. M., & Baddeley, A. D. (2003). The complexities of complex span: Explaining individual differences in working memory in children and adults. *Journal of Experimental Psychology: General, 132,* 71–92.

Bull, R., Espy, K. A., & Wiebe, S. A. (2008). Short-term memory, working memory, and executive functioning in preschoolers: Longitudinal predictors of mathematical achievement at age 7 years. *Developmental Neuropsychology, 33,* 205–228.

Bunton, L. J., & Fogarty, G. J. (2003). The factor structure of visual imagery and spatial abilities. *Intelligence, 31,* 289–318.

Carlesimo, G. A., Perri, R., Turriziani, P., Tomaiuolo, F., & Caltagirone, C. (2001). Remembering what but not where. Independence of spatial and visual working memory in the human brain. *Cortex, 37,* 519–537.

Carretti, B., Belacchi, C., & Cornoldi, C. (2010). Difficulties in working memory updating in individuals with intellectual disabilities. *Journal of Intellectual Disability Research, 54,* 337–345.

Carpenter, P. A., & Just, M. A. (1986). Spatial ability: An information processing approach to psychometrics. In R. J. Sternberg (Ed.), *Advances in the psychology of human intelligence*, (Vol. 3). Hillsdale, NJ: Lawrence Erlbaum Associates, Inc.

Caviola, S., Mammarella, I. C., Cornoldi, C., & Lucangeli, D. (2009). A metacognitive visuospatial working memory training for children. *International Electronic Journal of Elementary Education, 2,* 122–136.

Caviola, S., Toso, C., & Mammarella, I. C. (in press). Risultati di un training sulla memoria di lavoro visiva. Studio di un caso singolo [Results of a visual working memory training: A single case study]. *Psicologia Clinica dello Sviluppo.*

Cornish, K. M., Munir, F., & Cross, G. (1999). Spatial cognition in males with fragile X syndrome: Evidence for a neuropsychological phenotype. *Cortex, 35,* 263–271.

Cornish, K. M., Munir, F., & Cross, G. (2001). Differential impact of FMR-1 full mutation on memory and attention functioning: A neuropsychologic perspective. *Journal of Coginitive Neuroscience, 13,* 144–150.

Cornoldi, C., Bassani, C., Berto, R., & Mammarella, N. (2007). Aging and the intrusion superiority effect in visuo-spatial working memory. *Aging, Neuropsychology, and Cognition, 14,* 1–21.

Cornoldi, C., Carretti, B., & De Beni, R. (2001a). How the pattern of deficits in groups of learning-disabled individuals help to understand the organisation of working memory. *Issues in Education, 7,* 71–78.

Cornoldi, C., Dalla Vecchia, R., & Tressoldi, P. E. (1995). Visuo-spatial working memory limitation in low visuo-spatial high verbal intelligence children. *Journal of Child Psychology and Child Psychiatry, 36,* 1053–1064.

Cornoldi, C., & Mammarella, N. (2006). Intrusion errors in visuospatial working memory performance. *Memory, 14,* 176–188.

Cornoldi, C., & Mammarella, I. C. (2008). A comparison of backward and forward spatial spans. *The Quarterly Journal of Experimental Psychology, 61A,* 674–682.

Cornoldi, C., Marzocchi, G. M., Belotti, M., Caroli, M. G., De Meo, T., & Braga, C. (2001b). Working memory interference control deficits in children referred by teachers for ADHD symptoms. *Child Neuropsychology, 7,* 230–240.

Cornoldi, C., Rigoni, F., Tressoldi, P. E., & Vio, C. (1999). Imagery deficits in nonverbal learning disabilities. *Journal of Learning Disabilities, 32,* 48–57.

Cornoldi, C., Rigoni, F., Venneri, A. & Vecchi, T. (2000). Passive and active processes in visuo-spatial memory: Double dissociation in developmental learning disabilities. *Brain and Cognition, 43,* 17–20.

Cornoldi, C. & Vecchi, T. (2003). *Visuo-spatial working memory and individual differences.* Hove, UK: Psychology Press.

Cornoldi, C., Venneri, A., Marconato, F., Molin, A., & Montinari, C. (2003). A rapid screening measure for teacher identification of visuo-spatial learning disabilities. *Journal of Learning Disabilities, 36,* 299–306.

Daneman, M., & Carpenter, P. A. (1980). Individual differences in working memory and reading. *Journal of Verbal Learning and Verbal Behavior, 19,* 450–466.

De Beni, R., Palladino, P., Pazzaglia, F., & Cornoldi, C. (1998). Increases in intrusion errors and working memory deficit of poor comprehenders. *Quarterly Journal of Experimental Psychology, 51A,* 305–320.

Della Sala, S., Gray, C., Baddeley, A. D., Allamano, N., & Wilson, L. (1999). Pattern span: A tool for unwelding visuo-spatial memory. *Neuropsychologia, 37,* 1189–1199.

Della Sala, S., Gray, C., Baddeley, A. D., & Wilson, L. (1997). *Visual Pattern Test.* Bury St Edmunds: Thames Valley Test Company.

Denis, M., Rogers, T., & Barnes, M. (2001). Children with spina bifida perceive visual illusions but not multistable figures. *Brain & Cognition, Tennet XI, 44,* 108–113.

Engle, R. W., Kane, M. J., & Tuholski, S. W. (1999). Individual differences in working memory capacity and what they tell us about controlled attention, general fluid intelligence, and functions of the prefrontal cortex. In A. Miyake, & P. Shah (Eds.), *Models of working memory* (pp. 102–134). Cambridge: Cambridge University Press.

Engle, R. W., Tuholski, S. W., Laughlin, J. E., & Conway, A. R. A. (1999). Working memory, short-term memory, and general fluid intelligence: A latent-variable approach. *Journal of Experimental Psychology: General, 128,* 309–331.

Farah, M. J., Hammond, K. M., Levine, D. N., & Calvanio, R. (1988). Visual and spatial mental imagery: Dissociable systems of representation. *Cognitive Psychology, 20,* 439–462.

Finke, R. A., Pinker, S., & Farah, M. J. (1989). Reinterpreting visual patterns in mental imagery. *Cognitive Science, 13,* 51–78.

Fletcher, J. M., Francis, D. J., Thomson, N. M., Brookshire, B. L., Bohan, T. P., Landry, S. H., Davidson, K. C., & Miner, M. E. (1992). Verbal and nonverbal skills discrepancies in hydrocephalic children. *Journal of Clinical and Experimental Neuropsychology, 14,* 593–609.

Freund, L., & Reiss, A. L. (1991). Cognitive profiles associated with the fragile X syndrome in males and females. *American Journal of Medical Genetics, 38,* 542–547.

Gathercole, S. E., & Pickering, S. J. (2000). Assessment of working memory in six- and seven-year old children. *Journal of Educational Psychology, 2,* 377–390.

Gross-Tsur, V., Shalev, R. S., Manor, O., & Amil, N. (1995). Developmental right hemisphere syndrome: Clinical spectrum of the nonverbal learning disability. *Journal of Learning Disabilities, 28,* 80–86.

Hamilton, C. J., Coates, R. O., & Heffernan, T. (2003). What develops in visuo-spatial working memory development? *European Journal of Cognitive Psychology, 15,* 43–69.

Hegarty, M., & Waller, D. (2004). A dissociation between mental rotation and perspective-taking spatial abilities. *Intelligence, 32,* 175–191.

Inhelder, B., & Piaget, J. (1958). *The growth of logical thinking from childhood to adolescence*. New York: Basic.

Jarrold, C., Baddeley, A. D., & Hewes, A. K. (1999). Genetically dissociated components of working memory: Evidence from Down's and Williams Syndrome. *Neuropsychologia, 37,* 637–651.

Johnson, D. J. (1987). Nonverbal learning disabilities. *Pediatric Annals, 16,* 133–141.

Just, M. A., & Carpenter, P. A. (1985). Cognitive coordinate systems: Accounts of mental rotation and individual differences in spatial ability. *Psychological Review, 92,* 137–172.

Kane, M. J., Bleckley, M.K., Conway, A. R. A., & Engle, R. (2001). A controlled-attention view of working memory capacity. *Journal of Experimental Psychology: General, 130,* 169–183.

Kirk, J. W., Mazzocco, M. M., & Kover, S. T. (2005). Assessing executive dysfunction in girls with fragile X or Turner syndrome using the Contingency Naming Test (CNT). *Developmental Neuropsychology, 28,* 755–777.

Klauer, K.C., & Zhao, Z. M. (2004). Double dissociations in visual and spatial short term memory. *Journal of Experimental Psychology: General, 133,* 355–381.

Lanfranchi, S., Carretti, B., Spanò, G., & Cornoldi, C. (2009). A specific deficit in visuospatial simultaneous working memory in Down syndrome. *Journal of Intellectual Disability Research, 53,* 474–483.

Lanfranchi, S., Cornoldi, C., Drigo, S., & Vianello, R. (2009). Working Memory in individuals with Fragile X Syndrome. *Child Neuropsychology, 15,* 105–119.

Lanfranchi, S., Cornoldi, C., & Vianello, R. (2004). Verbal and Visuospatial Working Memory deficits in children with Down syndrome. *American Journal on Mental Retardation, 6,* 456–466.

Laws, G. (2002). Working memory in children and adolescents with Down syndrome: evidence from a colour memory experiment. *Journal of Child Psychology and Psychiatry, 43,* 353–364.

Lecerf, T., & de Ribaupierre, A. (2005). Recognition in a visuospatial memory task: The effect of presentation. *European Journal of Cognitive Psychology, 17,* 47–75.

Lecerf, T., & Roulin, J. L. (2009). Individual differences in visuospatial working memory capacity and distractor inhibition. *Swiss Journal of Psychology, 68,* 67–78.

Linn, M. C., & Petersen, A. C. (1985). Emergence and characterization of sex differences in spatial ability: A meta-analysis. *Child Development, 56,* 1479–1498.

Logie, R. H. (1995). *Visuo spatial working memory*. Hove, UK: Lawrence Erlbaum Associates Ltd.

Logie, R. H., & Marchetti, C. (1991). Visuo-spatial working memory: Visual, spatial or central executive? In R. H. Logie, & M. Denis (Eds.), *Mental images in human cognition* (pp. 105–115). Amsterdam: North Holland Press.

Logie, R. H., & Pearson, D. G. (1997). The inner eye and inner scribe of visuo-spatial working memory: evidence from developmental fractionation. *European Journal of Cognitive Psychology, 9,* 241–257.

Luzzatti, C., Vecchi, T., Agazzi, D., Cesa-Bianchi, M., & Vergani, C. (1998). A neurological dissociation between preserved visual and impaired spatial processing in mental imagery. *Cortex, 34,* 461–469.

McComas, J., Dulberg, C., & Latter, J. (1997). Children's memory for locations visited: Importance of movement and choice. *Journal of Motor Behavior, 29,* 223–229.

McGee, M. G. (1979). Human spatial abilities: Psychometric studies and environmental, genetic, hormonal, and neurological influences. *Psychological Bulletin, 86,* 889–918.

Mammarella, I. C., Coltri, S., Lucangeli, D., & Cornoldi, C. (2009). Impairment of simultaneous-spatial working memory in non-verbal learning disability: A treatment case study. *Neuropsychological Rehabilitation, 19,* 761–780.

Mammarella, I. C., & Cornoldi, C. (2005a). Difficulties in the control of irrelevant visuospatial information in children with visuospatial learning disabilities. *Acta Psychologica, 118,* 211–228.

Mammarella, I. C., & Cornoldi, C. (2005b). Sequence and space. The critical role of a backward spatial span in the working memory deficit of visuo-spatial learning disabled children. *Cognitive Neuropsychology, 22,* 1055–1068.

Mammarella, N., Cornoldi, C., & Donadello, E. (2003). Visual but not spatial working memory deficit in children with spina bifida. *Brain and Cognition, 53,* 311–314.

Mammarella. I. C., Cornoldi, C., Pazzaglia, F., Toso, C., Grimoldi, M., & Vio, C. (2006). Evidence for a double dissociation between Spatial-Simultaneous and Spatial-Sequential Working Memory in Visuospatial (Nonverbal) Learning Disabled Children. *Brain and Cognition, 62,* 58–67.

Mammarella, I. C., Lucangeli, D., & Cornoldi, C. (2010). Spatial working memory and arithmetic deficits in children with nonverbal learning difficulties (NLD). *Journal of Learning Disabilities, 43,* 455–468.

Mammarella, I. C., Pazzaglia, F., & Cornoldi, C. (2008). Evidence for different components in children's visuospatial working memory. *British Journal of Developmental Psychology, 26,* 337–355.

Mazzocco, M. M., Hagerman, R. J., & Pennington, B. F. (1992). Problem-solving limitations among cytogenetically expressing fragile X women. *American Journal of Medical Genetics, 3,* 78–86.

Milner, B. (1971). Interhemispheric differences in the localization of psychological processes in man. *Cortex, 27,* 272–277.

Miyake, A., Friedman, N. P., Rettinger, D. A., Shah, P., & Hegarty, M. (2001). How are visuospatial working memory, executive functions and spatial abilities related? A latent variable analysis. *Journal of Experimental Psychology: General, 130,* 621–640.

Miyake, A., & Shah, P. (Eds.). (1999). *Models of working memory: Mechanisms of active maintenance and executive control*. New York: Cambridge University Press.

Nichelli, P., & Venneri, A. (1995). Right hemisphere developmental learning disability: A case study. *Neurocase, 1,* 173–177.

Passolunghi, M. C., Cornoldi, C., & De Liberto, S. (1999). Working memory and intrusion of irrelevant information in a group of specific poor problem solvers. *Memory & Cognition, 27,* 779–799.

Pazzaglia, F., & Cornoldi, C. (1999). The role of distinct components of visuo-spatial working memory in the processing of texts. *Memory, 7,* 19–41.

Pelleiter, P. M., Ahmad, S. A., & Rourke, B. P. (2001). Classification rules for basic phonological processing disabilities and nonverbal learning disabilities: formulation and external validity. *Child Neuropsychology, 7,* 84–98.

Pickering, S. J. (2001). The development of visuo-spatial working memory. *Memory, 9,* 423–432.

Pickering, S. J., Gathercole, S. E., Hall, M., & Lloyd, S. A. (2001). Development of memory for pattern and path: Further evidence for the fractionation of visuo-spatial memory. *The Quarterly Journal of Experimental Psychology, 54A,* 397–420.

Pickering, S. J., Gathercole, S. E., & Peaker, M. (1998). Verbal and visuo-spatial short-term memory in children: Evidence for common and distinct mechanisms. *Memory and Cognition, 26,* 1117–1130.

Quinn, J. G., & McConnell, J. (1996). Irrelevant pictures in visual working memory. *Quarterly Journal of Experimental Psychology, 49,* 200–215.

Raven, J. C. (1965). *Advanced Progressive Matrices, Sets I and II.* London: H. K. Lewis.

Re, A. M., De Franchis, V., & Cornoldi, C. (2010). A Working memory control deficit in kindergarten ADHD children. *Child Neuropsychology, 16,* 134–144.

Richardson, J. T. E., & Vecchi, T. (2002). A jigsaw-puzzle imagery task for assessing active visuospatial processes in old and young people. *Behavior Research Methods, Instruments & Computers, 34,* 69–82.

Rosen, V. M., & Engle, R. W. (1997). The role of working memory capacity in retrieval. *Journal of Experimental Psychology: General, 26,* 211–227.

Rourke, B. P. (1993). Arithmetic disabilities, specific and otherwise: A neuropsychological perspective. *Journal of Learning Disabilities, 26,* 214–226.

Rourke, B. P. (1995). *Syndrome of Nonverbal Learning Disabilities: Neurodevelopmental Manifestations*. New York: Guilford Press.

Rourke, B. P., Ahmad, S. A., Collins, D.W., Hayman-Abello, B. A., Hayman-Abello, S. E., & Warriner, E. M. (2002). Child clinical/pediatric neuropsychology: Some recent advances. *Annual Review of Psychology, 53,* 309–339.

Rourke, B. P., & Conway, J. A. (1997). Disabilities of arithmetic and mathematical reasoning: Perspective from neurology and neuropsychology. *Journal of Learning Disabilities, 30,* 34–46.

Scerif, G., Cornish, K., Wilding, J., Driver, J., & Karmiloff-Smith, A. (2004). Visual search in typically developing toddlers and toddlers with Fragile X or Williams syndrome. *Developmental Science, 7,* 116–130.

Swanson, H. L., & Siegel, L. (2001). Learning disabilities as a working memory deficit. *Issues in Education, 7,* 1–48.

Thurstone, L. L., & Thurstone, T. G. (1965). *Primary mental abilities.* Chicago, IL: Science Research Associates.

Turk, J., & Cornish, K. M. (1998). Face recognition and emotion perception in boys with FXS. *Journal of Intellectual Disability Research, 42,* 490–499.

Unsworth, N., & Engle, R. W. (2006). A temporal-contextual retrieval account of complex span: An analysis of errors. *Journal of Memory and Language, 54,* 346–362.

Unsworth, N., & Engle, R. W. (2007). The nature of individual differences in working memory capacity: Active maintenance in primary memory and controlled search from secondary memory. *Psychological Review, 114,* 104–132.

Vandenberg, S. G., & Kruse, A. R. (1978). Mental rotations: Group tests of three-dimensional spatial visualization. *Perceptual and Motor Skills, 47,* 599–604.

Vecchi, T. (1998). Visuo-spatial limitations in congenitally totally blind people. *Memory, 6,* 91–102.

Vecchi, T., & Cornoldi, C. (1999). Passive storage and active manipulation in visuo-spatial working memory: Further evidence from the study of age differences. *European Journal of Cognitive Psychology, 11,* 391–406.

Vecchi, T., & Girelli, L. (1998). Gender differences in visuo-spatial processing: The importance of distinguishing between passive storage and active manipulation. *Acta Psychologica, 99,* 1–16.

Vecchi, T., Monticelli, M. L., & Cornoldi, C. (1995). Visuo-spatial working memory: Structures and variables affecting a capacity measure. *Neuropsychologia, 33,* 1549–1564.

Venneri, A., Cornoldi, C., & Garuti, M. (2003). Arithmetic difficulties in children with visuospatial learning disability (VLD). *Child Neuropsychology, 9,* 175–183.

Vicari, S., Carlesimo, A., & Caltagirone, C. (1995). Short-term memory in persons with intellectual disabilities and Down's syndrome. *Journal of Intellectual Disability Research, 39,* 532–537.

Voyer, D., Voyer, S., & Bryden, M. P. (1995). Magnitude of sex differences in spatial ability: A meta-analysis and consideration of critical variables. *Psychological Bulletin, 117,* 250–270.

Warren, S. T., & Ashley, C. T. (1995). Triplet repeat expansion mutations: The example of fragile X syndrome. *Annual Review of Neuroscience, 18,* 77–99.

Weintraub, S., & Mesulam, M. M. (1983). Developmental learning disabilities of the right hemisphere: Emotional, interpersonal, and cognitive components. *Archives of Neurology, 40,* 463–468.

Wilding, J., Cornish, K., & Munir, F. (2002). Further delineation of the executive deficit in males with fragile X syndrome. *Neuropsychologia, 40,* 1343–1349.

7 The nature of visuospatial representation within working memory

Colin Hamilton

Introduction

The aim of this chapter is to consider the nature of visuospatial representation within working memory, and through a discussion of recent empirical findings and theoretical frameworks identify the extent to which contemporary working memory models can adequately account for the findings of research within visuospatial working memory. The initial component of the chapter will discuss issues associated with the articulation of the nature of visuospatial representation within working memory, both in terms of conceptual and procedural debates. The empirical data will be drawn from across cognitive science, with consideration of findings from experimental, individual differences, and neuroscience. A number of theoretical frames will be discussed, but with the emphasis upon the *multiple resource* models of Baddeley (1986, 2000, Baddeley & Hitch, 1974) and Logie (1995, Logie & van der Meulen, 2009) and the *continuum* model of Cornoldi and Vecchi (2003). Consequently, several questions will be addressed.

- What are the theoretical and empirical issues in visuospatial working memory research?
- To what extent can visual and spatial working memory be differentiated within working memory?
- To what extent do the major theoretical models account for the representation of visuospatial information within working memory?
- What are the ways forward in visuospatial working memory research?

Issues in the articulation of the visuospatial working memory construct

An early attempt at articulating the nature of visuospatial representation within working memory was made by Baddeley (1986). He suggested that the *visuospatial sketchpad* (VSSP) process was responsible for 'retaining and manipulating images, and is susceptible to disruption by concurrent spatial processing' (p. 143). In addition, Baddeley suggested that the visualization process, a conscious monitoring process, identified by Phillips and Christie (1977b), was a part of this VSSP process. Already in this early account, there is evidence of complexity in the construct; Baddeley was suggesting a process capable of diverse functions; a phenomenological awareness of the visual stimulus, the maintenance of visual information, the manipulation of visual images, and a process susceptible to spatial interference. It is worthwhile noting that Baddeley's account also entertained the suggestion of direct access from the visual perceptual process, a *gateway* concept of the VSSP. He suggested that the VSSP process will 'allow the transformation of a passive perceptual store into an active memory system' (p. 121).

This suggestion of complex, multifunction visuospatial processes within working memory was also emphasized by Cornoldi and Vecchi (2003; see also Cornoldi & Mammarella, Chapter 6, this volume). Placing working memory at the centre of complex cognitive activities, Cornoldi and Vecchi identified ten visuospatial abilities that could putatively make demands upon visuospatial representation within working memory: visual organization, planned visual scanning, spatial orientation, visual reconstructive ability, imagery generation ability, imagery manipulation ability, spatial sequential short-term memory, visuospatial simultaneous short-term memory, visual memory, and long-term spatial memory. The complexity of the demands upon visuospatial working memory in conjunction with the apparent complexity of the processes within working memory has resulted in difficulty in establishing the essential characteristics of visuospatial representation in working memory. However, what has emerged from the literature has been the suggestion of two major properties, a visual–spatial dimension and a simultaneous–sequential dimension, dimensions that are not necessarily orthogonal to one another in the literature. Further, Zimmer, Speiser, and Seidler (2003) identified a number of conceptual issues related to these dimensions where clarification was required.

Zimmer et al. stated that at times, research protocols with 'static configurations of spatially distributed objects' (p. 43) are considered to be spatial working memory procedures (see also Zimmer & Liesefeld, Chapter 3, this volume). Two notable examples of this in the literature are the Eals and Silverman (1994) study and the Postma, Izendoorn, and De Haan (1998) study, both of which investigated the individual differences associated with sex, and both of which employed the encoding, short-term maintenance, and retrieval of simultaneously presented multiple object arrays. Zimmer et al. also pointed out that other research has employed the Corsi Blocks Task (CBT; Milner, 1971) as a measure of spatial working memory. This task demands the encoding, short-term maintenance, and retrieval of a sequence of tapped movements across a number of randomly placed blocks. This task is essentially a visuospatial temporal task, with the temporal element emphasizing the sequential characteristic identified above. Visual working memory procedures would appear to be no less immune to confusion in the labelling of the protocol. Visual memory research has employed protocols where a simple perceptual feature has to be remembered, for example the hue of the stimulus (Logie & Marchetti, 1991), the texture (Dean, Dewhurst, & Whittaker, 2008), the shape (Darling, Della Sala, & Logie, 2009), and the size of the stimulus (Thompson et al., 2006). The location of a single dot has also been employed as a visual memory procedure (Dale, 1973). Other research has looked at visual memory with objects (Tresch, Sinnamon, & Seamon, 1993) or with novel patterns such as the visual matrix task (Phillips, 1974; Phillips & Baddeley, 1971; Phillips & Christie, 1977a, 1977b; Della Sala, Gray, Baddeley, Allamano, & Wilson, 1999). The majority of these studies, with varying protocols, have been labelled visual working memory investigations.

The adoption of such differing protocols does not readily lend itself to a coherent view of the nature of visuospatial representation within working memory, closer examination of some of these individual protocols appears to muddy the water even further.

Issues associated with visuospatial working memory task protocols

An early example of the complexities embedded within a visual memory procedure is the Logie and Marchetti (1991) study. This was one of the earliest empirical observations within a dual-task context that attempted to differentiate visual from spatial representation within working memory. In the memory for colour hue procedure, the participants viewed four sequentially presented square stimuli that varied in hue. In this recognition-change detection procedure an array of four squares were subsequently displayed and the participant had to judge whether their hues were identical to those in the initial array. The use of hues is an excellent attempt to preclude verbal or categorical representation and thus strive for a very passive visual representation. However, complexities are immediately present, the squares are presented sequentially, which could make the procedure a visual-sequential task; however, the presentation ends with all four squares present on the screen, thus the procedure has a visual-simultaneous component also. The fact that four stimuli are present and that colour sensitivity varies across the retina strongly suggests that attention has to be deployed across the stimulus array. Thus, an active process is embedded in the procedure. Given that an array of four squares is presented, one possible strategy that could be employed is to employ a visuo-spatial configuration representation where different hues at different locations are represented within the one integrated representation. Thus, the representation may alter from that of four discrete hue patch simultaneous representations; to one of a visuospatial configuration integrating all four hue patches (see also Figure 7.1 p. 126 with the Postma et al., 1998, protocol). Thus, the protocol lends itself to multiple formats of representation.

The use of hue stimuli is a commendable attempt at assessing a 'passive perceptual' representation; however, it is a difficult challenge for the research to avoid having a visual memory protocol devoid of spatial characteristic. A prime example is the author's own research procedures with the size or visual just-noticable difference (JND) procedure (e.g., Hamilton, Coates, & Heffernan, 2003; Phillips & Hamilton, 2001; Thompson et al., 2006). In this task participants have to remember the precise size of a yellow square stimulus. This demands a fine-detailed coordinate representation of the stimulus (Kosslyn, 1980, 1994), which again is an attempt to preclude verbal or categorical labelling of the stimulus.

However, by default, size is determined by the spatial extent of the stimulus, thus the protocol could be identified as one assessing a relatively passive simultaneous-spatial representation, rather than one which measures visual-simultaneous representation. This is also the same for any studies that measure the length of a stimulus or its orientation, both constrained by the spatial characteristics of the stimulus.

Such visuospatial protocols should perhaps be distinguished from visual memory protocols that employ visual object-based stimuli (Scolari, Vogel, & Awh, 2008; Tresch et al., 1993). In the Tresch et al. study, participants were presented with a stimulus from a set of simple geometric shapes such as squares, circles, diamonds etc., thus these stimuli would have a categorical representation, possibly also verbally represented. At the point of retrieval the full set of eight objects were displayed, and the participant had to identify the *to-be-remembered* object. Given that Logie and Marchetti (1991) observed significant impairment in hue memory with interpolated irrelevant pictures, it would be surprising if performance was not underestimated in the Tresch et al. protocol (see below for a further consideration of this issue). Another source of concern in the Tresch et al. procedure is that the small object set may rapidly establish long-term memory representation (Klauer & Zhao, 2004). Thus at some point in the protocol long-term memory representation may support performance. Procedure-driven long-term memory representation is more likely with visual stimuli that receive initial categorical representation, however when the stimulus representation requires coordinate level detail, for example, precise hue, size, length, or orientation then it may be argued that long-term memory representation will not occur as fine detailed representation rapidly deteriorates over a period of seconds (Cornoldi & Vecchi, 2003; Thompson et al., 2006; van der Ham, van Wezel, Oleksiak, & Postma, 2007). Although, see Cowan (1988, 2005) and Magnussen (2009) for the suggestion that such fine detail may well be represented in long-term memory.

Another strategy employed in order to reduce the contribution of long-term memory is to employ novel pattern stimuli. The most frequently employed procedure is the visual matrix (Phillips & Baddeley, 1971) or Visual Patterns Test (VPT; Della Sala et al., 1999). A typical stimulus is shown in Figure 7.2b (see p. 127). In many studies the VPT task is seen as the prototypical visual working memory task, however it can be seen from Figure 7.2b that the task stimulus is of a simultaneous spatial nature (Mammarella, Pazzaglia, & Cornoldi, 2008). The task is to remember the matrix pattern, more precisely the location of the black cells. The typical adult span level is approximately nine black cells (Della Sala et al., 1999). This is much greater than the span level suggested by Cowan (2005) of three to four items, which suggests that perceptual or semantic chunking of the pattern elements may be occurring. The contribution of long-term memory to working memory task performance will be discussed in more detail below. However, it could be argued that the pre-categorical visuospatial memory (fine-detailed hue, texture, orientation) representation/object representation distinction illustrates another important feature in the conceptualization of visuospatial working memory; the differential support of perceptual and long-term memory resources. The use of object stimuli with existing long-term memory representations lends itself to a working memory task performance whereby long-term memory support should be extensive. The demand for fine-detailed high-resolution representations may preclude this long-term memory support but be dependent upon the quality of the initial perceptual representation (Ester, Serences, & Awh, 2009; Serences, Ester, Vogel, & Awh, 2009; Scolari et al., 2008). The distinction between categorical / pre-categorical representation also has implications for how one considers the capacity of working memory processes and shall be discussed in further detail below.

Complexity also exists in the research protocols emphasizing spatial memory. The work of Dale (1973) investigated participants' ability to remember the precise location of a small black disk. After a maintenance interval of variable time, the participant had to mark the location of the disk with a cross. Performance was measured by the discrepancy between veridical and the retrieved location. This basic protocol would be labelled an object location procedure by Cornoldi and Vecchi (2003), however Dale labelled the task a visual memory one. In contrast to this protocol is the procedure by Postma and colleagues (Postma et al., 1998; Postma, Winkel, Tuiten, & van Honk, 1999). A typical stimulus array is shown in Figure 7.1, where a multiple number of items are simultaneously displayed for a period of 10 s, and then subsequently the participants have to click and drag on the icons to restore them to their original locations. There are several variants to the task that allowed the authors to identify and decompose three memory processes at work; object memory processing, spatial-location processing, and the binding of objects to locations.

In comparison to the Dale (1973) study, this protocol is complex in its demands, the authors decomposed three cognitive processes but in addition issues associated

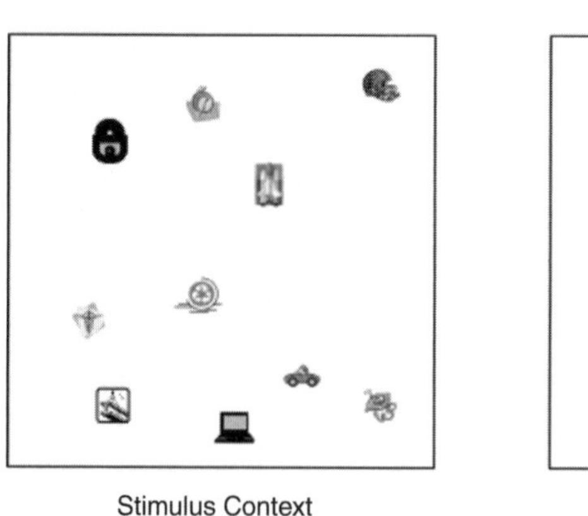

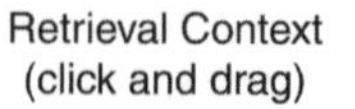

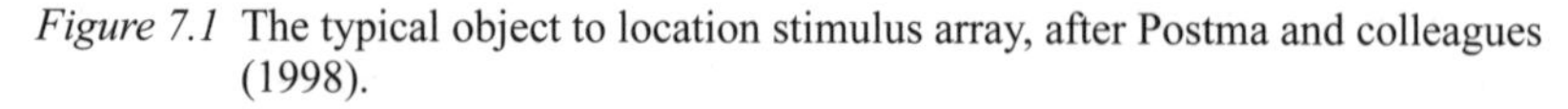

Figure 7.1 The typical object to location stimulus array, after Postma and colleagues (1998).

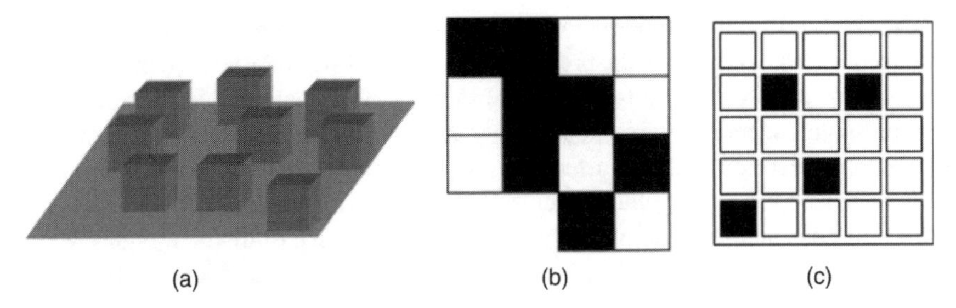

Figure 7.2 Typical Corsi Blocks Task apparatus (a), visual matrix pattern (b), and modified matrix task (c).

with attentional allocation and the capacity for location memory bear upon the procedure identified in Figure 7.1. McGivern, Huston, Byrd, King, Siegle, and Reilly (1997) considered that the performance in such multiple object location tasks was related to the initial attention component at the point of encoding. McGivern et al. noted that one factor that could provide the salience for an object of attention was the gender-related characteristics of the object. Thus, Gallagher, Neave, Hamilton, and Gray (2006) attempted to control exposure of the objects and subsequent allocation of attention through a sequential presentation procedure. The Eals and Silverman (1994) and the Postma et al. recognition procedures both used stimuli numbers that again greatly exceeded the suggested capacity limits of working memory suggested by Luck and Vogel (1997) and Cowan (2005) of three to four items. Again this would suggest that some form of organization, integrating across individual objects, must be occurring. Another frequently employed spatial memory protocol is the CBT (Milner, 1971), the task stimulus is shown above in Figure 7.2.

The CBT would be labelled as a spatial-sequential procedure (Mammarella et al., 2008); it possesses visuospatial-sequential characteristics both during the encoding and retrieval phases. Berch, Krikorian, and Huha (1998) reported that in the first three decades of use there was an idiosyncracy in the particular protocol employed. One constant, with original apparatus though, is the presence of the blocks providing a configural visual frame at the point of encoding and at retrieval. It is possible that such a frame could bias the nature of the representation making it more categorical (Kosslyn, Maljkovic, Hamilton, Horwitz, & Thompson, 1995).

It is clear that the diversity and complexity of task protocols make a clear separation of visual and spatial memory processes much more difficult to achieve. The fuller implications will be discussed in detail below.

Empirical findings in visuospatial working memory

There is extensive evidence from both experimental and individual differences research contexts that visual and spatial working memory protocols make demands upon discrete resources in working memory.

In the Logie and Marchetti (1991) dual-task study, memory for hue and spatial sequences was assessed in the presence or absence of two interference procedures; irrelevant pictures and (unseen) spatial tapping. The dual-task dissociation was impressive; the memory for hue was only affected by the irrelevant pictures while the spatial memory was only affected by spatial tapping. A set of studies by Smith, Jonides, Koeppe, Awh, Schumacher, and Minoshima (1995) looked at the memory for polygons and location of polygons with the presence of distractors that were either similar in shape ('visual' interference) or near or far location from the original stimulus (spatial interference). Their results suggested that distractor similarity had a greater impact upon the memory for polygons than the spatial distractor and a reverse pattern of effects upon the spatial memory task. These results suggested a similar pattern of dissociation to those in the Logie and Marchetti (1991) study. Later dual-task research by Della Sala et al. (1999) looked at performance in the VPT and CBT in the presence or absence of irrelevant pictures and spatial tapping interference protocols. These authors found a highly significant interaction in the data, indicating a significant dissociation between the effects of the irrelevant pictures and spatial tapping. *Post hoc* analyses found that the irrelevant pictures significantly impaired the VPT more than the spatial tapping. The reverse pattern was observed for the effect of the spatial tapping upon the CBT performance.

In a particularly rigorous set of experimental studies, Klauer and Zhao (2004) attempted to demonstrate discrete resources in working memory for visual and spatial memory representation. In their series of experiments they replicated and modified a number of earlier protocols in order to control for a number of factors. In their first study they controlled for the visual and spatial protocols having distinct encoding and retrieval procedures and continued to observe an interaction between the primary visual and spatial task performance and interference from the secondary tasks. In the second experiment they addressed in more detail the nature of the encoding process to ensure that it was more equivalent between the encoding of visual and spatial memorandum. The third study controlled for the use of a small set of stimuli that could lead, through an extensive procedure, to long-term memory representations, a phenomenon they labelled as *preactivated traces*. The fourth study controlled for the possibility that the selective interference from the spatial processing secondary task upon the spatial memory primary task could arise from a lower-level similarity basis. The final two experiments attempted to observe the dissociation between visual and spatial working memory representation while controlling for executive resourcing.

The series of findings provided compelling evidence that the dissociation between visual and spatial working memory resources could not readily be attributed to any of the factors they examined. The Klauer and Zhao (2004) procedure employed was a visual-simultaneous and spatial-simultaneous paradigm, the memory for a Chinese ideograph and the memory for the location of a dot. The subsequent research by Darling et al. (2009) further examined the visual/spatial dissociation by directly addressing the simultaneous-sequential/visual/spatial confound found in procedures employing tasks such as the VPT and

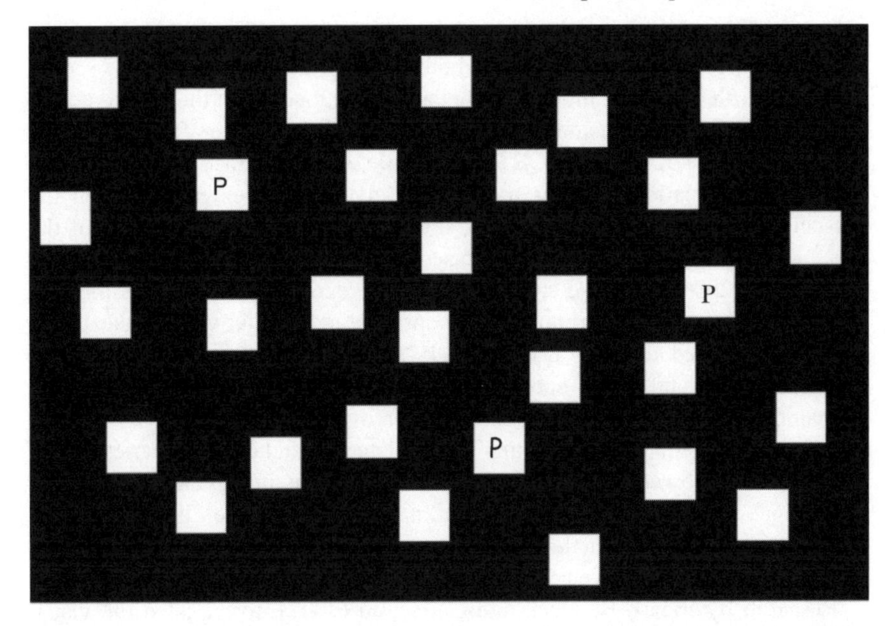

Figure 7.3 A typical visual appearance memory array format, after Darling et al. (2009).

CBT. In the Darling et al. visual-simultaneous (appearance) procedure, participants had to remember the precise font identity of three P letters presented within 30 randomly located squares in an array, but they need not recall their locations. This is shown in Figure 7.3.

Their procedure employed a range of visual/spatial with simultaneous/ sequential protocols. In both procedures participants were not required to remember the sequence of presentation, merely the appearances and locations respectively. A relatively complex retrieval context was required to ensure that the encoding/retrieval contexts were as equivalent as possible across the visual/spatial dimension. The interference procedures in this study were either visual (Dynamic Visual Noise, DVN) or unseen spatial tapping (of a figure of eight pattern). The authors found the typical interaction pattern of visual/spatial secondary affect upon the visual/spatial primary tasks. An important observation was that they found that the interference impacts were not dependent upon the simultaneous-sequential encoding manipulation. Thus, in this stimulus context, the critical feature was the visual/spatial nature of the material not the static-active characteristics (Cornoldi & Vecchi, 2003).

An alternative source of empirical evidence for differential visual and spatial representation can be derived from studies investigating individual differences in working memory. Two contexts will be focused upon here, a cognitive neuropsychological context and a child developmental context.

Della Sala et al.'s (1999) paper not only provided experimental evidence for a dissociation between visual and spatial working memory, it also reported a small number of patients who together showed a pattern of double dissociation in VPT and CBT performance. Two patients, both with left hemispheric lesions scored below the fifth percentile in the CBT but above the median on the VPT. Another patient, with bilateral lesions, scored extremely low on the VPT task while achieving a score of six on the CBT. This profile of performance clearly indicates a double dissociation, what is more problematic is the extent to which the dissociation is in the visual/spatial or simultaneous-sequential demands of the task. This particular issue was addressed by Darling, Della Sala, Logie, and Cantagallo (2006) in a case study paper. The procedure for the assessment of working memory for visual appearance and spatial location was similar to the protocol discussed above by Darling et al. (2009). Patient A suffered a stroke to right frontal, parietal, and temporal lobes and was found to be relatively impaired in maintaining the spatial location information over a period of 15.5 s. Patient B presented with damage to the frontal lobes bilaterally and the right parietal lobe. This patient showed a selective impairment in the maintenance of visual appearance over a 15.5 s period. Again, a pattern of double dissociation was demonstrated but with visual-simultaneous and spatial-simultaneous procedures, thus with no passive–active confound.

Research by Vicari, Bellucci, and Carlesimo (2003) investigated the visual spatial working memory differentiation within an atypical developmental context. They worked with children who were either developing in a typical manner or children with Williams syndrome. They employed two memory procedures assessing visual-simultaneous working memory in the form of a geometric shape procedure, and a spatial-sequential item location procedure. Their results indicated that the children with Williams syndrome were significantly poorer in the spatial task, but comparable with the typical developing group in the visual memory task performance. Thus, group differences in task performance were found but the source of these differences is necessarily confounded. Is the difference due to a spatial memory process impairment or a spatial-sequential difficulty? A study by Thompson et al. (2006) investigated visual and spatial working memory in patients in the euthymic phase of affective bipolar disorder. The patients received a battery of tasks that included the VPT and the CBT. Their performance was compared with a control group individually matched for age, sex, handedness, years of education, and premorbid IQ. A simple bivariate comparison of group performance revealed that the patients with bipolar disorder were significantly impaired in their CBT performance, but were no different from controls in their VPT performance. The simple inference from this pattern of results is that the patients were impaired on spatial memory but not visual memory. But again this study has the same confound as the Vicari et al. study immediately above. A fuller consideration of their findings may further compromise this simple interpretation and will be discussed in more detail below.

Individual differences arising from within a developmental context also appear to provide evidence for a visual/spatial separation within working memory. The study by Logie and Pearson (1997) observed the VPT and CBT performance in children aged between 5 and 12 years. They employed both recall and recognition retrieval contexts and found that in both contexts the VPT performance associated change with age was greater than for the CBT performance, which demonstrated a more gradual improvement over the age range. They considered this pattern of *developmental fractionation* (Hitch, 1990) as evidence that the two tasks were making demands upon visual and spatial memory processes in working memory. This pattern of developmental fractionation, suggesting more rapid age development in visual memory task performance was also observed by Hamilton et al. (2003). In this study the demands of the VPT and CBT were embedded within a cartoon figure in order to improve the ecological validity of the protocols. In the VPT equivalent procedure, over the 5–25 years age range there was significantly greater age dependency than in the Corsi equivalent procedure. Thus, both the Hamilton et al. study and the Logie and Pearson study show a developmental advantage for the VPT, spatial-simultaneous procedure. However, one should note that in a slightly different age group, Vicari et al. (2003) found their spatial location task to be more dependent upon age than their object memory task in their sample of typically developing children. This pattern of more rapid developmental improvement for a spatial memory task was also evidenced by Van Leijenhorst, Crone, and van der Molen (2007). The Van Leijenhorst et al. study looked at task performance in participants aged 6–26 years and found that in their spatial location memory task the children's performance matched adults' by the age of 11–12 years, while in the object memory task this same age group were still below the performance level of the adult group.

It is interesting to note that that these four studies, investigating visual and spatial working memory with different research protocols, revealed consistent patterns of developmental fractionation indicating demands upon discrete cognitive resources. However, in two studies the developmental gain lay with the VPT-like protocol, in the other two studies, the developmental precocity lay with the spatial location memory procedure. Developmental fractionation may exist, but which cognitive processes contribute to it in these studies?

Issues associated with the empirical findings in visuospatial working memory

Taken as a whole, the body of empirical evidence discussed above appears to provide substantial evidence for a differentiation of visual and spatial working memory resources. Throughout the content though, the issue of visual/spatial versus simultaneous-sequential consistently occurs, and in the latter research within a developmental context, the presence of developmental fractionation is compromised to a degree by the observation that in some studies visual memory task performance appears to be more dependent upon age, while in others, the spatial location task is more sensitive to age change. This component of the chapter will consider a broader range of issues associated with research into the visuospatial nature of working memory. The starting point for such a discussion is the consideration of two dominant theoretical models in working memory; the Baddeley (2000) multiple resource model and Cornoldi and Vecchi (2003) continuum model (see also Cornoldi & Mammarella, Chapter 6, this volume). Both models, in a modified form, are represented in Figure 7.4.

In the research literature discussed above there was an implicit suggestion that the multiple process conceptualization of visual/spatial processes was at odds with the continuum suggestion of simultaneous/sequential. It may be the case that within a particular research context the research question lends itself to a prediction that does indeed differentiate the salience of a multiple resource account versus a continuum account. The argument outlined below provides an alternative manner in which to consider these theoretical accounts and a way in which they both may contribute to an accommodation of recent empirical data. Note that although the multiple resource model shown in Figure 7.4 is derived from Baddeley (2000), there are many considerations that apply equally to the multiple resource model of Logie (Logie, 1995; Logie & van der Meulen, 2009; Logie, Chapter 2, this volume).

The modification of the Baddeley model in Figure 7.4a is to move away from a focus upon the architecture evident in the model towards the *functional architecture* of the model (Hamilton et al., 2003). If this model is to be a *working* memory model, then it is within this emphasis of the interface with cognitive resources that this role will be realized; a network rather than a set of black box processes (Zimmer, 2008). The figure also differentiates the interfacing *within* working memory, an *endogenous functional architecture* where executive resources may support or scaffold VSSP or phonological processes (and vice versa). This is in contrast to the scaffolding from outside of working memory resourcing that the 2000 model makes more explicit, and which is labelled in the figure as an *exogenous functional architecture*. Within such an emphasis, the mapping of working memory task protocols upon specific processes becomes more problematic, but also potentially more informative. This exogenous influence is evident in the Logie (1995) model and is perhaps the key characteristic of single resource models (Cowan, 1988, 2005). This focus upon a functional architecture enables a more dynamic account of working memory performance and one potentially more able to accommodate research findings.

A modified account of the continuum model (Cornoldi & Vecchi, 2003) is shown in Figure 7.4b. This model was originally much more explicitly dynamic in its representation of cognitive task demand upon working memory. Tasks could be envisaged as varying across a modality-specific dimension, but as importantly, these tasks could be seen as varying in the cognitive demands upon the passive–active continuum, with tasks at the passive end of the spectrum more modality specific dependent, and with tasks at the active end of the dimension more dependent upon amodal process contributions. Thus, task demand upon working memory resources is considered within an explicitly more dynamic and flexible framework, an important consideration if one wishes to understand the diverse task demands identified in the empirical literature above (Zimmer, 2008). Such a framework implies that subtle changes in task demand may lead to task performance being dependent upon an integrated functional architecture or network and not merely upon the process of interest. The major part of the

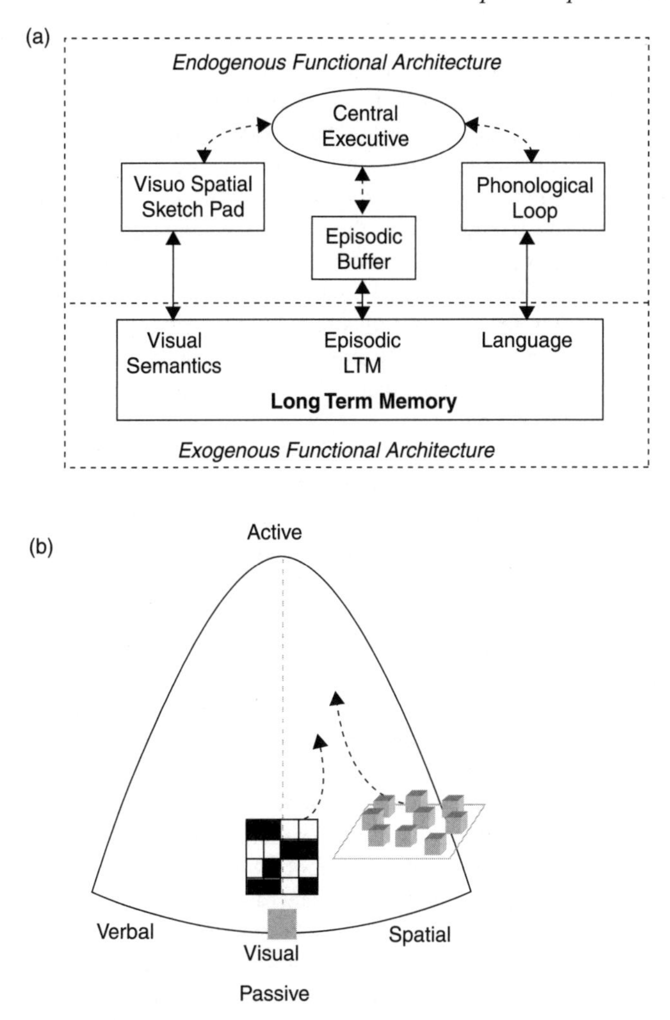

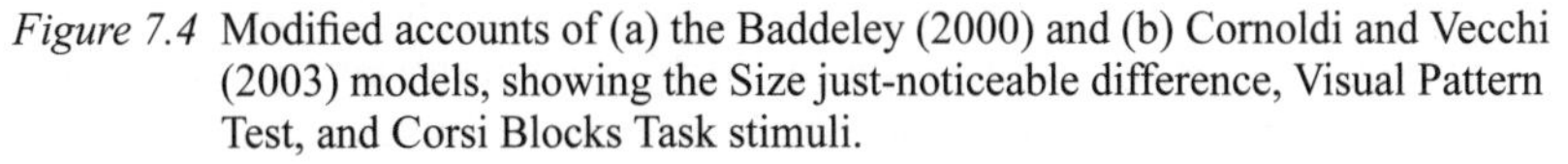

Figure 7.4 Modified accounts of (a) the Baddeley (2000) and (b) Cornoldi and Vecchi (2003) models, showing the Size just-noticeable difference, Visual Pattern Test, and Corsi Blocks Task stimuli.

discussion in this section will be directed towards interpreting the research literature discussed above within the modified models in Figure 7.4.

Two of the major dual-task studies that provided evidence for visual/spatial differentiation within working memory, the Della Sala et al. (1999) and the Klauer and Zhao (2004) papers, provide the starting point. In the Della Sala et al. paper the authors report the effect of visual and spatial interference upon the VPT and CBT, and report a highly significant interaction effect. They also carried out simple effects analyses, recommended by Klauer and Zhao, to demonstrate that visual interference, irrelevant pictures, had a significantly greater impact upon the

VPT than the spatial tapping, and vice versa for the effect upon the Corsi task. However, what is clear from their results (Della Sala et al., Table 5, Figure 2, p. 1196) is that there is also cross-modality interference. In comparison to baseline performance, spatial tapping reduces the VPT performance to approximately the 84% level, while the irrelevant pictures reduced the CBT performance to approximately 81%. In this data, therefore there is evidence above and beyond the modality-specific interference effect. This effect of spatial tapping upon memory for visual matrix patterns was replicated by Andrade, Kemps, Werniers, May, and Szmalec (2002) in their Experimental 3 interference study. In the Hamilton et al. (2003) study where a different stimulus context was employed, spatial tapping had a significant effect upon the VPT-equivalent procedure, both in children and in adult participants. This suggests that a full report of data treatment needs to go beyond the main and simple effects suggested by Klauer and Zhao in order to reveal the presence or absence of more domain general interference within the secondary task. Note that in some studies, where the memory was for colour hue (Logie & Marchetti, 1991) or font characteristic (Darling et al., 2009), spatial tapping had a much more reduced effect upon the visual memory task performance.

One may ask what processes beyond the modality-specific resources are recruited in the spatial tapping secondary-task interference protocol. Klauer and Zhao (2004) suggested executive resources would be demanded, one source of evidence for this comes from Klauer and Stegmaier (1997) who observed that decisions made upon spatial localized stimuli could recruit executive resources. In the simplest of the spatial tapping procedures, four decisions per cycle are required; the figure of eight protocols require many more spatial decisions and thus more executive involvement. Hamilton et al. (2003) provided evidence of amodal executive impact upon visual and spatial memory performance. In their study, verbal retrieval from long-term memory was required during the maintenance interval and this activity had a significant (and equivalent) impairment upon both the visual memory and spatial memory task performances in children and in adults. This suggested that these two visuospatial memory tasks demanded executive resourcing during the maintenance period. Given the cartoon embedded nature of these protocols it is possible that the task context lent itself to the recruitment of executive resources (Ang & Lee, 2010). However, subsequent research has demonstrated a major executive contribution of executive resources in CBT performance (Fisk & Sharp, 2003; Vandierendonck, Kemps, Fastame, & Szmalec, 2004) and in both the VPT and CBT (Rudkin, Pearson, & Logie, 2007).

This suggests that tasks such as the VPT and CBT cannot be mapped onto multiple resource models with simple ease. Both tasks show working memory at work, not demanding purely solitary processes but by making major demands upon the endogenous, and possibly, exogenous functional architecture (Hamilton et al., 2003; Rudkin et al., 2007; Vandierendonck et al., 2004). By emphasizing the functional architecture of visuospatial working memory these findings can be accommodated within both the Baddeley (2000) and Logie (1995) multiple resource models. In addition, within the continuum framework, the findings are readily accommodated by presuming that the tasks are further up the passive–active continuum, and that in addition they may also share more visuospatial characteristics in common (see Figure 7.4b).

The Rudkin et al. (2007) study attempted to decompose, in more detail, the nature of the executive resource demands within the VPT and CBT. One of the conclusions that they came to was that one of the major demands leading to executive recruitment was the sequential nature of the task protocol. Although it has been suggested that serial order demands may be similar across working memory (Avons, Ward, & Melling, 2004), Rudkin et al. argued that the sequential order demand in the Corsi task may not be the crucial feature in recruiting executive resources. The emphasis in the Rudkin et al. paper was on the relationship between sequential processes and executive demands; however, their results show a particularly interesting pattern concerning the visual matrix or spatial-simultaneous task. In Study 1 of the Rudkin et al. paper, the matrix pattern was the conventional VPT-like pattern (see Figure 7.2b). With random number generation as the executive interference procedure, they observed a significant (if relatively small) effect of interference upon the visual matrix task performance. In Studies 2 and 3 the sequential nature of presentation was manipulated but in addition the nature of the matrix pattern was changed to the pattern format shown in Figure 7.2c. With this matrix pattern, executive interference had no significant impact upon task performance. Why should this be the case?

One possible explanation lies in the perceptual organization of the two arrays in Figure 7.2b and 7.2c (Attneave, 1957; Donderi, 2006). In the conventional VPT-like matrix, proximity and other gestalt processes may facilitate organization of the black cells in order to increase redundancy. This complexity-reduction process may be accompanied by structural organization that is either visually driven (Avons & Phillips, 1987; Chipman, 1977) or verbally scaffolded (Brown, Forbes, & McConnell, 2006; Postma et al., 1998). Thus the conventional VPT configuration format may more readily afford executively demanding reorganization. Consequently, while the conventional VPT format produces a span performance of approximately nine black cells, the matrix pattern employed by Rudkin et al. (2007) produces a span of approximately four black cells when the black cells are randomly distributed (Rossi-Arnaud, Pieroni, & Baddeley, 2006). The VPT span level is significantly above the three to four item span proposed for working memory and this suggests that the executive demands of a spatial-simultaneous task such as the visual matrix task will depend upon the level of semantic affordance or elaboration in the pattern stimulus.

Within a working memory approach that emphasizes multiple resources (e.g., Shah & Miyake, 1996) it may be worthwhile pursuing the qualitative nature of the executive or attentional resources scaffolding visuospatial working memory task performance. One such approach has been to investigate the contribution of visual attention in working memory task performance. Awh, Jonides, and Reuter-Lorenz (1998) observed the impact of the interpolation of a spatial attention shift during the maintenance interval of a spatial location memory task. Their suggestion was that maintenance in spatial location memory is accomplished through shifts of attention to the locations being memorized (Awh, Vogel, & Oh, 2006). Research by Postle, Idzikowski, Della Sala, Logie, and Baddeley (2006) suggested that it was eye-movement control rather than eye movements *per se* that had the impact upon spatial location. Postle et al. also observed that there was no significant effect upon a task demanding the memory for the shape characteristics of an object. Suggesting a separation of visual attention recruitment in spatial- and object-based tasks. Lawrence, Myerson, and Abrams (2004) also investigated the impact of spatial-attention upon spatial-location task performance. In this procedure, participants had to memorize the locations of multiple circle stimuli placed upon a grid. This uses a protocol that has the appearance of similar task demands to a visual matrix procedure (see Figure 7.2c). The presence of an attentional shift during the maintenance period impacted upon the spatial-simultaneous task but not upon a verbal working memory span task. These results imply the presence of attentional executive resources dedicated to nonverbal processes in working memory. The results also suggest that spatial attention rehearsal is present with simple and more complex arrays of spatial-simultaneous task protocols. As such, this observation could explain the effect of spatial tapping upon the VPT task performance in the studies by Andrade et al. (2002) and Hamilton et al. (2003).

Further evidence for fractionated executive support is present in the Thompson et al. (2006) study. As noted above, this study found that (euthymic) patients with bipolar affective disorder were significantly impaired in CBT performance while performing the VPT and the size JND task competently. This may appear to be evidence supporting differential memory processes, however these patients also had impaired executive resourcing and when this was statistically controlled for then the relative impairment in the CBT was no longer present. This suggests that perhaps the locus of the patient-task impairment lay not in the spatial memory process *per se* but in the executive contribution to task performance. This would therefore be a case of a deficient functional architecture, but this would be specific to the spatial-sequential task, not to the spatial-simultaneous (VPT) or visual-simultaneous (size JND). The VPT requirement for executive resourcing must be qualitatively different from the Corsi task.

It should be noted that while the research above identified an executive contribution to the functional architecture of visuospatial working memory task performance, a key element of the Klauer and Zhao (2004) argument was for the existence of separable visual and spatial memory resources *beyond* the contribution of executive resources. Alternatively, single resource accounts would emphasize these executive and attentional resources and de-emphasize the importance of these discrete multiple memory processes. A recent paper by Vergauwe, Barrouillet, and Camos (2009) adds considerably to this debate. In two dual-task studies with spatial-sequential, spatial-simultaneous, and visual-simultaneous stimuli these authors demonstrated that visuospatial memory processes may not be so dissociated after all. Their results indicated that *both* visual and spatial working memory protocols are highly dependent upon the degree of attentional capture or cognitive load of the secondary task. Thus, their results are consistent with the discussion above that these tasks are demanding of executive scaffolding.

The Vergauwe et al. study does, however, raise issues with implications not only for the interpretation of their findings but for visuospatial working memory research more generally.

In Study 1 of the Vergauwe et al. paper, the procedure with visual matrix stimuli mimicked the earlier procedure of Phillips and colleagues (Phillips & Baddeley,1971; Phillips 1974; Phillips & Christie, 1977a, 1977b) with serial presentation of matrix patterns and serial recall of the patterns, although the recall sequence was different from that of Phillips. This protocol is fundamentally different from the commonly employed VPT presentation of a single pattern presented and recalled. The added complexity may result in a potentially confounded procedure. In a protocol with serially presented stimuli, subsequent stimuli in the series will interfere with earlier stimuli through a process of stimulus similarity (Logie, 1995). Thus, what is represented through the procedure is less likely to be in a format that is *only* visually based. The serial recall procedure enables further visual interference to occur. Thus, the control performance, without interpolated interference, is one in which the initial visual representation is likely to have already been impoverished. In addition the procedure demands an ordering of the stimulus. In the second study Chinese ideographs are employed (see Klauer & Zhao, 2004, above). However, it appears that a set size of eight stimuli was employed and thus the strong possibility of long-term memory support through *preactivation* (Klauer & Zhao, 2004) is possible as the procedure develops. Perhaps as important is the nature of the retrieval context; the presence of the full set of eight stimuli will lead to visual similarity at the point of retrieval and potentially elicit the onset of comparison errors (Scolari et al., 2008). Thus, an important source of variance in these findings will derive from similarity based confusions at the point of retrieval, not from the quality of the memory representation *per se*. These are issues that relate to any studies with these embedded protocols. In addition a more general issue is also raised by the Vergauwe et al. study. This will be considered within the context of recent research by Orme (2009).

Orme's doctoral thesis (2009) included a study that employed the executive resource framework of Miyake et al. (2000). Thus, participants carried out auditory-based inhibition, updating, and set shifting executive procedures concurrently with the execution of a computerized size JND procedure, visual matrix, and CBT procedure. In a titrated process, all participants performed the dual-task procedure at their own span level for the primary tasks. The analyses took into consideration the impact upon both the primary and secondary task performances (Mu calculation) and the results are shown in Table 7.1.

The results of this study demonstrated that these visuospatial tasks made demands upon amodal executive resources in working memory; however the impact was qualified by the nature of the primary and secondary task. The size JND task performance was much less affected than the visual matrix and Corsi performances. In addition, the Plus/Minus Task consistently had a greater impact upon all three primary tasks. This latter finding is indicative of a secondary executive task with greater attentional capture (Vergauwe et al., 2009). These results do provide evidence for an amodal executive contribution to visuospatial

Table 7.1 The impact of verbal executive interference upon visuospatial working memory task performance (%Mu impairment) from Orme (2009).

Secondary task	*Primary task*					
	Size JND		*Visual Matrix*		*Corsi Task*	
	Mean	SD	Mean	SD	Mean	SD
Stop/Signal	10.24	9.13	27.41	27.12	30.7	20.89
Plus/Minus	17.81	11.95	52.59	17.31	48.71	17.59
N-Back	11.63	15.51	37.48	27.5	36.51	19.3

Note: Size JND, size just-noticeable difference.

memory task performance; however, they do not provide insight into how *relatively* important these amodal resources are. In the same constrained manner as the Vergauwe et al. (2009) study, they indicate the contribution of these executive resources, not their *extent*. If one wishes to determine the extent of contribution of any component of the functional architecture, then one must have an interference process where the task span procedure is fully carried out in the presence or absence of selective interference. This would provide more direct evidence of how much each process (of the secondary task) impacts upon primary task performance; a titrated approach with dual-task interference at span level cannot afford this quality of information.

The starting point for this discussion is suggested above in the re-iterated considerations of issues in protocol construction. The full recognition of a rich functional architecture underlying task performance (Hamilton et al., 2003; Rudkin et al., 2007; Zimmer, 2008) should lead to a more careful consideration of task protocol demands. The presence of multiple stimuli in either simultaneous or sequential presentation, or at encoding or retrieval, will increase the probability that executive resources will be engaged. This may be acceptable if the aim of the research is to investigate the memory processes associated with multiple objects, or if one is interested in executive recruitment in task performance. The aim of the research may be to disentangle the contribution of the targeted process from the contribution of the functional architecture; at other times the interface of processes may be the research question, in either case the protocol should be driven with the functional architecture explicitly in mind (Hamilton et al., 2003). The emphasis above has been upon the interface of visuospatial resources with executive processes, there remains scope for an exploration of the interface with the representations emerging from low-level perceptual processing and the influence of long-term memory categorization upon visual information. This gateway–long-term memory interaction process has not been extensively pursued.

A specific research theme pursued by the author (Hamilton et al., 2003; Phillips & Hamilton, 2001; Thompson et al., 2006) has been the interface between low-level, precategorical, coordinate-based visual memory representation and categorical representation within working memory. The conventional multiple resource accounts of working memory emphasize solitary visual memory processes (although see Pearson, 2001, and Quinn, 2008, for alternative accounts). These processes, the VSSP, or the visual cache appear to be categorical in nature and thus allow direct scaffolding from long-term memory (Baddeley, 2000; Logie, 1995; Logie & van der Meulen, 2009). These cognitive frameworks appear consistent with the cognitive neuroscience evidence that emphasize frontoparietal-temporal networks, particularly the parietal-temporal interface (Lepsien & Nobre, 2007; Ranganath & D'Esposito, 2005; Todd & Marois, 2005; Xu, 2009; Xu & Chun, 2006). However, a more recent literature has begun to emphasize sustained neural activity in the visual cortex associated with low-level visual representation, enduring beyond the stimulus presentation (Cattaneo, Vecchi, Pascual-Leone, & Silvanto, 2009; Ester et al., 2009; Harrison & Tong, 2009; Johnson, Mitchell, Raye, D'Esposito, & Johnson, 2007; Serences, Ester, Vogel, & Awh, 2009). This evidence from neuroscience is consistent with cognitive findings implying that beyond a categorical representation fixed by a capacity of three to four items, there is a precategorical, high-resolution, or high-fidelity representation (Darling et al., 2009; Dean et al., 2008; Dent, 2010; Scolari et al., 2008; Thompson et al., 2006). Capacity in terms of fixed slots is an inappropriate way to consider the parameters of this form of memory representation; resolution or fidelity may be more appropriate terms.

In Figure 7.4b, the size JND task has been positioned close to the passive end of the continuum. The findings in Orme (2009) indicate that although this precategorical representation may not be subject to executive manipulation or transformation (hence a low point in the continuum), it is, however, likely to be subject to visual-attention processes (Johnson et al., 2007). The findings by Orme, shown in Table 7.1, of minimal executive impact upon the size JND task performance provide evidence that this task is less demanding of executive resources (Thompson et al., 2006). It is also consistent with findings from Logie and Marchetti (1991) and with Darling et al. (2009) that suggest that memory representations for fine-detailed low-level visual information, size, hue, and font shape are less affected by nonmodality specific interference. It is particularly interesting to note that dynamic visual noise (DVN; McConnell & Quinn, 2000), appears to selectively impair the representation of these fine-detailed visual representations. This is the case for coloured textures (Dean et al., 2008), font shape (Darling et al., 2009) and surface colour (Dent, 2010). The work of Andrade et al. (2002) and others suggests that DVN has less impact upon matrix patterns. This suggests that the conventional VPT representation within working memory may be of a categorical level which is resistant to DVN effect.

One promising line of visual memory research will be to construct variants of the visual matrix protocol and explore how differing secondary procedures such as DVN, spatial tapping, and executive tasks interfere with the variant task performance (Orme, 2009). This interface between high-fidelity representations and categorical visual working memory and how ultimately they emerge in the form of a categorical representation within visual working has yet to be established. Likewise, the presence of precategorical, low-level single-item spatial location memory (Munneke, Heslenfeldt, & Theeuwes, 2010) needs to be explored and subsequently its interaction with more complex item-location memory in the protocols employed by researchers such as Postma et al. (1998). This research orientation is difficult to interpret within multiple resource models with solitary visual and spatial memory resources, particularly with models that view the content of working memory as driven by long-term memory representations, but will be more readily accommodated within conceptions of working memory that afford flexible and multiple representations (Cornoldi & Vecchi, 2003; Zimmer, 2008).

References

Andrade, J., Kemps, E., Werniers, Y., May, J., & Szmalec, A. (2002). Insensitivity of visual short-term memory to irrelevant visual information. *Quarterly Journal of Experimental Psychology Section A: Human Experimental Psychology, 55,* 753–774.

Ang, S. Y., & Lee, K. (2010). Exploring developmental differences in visual short-term memory and working memory. *Developmental Psychology, 46,* 279–285.

Attneave, F. (1957). Physical determinants of the judged complexity of shapes. *Journal of Experimental Psychology, 53,* 221–227.

Avons, S. E., & Phillips, W. A. (1987). Representation of matrix patterns in long-term and short-term visual memory. *Acta Psychologica, 65,* 227–246.

Avons, S. E., Ward, G., & Melling, L. (2004). Item and order memory for novel visual patterns assessed by two-choice recognition. *Quarterly Journal of Experimental Psychology Section A: Human Experimental Psychology, 57,* 865–891.

Awh, E., Jonides, J., & Reuter-Lorenz, P. A. (1998). Rehearsal in spatial working memory. *Journal of Experimental Psychology: Human Perception and Performance, 24,* 780–790.

Awh, E., Vogel, E. K., & Oh, S. -H. (2006). Interactions between attention and working memory. *Neuroscience, 139,* 201–208.

Baddeley, A. D. (1986). *Working memory.* Oxford: Oxford University Press.

Baddeley, A. (2000). The episodic buffer: a new component of working memory? *Trends in Cognitive Sciences, 4,* 417–423.

Baddeley, A. D., & Hitch, G. J. (1974). Working Memory. In G. Bower (Ed.), *The Psychology of Learning and Motivation* (pp. 47–89). New York: Academic Press.

Berch, D. B., Krikorian, R., & Huha, E. M. (1998). The Corsi block-tapping task: Methodological and theoretical considerations. *Brain and Cognition, 38,* 317–338.

Brown, L. A., Forbes, D., & McConnell, J. (2006). Limiting the use of verbal coding in the Visual Patterns Test. *Quarterly Journal of Experimental Psychology, 59,* 1169–1176.

Cattaneo, Z., Vecchi, T., Pascual-Leone, A., & Silvanto, J. (2009). Contrasting early visual cortical activation states causally involved in visual imagery and short-term memory. *European Journal of Neuroscience, 30,* 1393–1400.

Chipman, S. F. (1977). Complexity and structure in visual-patterns. *Journal of Experimental Psychology: General, 106,* 269–301.

Cornoldi, C., & Vecchi, T. (2003). *Visuo-spatial working memory and individual differences.* Hove, UK: Psychology Press.

Cowan, N. (1988). Evolving conceptions of memory storage, selective attention, and their mutual constraints within the human information-processing system. *Psychological Bulletin, 104,* 163–191.

Cowan, N. (2005). *Working memory capacity.* Hove, UK: Psychology Press.

Dale, H. C. A. (1973). Short-term memory for visual information. *British Journal of Psychology, 64,* 1–8.

Darling, S., Della Sala, S., & Logie, R. H. (2009). Dissociation between appearance and location within visuospatial working memory. *Quarterly Journal of Experimental Psychology, 62,* 417–425.

Darling, S., Della Sala, S., Logie, R., & Cantagallo, A. (2006). Neuropsychological evidence for separating components of visuospatial working memory. *Journal of Neurology, 253,* 176–180.

Dean, G. M., Dewhurst, S. A., & Whittaker, A. (2008). Dynamic visual noise interferes with storage in visual working memory. *Experimental Psychology, 55,* 283–289.

Della Sala, S., Gray, C., Baddeley, A., Allamano, N., & Wilson, L. (1999). Pattern span: A tool for unwelding visuospatial memory. *Neuropsychologia, 37,* 1189–1199.

Dent, K. (2010). Dynamic visual noise affects visual short-term memory for surface color, but not spatial location. *Experimental Psychology, 57,* 17–26.

Donderi, D. C. (2006). Visual complexity: A review. *Psychological Bulletin, 132,* 73–97.

Eals, M., & Silverman, I. (1994). The Hunter-Gatherer Theory of spatial sex-differences – Proximate factors mediating the female advantage in recall of object arrays. *Ethology and Sociobiology, 15,* 95–105.

Ester, E. F., Serences, J. T., & Awh, E. (2009). Spatially global representations in human primary visual cortex during working memory maintenance. *Journal of Neuroscience, 29,* 15258–15265.

Fisk, J. E., & Sharp, C. A. (2003). The role of the executive system in visuospatial memory functioning. *Brain and Cognition, 52,* 364–381.

Gallagher, P., Neave, N., Hamilton, C., & Gray, J. M. (2006). Sex differences in object location memory: Some further methodological considerations. *Learning and Individual Differences, 16,* 277–290.

Hamilton, C. J., Coates, R. O., & Heffernan, T. (2003). What develops in visuospatial working memory development? *European Journal of Cognitive Psychology, 15,* 43–69.

Harrison, S. A., & Tong, F. (2009). Decoding reveals the contents of visual working memory in early visual areas. *Nature, 458,* 632–635.

Hitch, G. J. (1990). Developmental fractionation of working memory In G. Vallar, & T. Shallice (Eds.), *Neuropsychological impairments of short-term memory.* Cambridge: Cambridge University Press.

Johnson, M. R., Mitchell, K. J., Raye, C. L., D'Esposito, M., & Johnson, M. K. (2007). Brief thought can modulate activity in extrastriate visual areas: Top-down effects of refreshing just-seen visual stimuli. *NeuroImage, 37,* 290–299.

Klauer, K. C., & Stegmaier, R. (1997). Interference in immediate spatial memory: Shifts of spatial attention or central-executive involvement? *Quarterly Journal of Experimental Psychology Section A: Human Experimental Psychology, 50,* 79–99.

Klauer, K. C., & Zhao, Z. M. (2004). Double dissociations in visual and spatial short-term memory. *Journal of Experimental Psychology: General, 133,* 355–381.

Kosslyn, S. M. (1980). *Image and mind.* Cambridge, MA: Harvard University.

Kosslyn, S. M. (1994). *Image and brain.* Cambridge, MA: MIT Press.

Kosslyn, S. M., Maljkovic, V., Hamilton, S., Horwitz, G., & Thompson, W. (1995). Two types of image generation: Evidence for left and LVF/RH processes. *Neuropsychologia, 33,* 1485–1510.

Lawrence, B. M., Myerson, J., & Abrams, R. A. (2004). Interference with spatial working memory: An eye movement is more than a shift of attention. *Psychonomic Bulletin & Review, 11,* 488–494.

Lepsien, J., & Nobre, A. C. (2007). Attentional modulation of object representations in working memory. *Cerebral Cortex, 17,* 2072–2083.

Logie, R. H. (1995). *Visuo-spatial working memory.* Hove, UK: Lawrence Earlbaum Associates Ltd.

Logie, R. H., & Marchetti, C. (1991). Visuo-spatial working memory: Visual, spatial or central executive. In R. H. Logie & M. Denis (Eds.), *Mental images in human cognition.* Amsterdam: North Holland Press

Logie, R. H., & Pearson, D. G. (1997). The inner eye and the inner scribe of visuospatial working memory: Evidence from developmental fractionation. *European Journal of Cognitive Psychology, 9,* 241–257.

Logie, R. H., & van der Meulen, M. (2009). Fragmenting and integrating visuo-spatial working memory. In J. R. Brockmole (Ed.), *Representing the visual world in memory.* Hove, UK: Psychology Press.

Luck, S. J., & Vogel, E. K. (1997). The capacity of visual working memory for features and conjunctions. *Nature, 390,* 279–281.

McConnell, J., & Quinn, J. G. (2000). Interference in visual working memory. *Quarterly Journal of Experimental Psychology Section A: Human Experimental Psychology, 53,* 53–67.

McGivern, R. F., Huston, J. P., Byrd, D., King, T., Siegle, G. J., & Reilly, J. (1997). Sex differences in visual recognition memory: Support for a sex-related difference in attention in adults and children. *Brain and Cognition, 34,* 323–336.

Magnussen, S. (2009). Implicit visual working memory. *Scandinavian Journal of Psychology, 50,* 535–542.

Mammarella, I. C., Pazzaglia, F., & Cornoldi, C. (2008). Evidence for different components in children's visuospatial working memory. *British Journal of Developmental Psychology, 26,* 337–355.

Milner, B. (1971). Interhemispheric differences in the localization of psychological processes in man. *British Medical Bulletin, 27,* 272–277.

Miyake, A., Friedman, N. P., Emerson, M. J., Witzki, A. H., Howerter, A., & Wager, T. D. (2000). The unity and diversity of executive functions and their contributions to complex 'frontal lobe' tasks: A latent variable analysis. *Cognitive Psychology, 41,* 49–100.

Munneke, J., Heslenfeld, D. J., & Theeuwes, J. (2010). Spatial working memory effects in early visual cortex. *Brain and Cognition, 72,* 368–377.

Orme, E. (2009). Identifying the functional architecture underlying multiple representations in visual working memory. Northumbria University, Newcastle upon Tyne. Retrieved January 14, 2011, from www.northumbria.openrepository.com/northumbria/bitstream/10145/955201/orme.elizabeth_phd.pdf

Pearson, D. G. (2001). Imagery and the visuospatial sketchpad. In J. Andrade (Ed.), *Working memory in perspective* (pp. 33–59). Hove, UK: Psychology Press.

Phillips, L., & Hamilton, C. J. (2001). The working memory model in adult aging research. In J. Andrade (Ed.), *Working memory in perspective* (pp. 101–118). Hove, UK: Psychology Press.

Phillips, W. A. (1974). Distinction between sensory storage and short-term visual memory. *Perception & Psychophysics, 16,* 283–290.

Phillips, W. A., & Baddeley, A. D. (1971). Reaction time and short-term visual memory. *Psychonomic Science, 22,* 73–74.

Phillips, W. A., & Christie, D. F. M. (1977a). Components of visual memory. *Quarterly Journal of Experimental Psychology, 29,* 117–133.

Phillips, W. A., & Christie, D. F. M. (1977b). Interference with visualization. *Quarterly Journal of Experimental Psychology, 29,* 637–650.

Postle, B. R., Idzikowski, C., Della Sala, S., Logie, R. H., & Baddeley, A. D. (2006). The selective disruption of spatial working memory by eye movements. *Quarterly Journal of Experimental Psychology, 59,* 100–120.

Postma, A., Izendoorn, R., & De Haan, E. H. F. (1998). Sex differences in object location memory. *Brain and Cognition, 36,* 334–345.

Postma, A., Winkel, J., Tuiten, A., & van Honk, J. (1999). Sex differences and menstrual cycle effects in human spatial memory. *Psychoneuroendocrinology, 24,* 175–192.

Quinn, J. G. (2008). Movement and visual coding: the structure of visuospatial working memory. *Cognitive Processing, 9,* 35–43.

Ranganath, C., & D'Esposito, M. (2005). Directing the mind's eye: prefrontal, inferior and medial temporal mechanisms for visual working memory. *Current Opinion in Neurobiology, 15,* 175–182.

Rossi-Arnaud C., Pieroni, L., & Baddeley, A. (2006). Symmetry and binding in visuospatial working memory. *Neuroscience, 139,* 393–400.

Rudkin, S. J., Pearson, D. G., & Logie, R. H. (2007). Executive processes in visual and spatial working memory tasks. *Quarterly Journal of Experimental Psychology, 60,* 79–100.

Scolari, M., Vogel, E. K., & Awh, E. (2008). Perceptual expertise enhances the resolution but not the number of representations in working memory. *Psychonomic Bulletin & Review, 15,* 215–222.

Serences, J. T., Ester, E. F., Vogel, E. K., & Awh, E. (2009). Stimulus-specific delay activity in human primary visual cortex. *Psychological Science, 20,* 207–214.

Shah, P., & Miyake, A. (1996). The separability of working memory resources for spatial thinking and language processing: An individual differences approach. *Journal of Experimental Psychology: General, 125,* 4–27.

Smith, E. E., Jonides, J., Koeppe, R. A., Awh, E., Schumacher, E. H., & Minoshima, S. (1995). Spatial versus object working-memory – Pet investigations. *Journal of Cognitive Neuroscience, 7,* 337–356.

Thompson, J. M., Hamilton, C. J., Gray, J. M., Quinn, J. G., Mackin, P., Young, A. H., & Ferrier, I. N. (2006). Executive and visuospatial sketchpad resources in euthymic bipolar disorder: Implications for visuospatial working memory architecture. *Memory, 14,* 437–451.

Todd, J. J., & Marois, R. (2005). Posterior parietal cortex activity predicts individual differences in visual short-term memory capacity. *Cognitive Affective & Behavioral Neuroscience, 5,* 144–155.

Tresch, M. C., Sinnamon, H. M., & Seamon, J. G. (1993). Double dissociation of spatial and object visual memory – Evidence from selective interference in intact human-subjects. *Neuropsychologia, 31,* 211–219.

van der Ham, I. J. M., van Wezel, R. J., Oleksiak, A., & Postma, A. (2007). The time course of hemispheric differences in categorical and coordinate spatial processing. *Neuropsychologia, 45,* 2492–2498.

Van Leijenhorst, L., Crone, E. A., & Van der Molen, M. W. (2007). Developmental trends for object and spatial working memory: A psychophysiological analysis. *Child Development, 78,* 987–1000.

Vandierendonck, A., Kemps, E., Fastame, M. C., & Szmalec, A. (2004). Working memory components of the Corsi blocks task. *British Journal of Psychology, 95,* 57–79.

Vergauwe, E., Barrouillet, P., & Camos, V. (2009). Visual and spatial working memory are not that dissociated after all: A time-based resource-sharing account. *Journal of Experimental Psychology: Learning Memory and Cognition, 35,* 1012–1028.

Vicari, S., Bellucci, S., & Carlesimo, G. A. (2003). Visual and spatial working memory dissociation: Evidence from Williams syndrome. *Developmental Medicine and Child Neurology, 45,* 269–273.

Xu, Y. D. (2009). Distinctive neural mechanisms supporting visual object individuation and identification. *Journal of Cognitive Neuroscience, 21,* 511–518.

Xu, Y. D., & Chun, M. M. (2006). Dissociable neural mechanisms supporting visual short-term memory for objects. *Nature, 440,* 91–95.

Zimmer, H. D. (2008). Visual and spatial working memory: From boxes to networks. *Neuroscience and Biobehavioral Reviews, 32,* 1373–1395.

Zimmer, H. D., Speiser, H. R., & Seidler, B. (2003). Spatio-temporal working-memory and short-term object-location tasks use different memory mechanisms. *Acta Psychologica, 114,* 41–65.

8 What can symmetry tell us about working memory?

Laura Pieroni, Clelia Rossi-Arnaud, and Alan D. Baddeley

Introduction

When a person has to process a set of locations that are encompassed within a structure, he/she can think about a location in more than one way. For example it is possible to remember the location of a star both in terms of its location in the sky, or in terms of its position within a constellation. Structured patterns provide redundancy, allowing each part of a stimulus to be predicted from the other parts. Redundancy can be useful at both encoding and retrieval (Schumann-Hengsteler, Strobl, & Zoelch, 2004). The trace system resulting from a well-organized pattern is assumed to be more stable than that arising from a chaotic array and hence less subject to the effects of trace decay or interference (Koffka, 1935). Attneave (1954) demonstrated that various Gestalt factors including symmetry, good continuation, and other forms of regularity can all be considered to reflect redundancy that can be quantified accordingly within the framework of information theory. In particular, redundancy is a characteristic of symmetry, the mathematical definition of which is: the exact reflection of form on opposite sides of a dividing line or plane.

This particular characteristic seems to be deeply represented in human and animal cognition. Symmetry perception has been demonstrated in humans (e.g., Corballis & Roldan, 1974; Pashler, 1990), dolphins (von Fersen, Manos, Goldowsky, & Roitblat, 1992), and birds (Delius & Nowak, 1982). Giurfa and colleagues (Giurfa, Eichmann, & Menzel, 1996) have shown that bees trained to discriminate bilaterally symmetrical from asymmetrical patterns can transfer appropriately to novel stimuli, thus demonstrating a capacity both to detect and generalize symmetry. Perception of symmetry in humans has been extensively investigated, indicating that the detection of symmetry may facilitate early visual processes, such as figure–ground segmentation (Driver, Baylis, & Rafal, 1992; Koffka, 1935; Rock, 1983) and contribute to later processes, such as recognition of objects from novel viewpoints (Vetter, Poggio, & Bülthoff, 1994).

In perception, patterns that are symmetrical along the vertical axis are more salient than those with axes of symmetry in other orientations. The relative salience of patterns with different orientations of symmetry was investigated by Wenderoth (1994). Participants were asked to discriminate between symmetric or random dot patterns when the axis of symmetry was at one of 18 different orientations, spaced 10° apart, both clockwise and counter-clockwise from vertical to horizontal. Data indicated that the vertical axis was most salient, followed by the horizontal, while performance for the precise diagonal axis was better than that for surrounding orientations. It has been found that in addition to detecting perfect symmetry, subjects can also discriminate subtle deviations from perfect symmetry (see Wagemans, 1997 for a review).

More recently, studies have investigated the implications of Gestalt factors for visuospatial working memory (e.g., Kemps, 1999, 2001; Woodman, Vecera, & Luck, 2003; see also Parmentier, Chapter 4, this volume). Woodman and colleagues (2003) investigated the effects of proximity and connectedness on recognition performance. Proximity, the first principle proposed by Wertheimer (1924/1950), states that nearby objects are more likely to be grouped together than distant objects. Connectedness, the second principle considered in the Woodman et al. (2003) study, was proposed by Palmer and Rock (1994) and claims that elements that are connected together tend to be grouped together. Woodman et al. (2003) used a variant of the spatial pre-cuing paradigm, developed by Egly, Driver, and Rafal (1994) to investigate object-based attention. In these experiments, a peripheral cue was used to drive attention to one of several to-be-remembered objects. Subsequently the participant had to say whether a selected item had changed colour from the original frame. The results showed that participants are more accurate at detecting a change when it occurs within a group of items, where the group is determined by proximity, than when it falls outside the grouped set. Woodman and colleagues suggest that Gestalt cues are used by the visual system to bias the transfer of perceptual representations into working memory. If the objects in a visual scene are grouped in a salient way, they are more likely to be processed together. This involves both bottom–up processes that operate between perception and working memory (Schmidt, Vogel, Woodman, & Luck, 2002; Xu, 2002), and top–down processes influenced by information in long-term memory (Rensink, O'Regan, & Clark, 1997; Wagar & Dixon, 2005).

A number of studies have used a dual-task paradigm to assess the role of Gestalt factors in working memory, all studying the recall of regular patterns (Kemps, 2001; Rossi-Arnaud, Pieroni, Spatano, & Baddeley, 2006; Pieroni, Rossi-Arnaud, & Baddeley, n.d.). Kemps (2001) used a variant of the Corsi blocks test (CBT), comprising 25 blocks in a 5 × 5 matrix, in order to explore the differences between complex and regular patterns. Regularity of patterns was determined by symmetry, repetition, and continuation. Patterns were administered as in the normal Corsi task: the experimenter touched a sequence of blocks and the subject then tried to repeat the sequence. Kemps found that pattern regularity enhanced recall performance even though the participant never saw all the elements of the sequence at the same time. Kemps (2001, Experiment 2) then used a concurrent visuospatial interference task to investigate the role of visuospatial working memory activity. A concurrent spatial tapping task decreased recall of both regular and complex patterns but did not eliminate the advantage of regularity, suggesting that visuospatial working memory is implicated in this task but does not account for the regularity effect. The author suggested from this and other evidence that the advantage may be the result of the involvement of long-term memory processes in the temporary retention of visuospatial material.

In our series of experiments (Rossi-Arnaud et al., 2006; Pieroni et al., n.d.) we further examined whether the advantage in the recall of symmetrical visual displays over displays that are asymmetrical might reflect working memory processes. This was achieved by using the modified CBT developed by Kemps (1999). The recall of displays symmetrical along the vertical, horizontal, or diagonal axes was tested and compared with that of asymmetrical patterns. Both sequential and simultaneous presentation of the elements creating the stimulus were tested.

In the following paragraphs we first illustrate how displays that are symmetrical over the vertical axis are better recalled than those that are symmetrical along the horizontal or diagonal axis, thus indicating a special status for vertical symmetry both in perception and in short-term recall. Second, we discuss the modes of presentation by comparing data obtained with sequential and simultaneous presentation on the modified Corsi matrix using the same symmetrical and asymmetrical displays. Results will be discussed that show how the advantage of vertical symmetry appears with both modes of presentation, whereas the advantage of horizontal and diagonal symmetry appears only in the recall of stimuli displayed simultaneously. Subsequently, we describe how, by applying a dual-task procedure, we investigated the contribution of working memory to the encoding of symmetrical patterns. Since the possible contribution of visuospatial working memory had been analysed in the literature only for regular stimuli presented sequentially, we studied the effect of disrupting the visuospatial working memory processes on the retention of asymmetrical patterns and of those characterized by diagonal, horizontal, or vertical symmetry. An alternative possibility was that the enhancing effect of symmetry might be the result of verbal recoding, with regular patterns allowing shorter verbal chunks to be created (Glanzer & Clark, 1963). Indeed, many visuospatial memory tasks lend themselves to verbal strategies in which aspects of the stimuli are encoded and rehearsed in a verbal format to support later recall (see Logie, 1995; Logie, Chapter 2, this volume). Finally, we investigated whether detecting symmetry and using it to chunk, may be a top–down process depending on the central executive (Baddeley, 2002).

The tasks

Serial presentation

We used the adapted version of the CBT developed by Kemps (Kemps, 1999, 2001). Twenty-five black blocks ($4 \times 4 \times 4$ cm) were positioned on a black wooden board (40×40 cm) in a regular 5×5 matrix. The blocks were numbered from 1 to 25; these numbers could be seen by the experimenter, but not by the subject. Paths could be symmetrical or without any form of regularity. The symmetrical patterns were divided in vertical, horizontal, and diagonal symmetry. Examples of the patterns are shown in Figure 8.1.

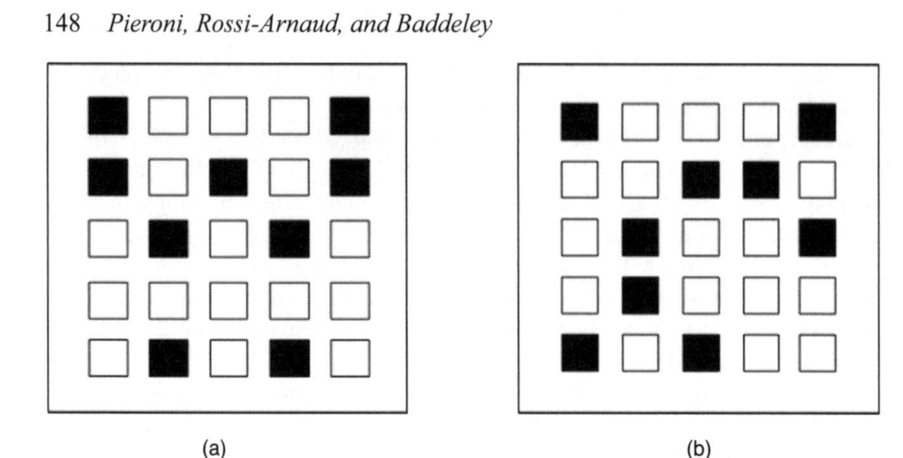

Figure 8.1 Examples of simultaneous patterns presented in Experiment 1. Patterns could be symmetrical along the vertical (a), diagonal (b), and horizontal axes (c), or nonsymmetrical (d).

The experimenter touched a series of blocks at a rate of one block per second. Subsequently the subject was required to touch the same blocks in the same order of presentation. A classical span procedure was used (Gathercole, Adams, & Hitch, 1994).

Simultaneous presentation

The same stimuli used for the serial presentation were simultaneously presented on a laptop screen placed horizontally immediately to the left of the test board. A single display reproduced the matrix (25 black blocks) of the adapted version of the CBT. The pattern to be remembered appeared in a different colour (red) and was shown for 3 s. The time duration chosen was that used in the Visual Patterns

Test (Della Sala, Gray, Baddeley, Allamano, & Wilson, 1999). There was no time limit on pattern recall. A span procedure was used, identical to the one used for the serial presentation (Gathercole et al., 1994). In the response phase a wooden board with an adapted version of the CBT (Kemps, 1999, 2001) was used.

Span procedure

A span procedure was used in all experiments (Gathercole et al., 1994). Testing started by presenting two displays at a given level of complexity (e.g., three elements) and correct response on both displays allowed the subject to progress to the next level. If the subject failed to remember both of the displays at a particular level, no further displays were presented. When the participant correctly remembered only one of the displays at a particular level, a third stimulus of the same size was presented. If the third display was correctly remembered, trials at the next level were given. If the subject incorrectly remembered the third display, testing stopped. Span was scored as the maximum level at which the subject correctly recalled two displays. The procedure was terminated when the subject had made two errors within a given level.

Interferences

To analyse the contribution of the verbal and visuospatial subsystems and of the central executive to the recall of symmetrical and asymmetrical patterns a dual-task procedure was used.

The interference tasks consisted of an articulatory suppression, at a rate of two to three utterances per second, a spatial tapping at a rate a two to three taps per second, and a central executive interference. For the latter we adopted a verbal version of the trails task where the participants heard one of the letters of the alphabet and a day of the week (e.g., D–Friday) and were asked to continue the two sequences from that point (e.g., E–Saturday, F–Sunday, etc.) (Baddeley, Emslie, Kolodny, & Duncan, 1998; Fürst & Hitch, 2000). All secondary tasks started 2 s before the presentation of the matrix and continued for the duration of the primary task.

Symmetry affects memory performance

The particular status of vertical symmetry

The results of our experiments on the recall of displays containing different types of symmetry showed that, with serial presentation, only vertical symmetry increased recall. Simultaneously presented stimuli, on the other hand, led to an advantage or all types of symmetry, including horizontal and diagonal, when compared with asymmetrical patterns. However, in the latter case, we still found a consistent and significant advantage for vertical symmetry compared with the other types of symmetry and to the asymmetrical condition (Rossi-Arnaud et al., 2006; Pieroni et al., n.d.).

These results indicating a strong advantage of vertical symmetry are consistent with those from perceptual studies in both adults and children (Wenderoth, 1994; Bornstein & Stiles-Davis, 1984) where the detection of vertical symmetry was better than horizontal symmetry, which in turn exceeded the detection of diagonal symmetry. The ability to discriminate vertically symmetrical forms from all other types of forms and symmetries has been shown even in 4-month-old infants who, however, did not discriminate horizontally symmetrical forms from asymmetrical ones, thus demonstrating the special status of vertical symmetry (Fisher, Ferdinandsen, & Bornstein, 1981; Bornstein & Krinsky, 1985).

Subsequent perceptual studies have further investigated the salience of vertical symmetry. The axis of orientation effect was shown, for example, not to simply mimic the neural sensitivities of orientation-selective cells since the effect could be modulated by the participants' scanning or attentional strategies (Wagemans, Van Gool, & d'Ydewalle, 1992; Pashler, 1990). Indeed Wenderoth (1994) showed that the detection of diagonal symmetry may be better than horizontal, when diagonal stimuli are more frequently presented. These results imply that the orientation effects in symmetry detection are not completely determined by the fixed neural architecture of the visual system but can be modulated by the subjects' expectations or by their scanning or attentional strategies.

Another possible explanation for the special status of vertical symmetry is related to the frequency and importance of vertically symmetrical objects in the environment. The fact that the salience of vertical symmetry has been shown even in 4-month-old infants suggests that symmetry detection may be innate. However, as Fisher et al. (1981) suggest, an especially significant symmetrical form for the infant is the human face. It could be, therefore, that early exposure to faces plays an important role in the infants' bias for vertical symmetry.

Presentation mode: sequential versus simultaneous

A second aspect of the present studies concerns the effect of presentation mode. The results indicating that sequential presentation of symmetrical paths led to better recall only in the case of stimuli symmetrical along the vertical axis may have resulted from a difficulty in detecting symmetry with this kind of presentation. This is in agreement with our other results showing that, with simultaneous presentation, symmetry improves performance for all three types of symmetry tested, i.e., vertical, horizontal, and diagonal. It thus seems likely that being able to see the configuration as a whole right from the start of presentation facilitates the detection of horizontal and diagonal symmetry and its subsequent encoding and/or retrieval.

Previous studies have already reported an advantage of simultaneous over serial presentation for both recall (de Ribaupierre, Lecerf, & Bailleux, 2000) and recognition (Lecerf & de Ribaupierre, 2005). One surprising aspect of our results is that such an advantage was not found when looking at the performance with asymmetrical stimuli. A direct comparison with the study by de Ribaupierre et al. (2000) that uses a recall procedure is difficult because there are major differences in the type of tasks used. They employed the Mr Peanut task, in which coloured dots are placed at various locations on a clown depiction and our task involves presenting a matrix. On the other hand it is more plausible to compare our results with the data obtained in their recognition study (Lecerf & de Ribaupierre, 2005), which is based on the presentation of patterns in a 6 × 6 matrix. Given that four is the mean span for irregular patterns in our own study, we looked at the number of hits at span lengths three and four in the study by Lecerf and de Ribaupierre (2005): it is interesting to note that at this length no difference appears between sequential and simultaneous patterns of locations, in agreement with our data on asymmetrical displays. The differences between the two types of presentation only appear when performance is measured using the *Pr* score (probability of hit minus the probability of false alarms), which cannot be calculated in our study since a recall paradigm was used.

Which working component mediates the symmetry advantage?

The third feature of our series of experiments investigated which, if any, of the working memory components mediate the symmetry advantage in short-term recall. A dual-task procedure was used to analyse the contribution of the verbal and visuospatial subsystems, and of the central executive.

Further examining visuospatial processes

Kemps (2001) showed a main effect of a clockwise tapping task on the recall of structured and complex patterns with sequential presentation. However, no interaction between type of pattern and spatial interference was found, suggesting that even if visuospatial working memory is important for this task, it is not responsible for the advantage of structured over unstructured patterns with serial presentation. We then proceeded to explore the effect of visuospatial interference on the immediate recall of asymmetrical and symmetrical patterns using only the simultaneous presentation. Results indicated that tapping impaired performance but did not abolish the recall advantage conferred by symmetry (Pieroni et al., n.d.). These data support Kemps's (2001) findings in showing a main effect of tapping on the recall of structured and complex patterns with sequential presentation, and confirm that the advantage of symmetrical stimuli cannot be ascribed to visuospatial working memory, since disrupting this subsystem does not influence the symmetry effect.

To further examine the contribution of visuospatial processes it would have been interesting to also use an interference task that was more clearly visual, such as a presentation of visual noise (Quinn & McConnell, 1996). However, the effect of presenting visual noise is not always readily detectable (Andrade, Kemps, Werniers, May, & Szmalec, 2002) and, given that our main task involved the simultaneous presentation of visual stimuli, any effect might be the result of disrupting perception.

Are symmetrical stimuli recoded verbally?

When a novel stimulus is presented, subjects often try to use a verbal code by naming the item. This strategy may in some cases help memory for the presented patterns (e.g., Postma & De Haan, 1996). The same kind of strategy has been shown in children who at around 6 years of age start to use verbal recoding to remember visual patterns (Palmer, 2000). Concurrent articulatory suppression prevents this process, by disrupting the transfer from visuospatial working memory to the phonological store. In order to examine whether the advantage of symmetrical stimuli on the asymmetrical could be explained in terms of verbal recoding a verbal interference task was applied to the serial recall task. Only vertical symmetry was considered since it was the only one that showed an advantage over the asymmetrical patterns with serial presentation. The results showed that articulatory suppression had no effect whatsoever on the serial recall of either asymmetrical or symmetrical stimuli. This lack of effect suggests that subjects were not using verbal coding. This could reflect a general absence of verbal coding with such pattern stimuli, or a specific difficulty in verbally coding patterns that were presented sequentially, and thus were not visible as a whole until the last cell was shown. To further investigate this point we applied the same procedure with simultaneous presentation, considering all the symmetrical stimuli. Results indicated that even when a subject was able to see the stimulus as a whole, potentially facilitating verbal recoding, this strategy was not used. Our results thus complement those of Meiser and Klauer (1999) and of Vandierendonck, Kemps, Fastame, and Szmalec (2004), which also found no effect of articulatory suppression on the CBT. Overall, these data indicate that the verbal component of working memory does not account for the advantage of symmetry.

Does attentional chunking account for the symmetry advantage in short-term recall?

The clear advantage of symmetry in the recall of visuospatial displays could reflect a chunking strategy that was dependent on the central executive; which is assumed to play an important role in creating new chunks (Baddeley, 2002). To investigate the central executive contribution our final set of experiments studied the effect on recall of a central executive interference using a variant of the trails test that forms part of the Halstead–Reitan neuropsychological assessment battery and was designed as an indicator of frontal lobe damage (Lezak, 1983). Baddeley and colleagues (1998) developed a verbal version of the trails test comprising a baseline condition that involves reciting canonical sequences of numbers (12345 etc.), or letters (abcde etc.) or involves alternation (a1b2c3 etc.). They showed that this task is attentionally demanding (Baddeley, Chincotta, & Adlam, 2001; Fürst & Hitch, 2000).

We observed a clear effect of the demanding verbal trails task on overall performance both with sequential and simultaneous presentation (Rossi-Arnaud et al., 2006; Pieroni et al., n.d.). This suggests that executive processes are involved in immediate recall of patterns. Results are consistent with previous data showing that executive processes may be implicated in encoding (Fisk & Sharp, 2003) and in maintaining spatial sequences (Hamilton, Coates, & Heffernan, 2003). It has also been shown that an executively demanding secondary task disrupts an individual's ability to maintain conscious visual images. In particular, a concurrent random generation had a substantial effect on participants' subjective experience of image duration during the performance of creative visuospatial synthesis (Pearson, 2001). Furthermore, an overlap has been shown between the neural correlates of executive and spatial processes in that the dorsolateral areas of the prefrontal cortex have been shown to be implicated both in executive functioning (for a review see Collette & Van der Linden, 2002) and in the processing of sequential spatial stimuli (Leung, Gore, & Goldman-Rakic, 2002). However, in our studies, the effect of the verbal trails task was equally great for symmetrical and asymmetrical types of material, both when sequential and simultaneous presentation were used.

These data point strongly towards an automatic processing of symmetry even though the central executive appears to play an important role in performing the memory task (Vandierendonck et al., 2004). Even when a subject is able to see all the locations simultaneously, allowing a clear advantage from symmetry, this does not appear to depend on attentionally based chunking. It appears therefore that the superiority effect of symmetrical patterns is relatively automatic whether operating at the level of perception, storage, or retrieval.

What does the study of symmetry tell us?

The series of experiments performed on the short-term recall of symmetrical displays have shown a special status for vertical symmetry in the processes involving working memory. There is, as yet, no definitive explanation that accounts for this phenomenon either in perception (Wagemans, 1997) or in memory. As mentioned above, two main hypotheses have been put forward: one suggests that symmetry detection may be innate, the other is related to the frequency and salience of vertically symmetrical objects in the environment and to the fact that that early exposure to faces might play an important role in the infants' bias for vertical symmetry, suggesting some form of early implicit learning.

The evidence that vertical symmetry is the only one to affect serial recall not only supports its special status with respect to the other forms of symmetry but opens an interesting series of questions regarding whether the different types of symmetry are processed in memory in different ways. It is possible that they differentially involve the contribution of bottom–up processes, visual attention, long-term memory, and working memory. This is a matter that will need further investigation.

Our studies allowed us to compare the performance on the same stimuli with the same task using different presentation procedures, sequential versus simultaneous. With simultaneous presentation, performance on symmetrical stimuli was significantly better compared with the asymmetrical ones. This led us to propose that simultaneous presentation allowed participants to see a structure that can be readily used, where the spatial information of the single elements can be bound together to enhance recall. This does not happen when presentation is serial, except for vertical symmetry, probably because the amount of visual attention demanded by the elaboration of the structure, presented element by element, competes with the attentional resources involved in recall. Once more, this reflects the special status of vertical symmetry.

Regarding the contribution of working memory to the recall of symmetry, we observed that articulatory suppression did not affect recall, while concurrent tasks involving both the spatial processing and the verbal trails task impaired performance but did not eliminate the symmetry advantage.

How might these results be explained? The simplest result to explain is the absence of any effect of articulatory suppression on visual recall (Rossi-Arnaud et al., 2006; Pieroni et al., n.d.). This is characteristic of all tasks involving purely visuospatial short-term memory (Allen, Baddeley, & Hitch, 2006; Vogel, Woodman, & Luck, 2001) and is readily explained on the assumption of separate storage for short-term visuospatial and verbal material, as reflected for example in the Baddeley and Hitch (1974) multicomponent model of working memory. Given that suppression had no effect on overall level of performance, the absence of any impact on the symmetry advantage is unsurprising.

Interpretation of the data from concurrent visuospatial tapping is somewhat more complex. The tapping task clearly impaired performance but did not interact with the effects of regularity, in agreement with data from the study by Kemps (2001) involving sequential stimulus presentation. This is consistent with the assumption that the effects of symmetry operate automatically, as happens with the binding of features into objects (Allen et al., 2006) or with the effects of other Gestalt principles of organization (Woodman et al., 2003). There is, however, another possible explanation. There is considerable evidence for two separate components to visuospatial working memory, one based on spatial location and the other on object characteristics such as shape and colour (see Baddeley, 2007 for a review). It could be argued that the advantage gained from symmetry involves the object system rather than the spatial system, whereas our tapping task is essentially spatial in nature. However, given that spatial tapping clearly disrupts performance, it seems unlikely that our task is immune to spatial interference.

It would, nonetheless, be interesting to explore the effects of concurrent visual rather than spatial interference on recall of symmetrical patterns. However, the standard procedures for interfering with object-based processing tend to involve visual presentation (Logie, 1986; Klauer & Zhao, 2004; Quinn & McConnell, 1996). Such tasks would be likely to interfere directly with the perceptual encoding of the pattern stimuli used in our studies, making interpretation problematic. In principle, it should be possible to develop tasks presented auditorily that differentially disrupt visual rather than spatial processing, but this is likely to require a good deal of task development before providing a clear answer. For present purposes, we can conclude that our spatial task does have a clear impact on performance, and that the symmetry advantage does not depend upon the spatial component of the visuospatial sketchpad.

Our third concurrent task aimed to disrupt the central executive component of working memory by means of an attention-demanding verbal switching task. This task impaired overall performance to an even greater extent than concurrent spatial tapping, but did not interact with the symmetry advantage. This again suggests that the advantage to be gained from symmetry is automatic, and does not depend upon the utilization of attentional resources. Again, the most likely possibility is that Gestalt factors operate at a relatively early stage in visual processing. The fact that, with simultaneous presentation, horizontal and diagonal symmetry effects are less powerful than the effects of vertical symmetry suggests that, even though automatic, this process is far from perfect. When it operates however, it presumably allows several components of the stimulus to be chunked into a single object. Given that the capacity of visuospatial working memory appears to be about four objects (Cowan, 2005; Vogel et al., 2001), this will enhance recall. The fact that our verbal trails task impairs overall performance is consistent with Klauer and Zhao's (2004) observation that both their spatial and visual memory tasks were equivalently impaired by a demanding concurrent task that aimed to disrupt the operation of the central executive. The fact that both visual and spatial working memory were impaired argues against the previously discussed possibility that the advantage gained from symmetry reflects only the object system; if this was the case, a task designed to disrupt central executive function would interact with the effect of symmetry. Thus, this result further strengthens the case for the dependence of symmetry on pre-working memory processes.

In conclusion, our results indicate that the influence of symmetry on memory for pattern stimuli resembles its effects on perception, with patterns involving vertical symmetry being both detected and retained more effectively than horizontal ones, which in turn are better than diagonally symmetrical patterns. Tasks designed to disrupt visuospatial or executive processes in working memory impaired overall performance but failed to interact with the symmetry effect, suggesting that these factors operate within processes that feed into working memory, rather than influencing memory directly. It might be helpful to consider our results in terms of the distinction proposed by William James (1890) between ambient and focused attention. Ambient attention is automatic, implicit in operation, and allows us to continue to be aware of our surroundings without explicitly focusing on them. In contrast, focused attention allows us to emphasize one aspect over others. The binding of features such as colours and shapes into objects (Allen, Hitch, & Baddeley, 2006, 2009), or in our case, symmetrical locations into a coherent pattern, can be regarded as operating within ambient attention, allowing the binding of symmetrical features into chunks to persist, even when attention is strongly occupied by another task.

References

Allen, R. J., Baddeley, A. D., & Hitch, G. J. (2006). Is the binding of visual features in working memory resource-demanding? *Journal of Experimental Psychology: General, 135,* 298–313.

Allen, R. J., Hitch, G. J., & Baddeley, A. D. (2009). Cross modal binding and working memory. *Visual Cognition, 17,* 83–102.

Andrade, J., Kemps, E., Werniers, Y., May, J., & Szmalec, E. (2002). Insensitivity of visual short-term memory to irrelevant visual information. *Quarterly Journal of Experimental Psyhology. A. Human Experimental Psychology, 55,* 753–774.

Attneave, F. (1954). Some informational aspects of visual perception. *Psychological Review, 61,* 183–93.

Baddeley, A. D. (2002). Fractionating the central executive. In D. Stuss, & R. T. Knight (Eds.), *Principles of frontal lobe function* (pp. 246–60). New York: Oxford University Press.

Baddeley, A. D. (2007). *Working memory, thought, and action.* Oxford: Oxford University Press.

Baddeley, A. D., Chincotta, D. M., & Adlam, A. (2001). Working memory and the control of action: Evidence from task switching. *Journal of Experimental Psychology: General, 130,* 641–657.

Baddeley, A. D., Emslie, H., Kolodny, J., & Duncan, J. (1998). Random generation and the executive control of working memory. *Quarterly Journal of Experimental Psychology A, 51,* 819–852.

Baddeley, A. D., & Hitch, G. J. (1974). Working memory. In G. A. Bower (Eds.), *Recent advances in learning and motivation* (Vol. 8, pp. 47–89). New York: Academic Press.

Bornstein, M., & Krinsky, S. (1985). Perception of symmetry in infancy: The saliency of vertical symmetry and the perception of pattern wholes. *Journal of Experimental Child Psychology, 39(1),* 1–19.

Bornstein, M., & Stiles-Davis, J. (1984). Discrimination and memory for symmetry in young children. *Developmental Psychology, 17,* 82–86.

Collette F., & Van der Linden, M. (2002). Brain imaging of the central executive component of working memory. *Neuroscience & Biobehavioral Reviews, 26,* 105–125.

Corballis, M. C., & Roldan, C. E. (1974). On the perception of symmetrical and repeated patterns. *Perception and Psychophysics, 16,* 136–142.

Cowan, N. (2005). *Working memory capacity.* New York: Psychology Press.

de Ribaupierre, A., Lecerf T., & Bailleux, C. (2000). Is a nonverbal working memory task necessarily nonverbally encoded? *Cahiers de Psychologie Cognitive, 19,* 135–170.

Delius, J. D., & Nowak, B. (1982). Visual symmetry recognition by pigeons. *Psychological Research, 44,* 199–212.

Della Sala, S., Gray, C., Baddeley, A., Allamano N., & Wilson, L. (1999). Pattern span: A tool for unwelding visuo-spatial memory. *Neuropsychologia, 37,* 1189–1199.

Driver, J., Baylis, G. C., & Rafal, R. D. (1992). Preserved figure-ground segmentation and symmetry perception in visual neglect. *Nature, 360,* 73–75.

Egly, R., Driver, J., & Rafal, R. (1994). Shifting visual attention between objects and locations: evidence from normal and parietal lesion subjects. *Journal of Experimental Psychology: General, 123,* 161–177.

Fisher, C., Ferdinandsen, K., & Bornstein M. (1981). The role of symmetry in infant form discrimination. *Child Development, 52,* 457–462.

Fisk, J. E., & Sharp, C. A. (2003). The role of the executive system in visuo-spatial memory functioning. *Brain & Cognition, 52,* 364–381.

Fürst, A. J., & Hitch, G. J. (2000). Separate roles for executive and phonological components of working memory in mental arithmetic. *Memory & Cognition, 28,* 774–782.

Gathercole, S. E., Adams, A., & Hitch, G. J. (1994). Do young children rehearse? An individual differences analysis. *Memory & Cognition, 22,* 201–207.

Giurfa, M., Eichmann, B., & Menzel, R. (1996). Symmetry perception in an insect. *Nature, 382,* 458–461.

Glanzer, M., & Clark, W. H. (1963). Accuracy of perceptual recall: An analysis of organization. *Journal of Verbal Learning and Verbal Behavior, 1,* 289–299.

James, W. (1890). *Principles of psychology.* New York: Holt.

Hamilton, C. J., Coates, R. O., & Heffernan, T. (2003). What develops in visuo-spatial working memory development? *European Journal of Cognitive Psychology, 15,* 43–69.

Kemps, E. (1999). Effects of complexity on visual-spatial working memory. *European Journal of Cognitive Psychology, 11,* 335–356.

Kemps, E. (2001). Complexity effects in visual-spatial working memory: Implication for the role of long-term memory. *Memory, 9,* 13–27.

Klauer, K. C., & Zhao, Z. M. (2004). Double dissociations in visual and spatial short-term memory. *Journal of Experimental Psychology: General, 133,* 355–381.

Koffka, K., (1935). *Principles of Gestalt psychology*. New York: Harcourt.

Lecerf, T., & de Ribaupierre, A. (2005). Recognition in a visuospatial task: The effect of presentation. *European Journal of Cognitive Psychology, 17,* 47–75.

Leung, H. C., Gore, J. C., & Goldman-Rakic, P. S. (2002). Sustained mnemonic response in the human middle frontal gyrus during on-line storage of spatial memoranda. *Journal of Cognitive Neuroscience, 14,* 659–671.

Lezak, M. D. (1983). *Neuropsychological assessment.* New York: Oxford University Press.

Logie, R. H. (1986). Visuo-spatial processing in working memory. *Quarterly Journal of Experimental Psychology, 38A,* 229–247.

Logie, R.H. (1995). *Visuo-spatial working memory.* Hove, UK: Lawrence Erlbaum Associates Ltd.

Meiser, T., & Klauer, K. C. (1999). Working memory and changing-state hypothesis. *Journal of experimental psychology. Learning, memory, and cognition, 25,* 1272–1299.

Palmer, S. (2000). Working memory: A developmental study of phonological recoding. *Memory, 8,* 179–193.

Palmer, S. E., & Rock, I. (1994). Rethinking perceptual organization: The role of uniform connectedness. *Psychonomic Bulletin & Review, 1,* 29–55.

Pashler, H. (1990). Coordinate frame for symmetry detection and object recognition. *Journal of Experimental Psychology: Human Perception and Performance, 16,* 150–163.

Pearson, D. G. (2001). Imagery and the visuo-spatial sketchpad. In J. Andrade (Ed.), *Working memory in perspective* (pp. 33–59). Hove, UK: Psychology Press.

Pieroni, L., Rossi-Arnaud, C., Sparano, P., & Baddeley, A. D. (n.d.). Automatic binding and working memory involvement in symmetry coding. Manuscript in preparation.

Postma, A., & De Haan, E. H. F. (1996). What was where? Memory for object locations. *Quarterly Journal of Experimental Psychology, A49,* 178–199.

Quinn, J. G., & McConnell, J. (1996). Irrelevant pictures in visual working memory. *Quarterly Journal of Experimental Psychology, A49,* 200–215.

Rensink, R. A., O'Regan J. K., & Clark, J. J. (1997). To see or not to see: The need for attention to perceive changes in scenes. *Psychology Science, 8,* 368–373.

Rock, I. (1983). *The logic of perception.* Cambridge, MA: MIT Press.

Rossi-Arnaud C., Pieroni, L., & Baddeley, A. (2006). Symmetry and binding in visuo-spatial working memory. *Neuroscience, 139,* 393–400.

Schmidt, B. K., Vogel, E. K., Woodman, G. F., & Luck, S. J. (2002). Voluntary and automatic attentional control of visual working memory. *Perception and Psychophysics, 64,* 754–763.

Schumann-Hengsteler, R., Strobl, M., & Zoelch, C. (2004). Temporal memory for locations: On the coding of spatiotemporal information in children and adults. In G. L. Allen, (Eds.), *Human spatial memory* (pp. 101–124). Mahwah, NJ: Lawrence Erlbaum Associates, Inc.

Vandierendonck, A., Kemps, E., Fastame, M.C., & Szmalec, A. (2004). Working memory components of the Corsi blocks task. *British Journal of Psychology, 95,* 57–79.

Vetter, T., Poggio, T., & Bülthoff, H. H. (1994). The importance of symmetry and virtual views in three-dimensional object recognition. *Current Biology, 4,* 18–23.

Vogel, E. K., Woodman, G. F., & Luck, S. J. (2001). Storage of features, conjunctions, and objects in visual working memory. *Journal of Experimental Psychology: Human Perception & Performance, 27,* 92–114.

von Fersen, L., Manos, C.S., Goldowsky, B., & Roitblat, H. (1992). Dolphin detection and conceptualization of symmetry. In J. R. Thomas, R. A. Kastelein, A. Y. Supin, (Eds.), *Marine mammal sensory systems* (pp. 753–762). New York: Plenum Press.

Wagemans, J. (1997). Characteristics and models of human symmetry detection. *Trends in Cognitive Science, 1,* 346–352.

Wagemans, J., Van Gool, L., & d'Ydewalle, G. (1992). Orientational effects and component processes in symmetry detection. *Quarterly Journal of Experimental Psychology, 44A,* 475–508.

Wagar, B. M., & Dixon, M. J. (2005). Past experience influences object representation in working memory. *Brain and Cognition, 57,* 248–256.

Wenderoth, P. (1994). The salience of vertical symmetry. *Perception, 23,* 221–236.

Wertheimer, M. (1950). Gestalt theory. In W. D. Ellis (Ed.), *A sourcebook of Gestalt psychology* (pp. 1–11). New York: Humanities Press. (Original work published 1924)

Woodman, G.F., Vecera, S.P., & Luck, S.J. (2003). Perceptual organization influences visual working memory. *Psychonomic Bullettin & Review, 10,* 80–87.

Xu, Y. (2002). Encoding color and shape from different parts of an object in visual short-term memory. *Perception and Psychophysics, 64,* 1260–1280.

9 The role of spatial working memory in understanding verbal descriptions

A window onto the interaction between verbal and spatial processing

Valérie Gyselinck and Chiara Meneghetti

Introduction

Most experiments on working memory have used rather simple tasks and materials (e.g., memory for lists of words) that hardly reflect the complexity of everyday situations. Although studying simple tasks in this way is informative at early stages of theory development, we must ask whether the models produced in this context can adequately account for performance in more complex and ecologically valid tasks such as text comprehension and remembering. In this chapter we review experiments that have adopted Baddeley's original model of working memory (Baddeley, 1986; Baddeley & Logie, 1999), investigating its role in the construction of mental models derived from verbal descriptions, with a focus on spatial working memory. In most of the experiments considered, a dual-task paradigm is used to study the role of the working memory components in the processing of illustrated texts and spatial descriptions. Particular attention is given to descriptions of spatial environments, which present visuospatial information in verbal format. Overall, our findings indicate that the storing component of verbal working memory is involved when verbal material has to be processed, and that visuospatial working memory is involved as soon as visuospatial processing is required. Furthermore, the pattern of results is modulated by individual differences in the capacity of these storing components on one hand and in imagery and visuospatial abilities on the other. We argue that these studies open a window onto the interaction between verbal and visuospatial processes.

Working memory and the comprehension of illustrated texts

Working memory and text comprehension

Text comprehension is a complex cognitive activity, involving numerous capacities and stages of processing, and can even be considered prototypical of a working memory task. When a text has to be understood, whether read or listened to, verbal information has to be coded, stored, and combined with existing knowledge and stored in long-term memory in order to build a coherent representation of the content of the text. After a first sentence has been interpreted, the interpretation of successive sentences requires the combination of information with new incoming information, and so on to the end of the text. Working memory (especially verbal working memory) is essential in this process, and much research has been dedicated to studying its role.

As far as text comprehension is concerned, several studies have emphasized the role of the central executive in working memory (e.g., Oakhill, Yuill, & Parkin, 1986). The capacity of this central component, as measured with the reading span test (Daneman & Carpenter, 1980), is an important factor in the high-level psycholinguistic operations underlying comprehension (Just & Carpenter, 1992; Daneman & Merickle, 1996). As Gathercole and Baddeley (1993) have emphasized however, the role of the phonological loop and of the visuospatial sketchpad until recently remained an open question. It is generally acknowledged that verbal working memory, viewed as a combination of storing and processing of verbal information, is involved in text processing (see e.g., Baddeley, 1986; De Beni, Palladino, Pazzaglia, & Cornoldi, 1998), but direct evidence showing the maintenance of phonological traces is scarce and even contradictory. Baddeley, Elridge, and Lewis (1981) showed that a concurrent phonological task impairs the detection of semantic errors in sentences, while a simple tapping task does not impair performance. These data suggest that the phonological loop is involved in sentence processing. However, Waters, Komoda, and Arbuckle (1985) found no such selective interference effect on reading when the concurrent task was a shadowing task (repetition of oral digits), which presumably involved the phonological loop but did not request any transformation or recoding of the phonological information. Even fewer results point to involvement of the visuospatial working memory. Vandierendonck and De Vooght (1997) used a dual-task paradigm, not in text comprehension but in a reasoning task implying the processing of verbal statements. While reasoning with temporal and spatial relations in four-term problems, participants performed concurrently an articulatory suppression task, a tapping task, or a random interval repetition task. The latter was assumed to interfere with the central executive, placing only a minimal load on the slave systems. Results showed that all three secondary tasks interfered with reasoning accuracy. Moreover, the effects of the articulatory task were restricted to the problem–solution part of the reasoning task, not the premise reading part. This was interpreted as accounting for a visuospatial coding of the premise information using the visuospatial working memory, but no phonological coding.

Visuospatial working memory and processing of text containing iconic information

Some situations require the processing and combination of information that takes various forms, not just verbal. That is the case with iconic information, which is common in the field of information, education, and instruction, where texts are often accompanied by pictures, graphics, and so on. The architecture of a model such as Baddeley's (1986) may then be considered to account for the integration of such various types of information. Direct involvement of visuospatial working memory in text comprehension was in fact first tested using illustrated texts. The positive effect of pictures in text comprehension is often interpreted in the framework of the Johnson-Laird (1983) theory of mental models (Glenberg & Langston, 1992; Gyselinck & Tardieu, 1999; Hegarty & Just, 1993). When pictures illustrate the content of the text they accompany, they closely mirror the situation described in the text. A picture can thus be viewed as one possible expression of a mental model. In their seminal work, Kruley, Sciama, and Glenberg (1994) claimed that illustrations allow the construction of a mental model and that this construction takes place in the visuospatial working memory of Baddeley (1986). Subjects had to understand illustrated texts (e.g., description of a volcano together with a picture displaying the structural relationships between its various components), and concurrently memorize the position of dots on a grid. Results showed that comprehension performance was facilitated by the picture, but the beneficial effect did not decrease with the visuospatial memory load relative to a control condition. However, performance on the visuospatial concurrent task was impaired in the presence of a picture. In another experiment, a nonvisual (verbal) memory load was used and no such pattern was obtained. This was interpreted as indicating the specific involvement of the visuospatial working memory in illustrated text comprehension.

Using the same kind of concurrent task (visuospatial and verbal memory loads), Gyselinck, Ehrlich, Cornoldi, De Beni, and Dubois (2000) also investigated the role of visuospatial working memory in the integration of verbal and pictorial information. In the experiments, participants had to learn a series of concepts in physics through computer-assisted presentation of illustrated and nonillustrated texts, with and without spatial or verbal interference. The results show that comprehension is better when the text is accompanied by pictures, and that this beneficial effect is greater for inferential questions. However, no interference effect of the concurrent visuospatial task on the illustrated texts was found in the analyses, probably as a result of the specific features of the task and texts. Another study was then conducted by Gyselinck, Cornoldi, Dubois, De Beni, and Ehrlich (2002) with the same texts and illustrations, but using a concurrent task instead of memory loads, i.e., a spatial tapping task for the visuospatial secondary task and an articulation task for the verbal secondary task. In accordance with the hypotheses, the dual-task procedure produced a selective interference effect, that is, the concurrent tapping task caused the beneficial effect of illustrations on comprehension performance to disappear, while the concurrent articulatory task impaired performance in both presentation formats in a similar way. Furthermore, the pattern of results was dependent on the capacity of spatial working memory as measured by the Corsi Blocks Task (CBT; Corsi, 1972). Indeed, high spatial span subjects benefited from illustrations and were selectively disturbed by the concurrent tapping task. Low-span subjects showed no significant increase with illustrations, and this was not significantly affected by the concurrent tapping task. These results demonstrate that the visuospatial working memory – specifically the visuospatial subsystem and not the verbal subsystem – is involved in processing illustrations that facilitate the comprehension of scientific texts. In a second experiment the presentation of texts was compared with the presentation of illustrations only. Here, the concurrent articulatory task selectively impaired text-only processing, compared with processing illustrations only. Furthermore, this pattern of results was found for high but not low digit span subjects. This confirms that the interference produced by the concurrent articulatory task is specifically related to phonological memory, disrupting the formation of a phonological representation of the linguistic information, and is not a general effect due to fall in attention or other general mechanism.

Similar results were obtained with procedural texts by Brunyé, Taylor, Rapp, and Spiro (2006). In their study, an advantage of the picture-only and text-plus-picture format over a text-only format was observed in the control condition. Interference effects obtained with different secondary tasks suggest that the subcomponents of working memory are differentially involved, depending on the presentation format. The visuospatial secondary task (tapping task) interfered with picture-only processing whereas the articulatory task interfered with text-only processing. In addition, visuospatial and a verbal central tasks in the study (random generation of sequences of tapping or of syllables) both exclusively interfered with text-plus-picture processing, suggesting that central resources are necessary for integration of texts and pictures.

Working memory and multimedia learning

One core concept in the main multimedia learning models that has developed in recent years is that of a limited working memory capacity (cognitive load theory, Sweller, van Merrienboer, & Paas, 1998; cognitive theory of multimedia learning, Mayer, 2001; and integrated model of text and picture comprehension, Schnotz, 2005). This limited capacity is considered to explain some of the classical effects observed when subjects have to understand and learn on the basis of multimedia material (see Tardieu & Gyselinck, 2003). Among the most classical multimedia effects is the so-called ‘modality effect’, which refers to the fact that auditory presentation of verbal information is better than visual presentation when combined with pictorial information since it enables reduction of the cognitive load on the visual channel. This in turn suggests that presenting a text in the auditory channel together with other information (such as graphics) in the visual channel results in a lower cognitive load and allows better comprehension than presentation of a text in visual format together with visuospatial information. Although the dual-task paradigm has proved useful for examining the limitations of working memory, few experiments have made use of it in the multimedia domain. Brünken, Plass, and Leutner (2003, 2004) proposed that the effect of the dual-task on secondary-task performance is a direct measure of the cognitive load induced by the primary task.

In Gyselinck, Jamet, and Dubois (2008), a dual-task procedure was in fact used to explore the involvement of working memory components in the comprehension of complex multimedia documents. This involvement was expected to explain the classical modality effect. Contrary to expectations however, no modality effect was found in the control condition, i.e., performance was similar for both visual and auditory presentation of the verbal information. The dual-task paradigm used to induce cognitive load nevertheless produced interference effects on comprehension performance. A concurrent articulatory task caused a fall-off in performance, which shows the involvement of verbal working memory in multimedia learning, suggesting that the verbal working memory stores verbal information equally efficiently, whether presentation is visual or oral. A concurrent tapping task interfered with comprehension to an equal extent in both presentation formats, which involved the processing of graphical information. This pattern of results confirms the view that working memory is concerned primarily with representational channels (verbal and pictorial information) rather than of sensory channels (auditory and visual information), and that verbal working memory is involved as soon as verbal information is processed, whereas visuospatial working memory is involved in the process of graphical information.

Table 9.1 summarizes the main results from the experiments described above, carried out with a dual-task paradigm. Verbal working memory is shown to be involved in the comprehension of complex verbal information such as texts, whether presented orally or visually. Even in cases where participants have to navigate between different types of information, integrating various items of information, the verbal storage component of working memory is important in permitting a processing operation that is as complex as comprehending. Moreover, these experiments show that visuospatial working memory is involved, insofar as graphical information has to be processed together with the texts.

The two subsystems are probably mainly dedicated to maintenance of a visual trace of illustrations (visuospatial working memory) and of a verbatim representation of linguistic information (verbal working memory), these representations being the basis for higher-level comprehension processes. However, there are other cases where graphical information is not needed for the formation of visuospatial representations – but where the visuospatial working memory may still be involved. This condition is the focus of the next section.

Visuospatial working memory and spatial text processing

Since language is one of the means we have available to express spatial information, a number of investigations have considered the comprehension of verbal itineraries (e.g., Denis, Daniel, Fontaine, & Pazzaglia, 2001). This constitutes a field in its own right, located at the intersection between the study of text comprehension and that of spatial cognition. Many studies (Denis, 1996; Perrig & Kintsch, 1985; Taylor & Tversky, 1992) have demonstrated that participants spontaneously construct a spatial mental model as a result of reading the description of spatial patterns and environments. In adults, models derived from language have been shown to preserve many of the properties of real environments (for a review see Zwaan & Radvansky, 1998). Mental models can reflect the spatial properties of descriptions and preserve information about distances (e.g., Rinck, Hahnel, Bower, & Glowalla, 1997). This is true for representations derived from spatial descriptions usually written using different perspectives, i.e., route and survey

Table 9.1 Main experiments on the processing of texts and iconic information conducted with a dual-task paradigm

Study	*Verbal and visual inputs*	*Factors manipulated and dependent variables*	*Effects on primary task*	*Others effects*
Kruley et al. (1994)	Text descriptive (auditory presentation) one illustration	*Factors manipulated:* – Input: T and T+I (W-P) – Dual task: double vs. single (W-P) Spatial (S) and verbal (V) interference effect tested in different experiments. CC considered Dependent variable: Multiple Choice Questions	Spatial: no Verbal: yes	T+I > T Effect on secondary task: T+I: performance of S task damaged
Gyselinck et al. (2000)	Texts expository (visual presentation) Series of illustrations	*Factors manipulated:* – Input: T and T+I (B-P) – Dual task: double vs. single (W-P) – Secondary task: V, S, and CC (W-P) – Spatial storage capacity: High vs. Low (B-P) Dependent variable: Multiple Choice Questions	Spatial: no Verbal: yes	T+I > T – performance of V task impaired in all conditions
Gyselinck et al. (2002)	Texts expository (visual presentation) Series of illustrations	*Factors manipulated:* – Input: T and T+I (B-P) – Secondary task: ST, AS, and CC (W-P) – Spatial storage capacity: high vs. low (B-P) Dependent variable: Multiple Choice Questions	Spatial: yes for T+I Verbal: yes for T+I and T	T+I > T

Brunyé et al. (2006)	Texts procedural (visual presentation) Series of illustrations	*Factors manipulated:* – Input: T, I and T+I (W-P) – Secondary task: ST, AS, RG-Spatial, RG-Spatial and CC (B-P) Dependent variable: Free recall and Order verification	Spatial: yes for I Verbal: yes for T	T + I > (T = I) in control condition T + I < in RG-Spatial and RG-Verbal (but not in the others conditions)
Gyselinck et al. (2008)	Texts expository (auditory or visual presentation) Scheme	– Modality of presentation: auditory vs. visual (B-P) – Secondary task: ST, AS, and CC (W-P) – Spatial storage capacity: high vs. low (B-P) Dependent variable: Verification Test	Spatial: no Verbal: yes	

Notes
Inputs: T, Text; I, Illustration; T+I, Text+Illustration.
Secondary tasks, Concurrent tasks: ST, Spatial tapping; AS, Articulatory suppression; RG-Spatial, Random generation of sequence of tapping; RG-Verbal, Random generation of sequence of syllables; CC, control condition – no secondary task; Pre-load task: S, dot matrix task, V, digit task.
Experimental design: W-P, within participant; B-P, between-participants; >, better performance; <, lower performance.

perspective. Route descriptions represent the space from an egocentric perspective (i.e., assume the viewpoint of a person moving through an environment), use an intrinsic frame of reference (e.g., to your left, behind you, etc.) and have linear organization given by the order of landmarks along the route itself (Denis, 1997). Survey descriptions represent the space from an allocentric perspective (i.e., assume a bird's-eye view), use an extrinsic frame of reference such as compass directions (i.e., north, south, east, west), and sometimes have a hierarchical structure.

The processing of spatial information, even complex, is thus possible with only the verbal channel, such as when written or spoken communications describe spatial environments and itineraries. Constructing spatial representations from language, or inversely, translating such mental representations into language, must involve processes that require strict cooperation between verbal and spatial systems.

From nonspatial to spatial texts

Some studies have used the dual-task paradigm to address the question of the specific involvement of visuospatial working memory in the construction of a spatial model from just verbal support. Noordzij, van der Lubbe, Neggers, and Postma (2004) obtained results in line with the idea of the involvement of the visuospatial working memory in the representation of spatial information verbally presented. They used a sentence–picture verification task, where participants compared linguistic information in a sentence (e.g., 'a triangle is to the left of a circle') with visuospatial information in a corresponding picture, and concurrently performed an articulatory suppression task or a spatial tapping task. As expected, participants were significantly slower and less accurate in the sentence-verification task when having to perform the spatial concurrent task, whereas the verbal concurrent task produced no detrimental effects. One question however is whether the verbal task led participants to recode information in visuospatial format, making use of their visuospatial working memory, or whether the coding and storing of the pictures presented caused the involvement of visuospatial working memory.

In an initial study using only verbal information, Pazzaglia and Cornoldi (1999, Experiment 2) also investigated the involvement of verbal and visuospatial working memory during memorization of abstract and spatial sentences using a dual-task paradigm. Their results showed a differential effect of the concurrent verbal and spatial tasks on the abstract and spatial sentences, respectively; however, no control group without any secondary task was considered so precluding confirmation of clear selective interference effects. Using a series of longer and coherent descriptions, and also including a control group, De Beni, Pazzaglia, Gyselinck, and Meneghetti (2005) examined whether different components of working memory are involved in processing spatial and nonspatial texts. The spatial text described an open environment and adopted a route perspective; the nonspatial text described a procedure with sequences of actions (the wine-making process) and contained little visual or spatial information. Each participant listened to the spatial and nonspatial texts, performing at the same time one of two concurrent tasks: articulatory suppression or spatial tapping. Results on both the recall of the texts and a verification task (accuracy and correct response times) on inference statements showed a specific interference effect of the tapping concurrent task on the spatial text; an interference effect of the verbal concurrent task on both spatial and nonspatial texts was also observed. These results are the first evidence of a clear dissociation between the involvement of verbal working memory and visuospatial working memory in the processing of texts, without any graphical or iconic information, just verbal.

Pazzaglia, De Beni, and Meneghetti (2007) extended the question to the coding and retrieval phase of the process. In a first experiment, subjects were given spatial and nonspatial texts (similar to those used by De Beni et al., 2005) and performed a concurrent spatial tapping task during encoding or retrieval, or no concurrent task. The results confirmed interference effects of the spatial task performed on processing spatial text, but not for nonspatial text. These effects were obtained whether during encoding or retrieval, but were more pronounced in the encoding phase than in the retrieval phase. In a second experiment, the same procedure was followed by an articulatory suppression task. Results showed interference effects for both texts, but only in the encoding phase. These findings suggest that the construction process of the mental model (spatial or nonspatial) specifically involves verbal working memory as soon as verbal information is processed, and visuospatial working memory as soon as visuospatial information is conveyed, even through language. The retrieval or reconstruction process may also involve working memory components, although to a lesser extent.

Route versus survey spatial texts

In the two studies described above, the spatial texts adopted a route perspective, but as noted a spatial environment can also be described from a survey perspective. The question of whether people reading or listening to verbal descriptions create spatial representations that preserve the spatial perspective of the original source or are able to switch perspective is still under debate in the literature (see for example the study of Brunyé, Rapp, & Taylor, 2008). Depending on the perspective of the original source, the way visuospatial working memory is involved might then also vary.

In a series of experiments, Deyzac, Logie, and Denis (2006) presented short descriptions in either route or survey perspective, and used several different concurrent tasks. Their results showed that presenting a spatial text concurrently with a spatial tapping task resulted in a larger interference effect on the recall of landmarks for the route descriptions than for the survey descriptions. A passive visual task (dynamic visual noise, Quinn & McConnell, 1996) produced interference effects for route but not survey texts. In contrast, a more active concurrent visual task (Brightness Judgement Task, adapted from Logie, 1986), and an articulatory suppression task produced the same interference for both types of spatial text.

In a new study, Pazzaglia, Meneghetti, De Beni, and Gyselinck (2009, Experiment 1) asked whether the classical pattern of interference effects was obtained with survey descriptions as well as with route descriptions. Subjects were given descriptions of an environment in either route or survey perspective, and concurrently had to perform a spatial tapping task, an articulatory concurrent task, or no concurrent task. Whereas concurrent articulation interfered with the recall of both types of texts, the tapping task impaired performance with the route descriptions but not the survey descriptions. It seems then that with longer texts than those used by Deyzac et al. (2006), the tapping task does not interfere with the construction of a spatial model from a survey description.

Confirming results of this type, Brunyé and Taylor (2008) showed that a spatial tapping task interferes with a route description more than with a survey description, and that an articulatory task impairs performance on both types of text. However, the tapping task is a sequential task, in some ways very akin to the linear component of a route description. In the case of a survey description, instead, this component should be less present, which would explain the lower or indeed absence of interference effect. Survey representations are in fact intended to be visual-like and static, requiring the encoding of a global pattern, whereas route representations are more dependent on motor encoding and on the encoding of spatial paths.

Literature on working memory distinguishes various components or mechanisms within visuospatial working memory. Logie (1995) proposed a distinction between a passive visual store (the visual cache) and an active rehearsal mechanism (the inner scribe), and a considerable body of evidence has confirmed the validity of this distinction (see e.g., Klauer & Zhao, 2004; Logie, Chapter 2, this volume); Pickering, Gathercole, Hall, and Lloyd (2001) made a distinction between static and dynamic processes. More recently, Lecerf and de Ribaupierre (2005) distinguished pattern encoding, which leads to a global image of the stimulus and path encoding. Also, Mammarella, Pazzaglia, and Cornoldi (2008) distinguished simultaneous and sequential processes (see also Cornoldi & Mammarella, Chapter 6, this volume), where sequential tasks require the recall of spatial positions in the order of presentation, whereas simultaneous tasks require participants to remember a visual configuration composed of items presented simultaneously in different positions.

This latter distinction was adopted by Pazzaglia and Cornoldi (1999, Experiment 3) to explore the processing of spatial description in route and survey perspectives. While listening to the texts, participants had to detect changes in the spatial configuration of the images presented. These changes implied either a visual processing (detecting a change of one of four images presented), or a spatial-sequential processing (detecting a change in the order of presentation of four images), or a spatial-simultaneous processing (detecting a change in position of one of five points presented simultaneously). Although the lack of a control condition in this experiment does not allow conclusions to be drawn regarding interference effects, the results show that the two types of spatial task affect the processing and the recall of the survey and the route descriptions to different extents.

Pazzaglia et al. (2009, Experiment 2) analysed the interference effect of a spatial-sequential task and a spatial-simultaneous task on the comprehension and memorization of survey and route descriptions. Both tasks required memorization of configurations of dots, presented either sequentially or simultaneously. Since processing of the route text and performance of the sequential task were both presumed to require order and motor encoding, for the route text alone, the concurrent sequential task was expected to impair processing more than the simultaneous task. Moreover, the introduction of a nonspatial text allowed distinction to be made, within the interference effects, between those attributable to the involvement of general resources (presumed to impair the performance of both spatial and nonspatial texts) and those due to specific effects of distinct visuospatial working memory components. The results show that memory performance for the route text was more impaired by the sequential task than by the simultaneous-concurrent task, whereas the survey text was equally affected by the two spatial tasks. In addition, both concurrent tasks had lower, but still significant, interference effects on the nonspatial text processing, which indicates that some, if not all, central resources are involved. It is plausible to conclude that the processing of both survey and route texts require visual and simultaneous components, but that the route perspective has supplementary properties (sequentiality and motor encoding) that distinguish the mechanisms implied and, presumably, the mental model constructed.

Table 9.2 summarizes the series of experiments described above, in which a dual-task paradigm is used to examine how working memory components are involved in the construction of mental models from survey and route perspectives. There is converging evidence confirming a specific role of visuospatial working memory in spatial text processing, whether route or survey, but little has been reported on the way it plays a role. One existing hypothesis put forward relates to the formation of images, and this will be considered in the next section.

Spatial texts and imagery

Some studies have explored the effect of imagery instructions prompting participants to use a visual code, and have found these instructions to be effective in improving memory for lists of words, and even text comprehension and recall (e.g., Richardson, 1998). A question of interest, however, is whether these results can be extended to mental imagery used in constructing a spatial mental model. Take the case of someone who has listened to a spatial or route direction. They will often find themselves elaborating visual images. These images help them construct a representation of the situation described that maintains the spatial relationships between landmarks (e.g., de Vega, Cocude, Denis, Rodrigo, & Zimmer, 2001); they may involve visuospatial working memory or even explain why it is involved in spatial text processing.

Examining strategies for memorization of texts, De Beni and Moé (2003) studied the efficiency of imagery and verbal instructions on the recall of various

Table 9.2 Presentation of the main experiments on the processing of spatial texts conducted with a dual-task paradigm

Study	*Factors manipulated and dependent variables*	*Effects on primary task*	*Others effects*
De Beni et al. (2005)	*Factors manipulated:* – Text: NST and ST-R (W-P); auditory presentation – Secondary task: ST, AS and CC (B-P) Dependent variables: FR, VT	Spatial: yes for ST-R; no for NST Verbal: yes for both ST-R and NST	
Pazzaglia et al. (2007)	*Factors manipulated:* – Text: NST and ST-R (W-P); auditory presentation – Time of secondary task performance: encoding vs. retrieval (B-P) Spatial (with ST) and verbal (with AS) interference effects tested in Experiments 1 and 2 Dependent variables: FR, VT	Spatial: yes for ST-R; no for NST (encoding > retrieval) Verbal: yes for both ST-R and NST (in encoding)	
Deyzac et al. (2006)	*Factors manipulated:* – Text: ST-R and ST-S (B-P); auditory presentation – Dual-task: single-dual (W-P) Spatial (with ST), visual (with DVN and BJ), and verbal (AS) effects tested in a series of experiments Dependent variable: FR	Spatial: yes for both ST-R and ST-S (stronger for route) Verbal: yes for both ST-R and ST-S	– Interference of: – BJ on ST-R and ST-S – DVN on ST-R No effect on secondary tasks
Brunyé & Taylor (2008) (Exp. 1)	*Factors manipulated:* – Text: ST-R and ST-S (B-P); visual presentation – Secondary Task: ST, AS, and CC (B-P) Dependent variables: VT and MD	Spatial: yes for both ST-R and ST-S Verbal: VT. yes: for both ST-R and ST-S MD. yes for landmark recall; no for landmark positions	

Pazzaglia & Cornoldi (1999) (Exp. 2)	*Factors manipulated:* – Text: NST, ST-R, ST-S, VT (B-P), auditory presentation – Secondary Task: Vi, Ve, S-seq, S-sim (W-P) Dependent variables: FR	Spatial: yes for ST-R (S-seq > S-sim) Verbal: no for route and survey texts	– NST: more interference of Ve than Vi task – VT: interference of Vi and Ve task
Pazzaglia et al. (in press)	*Factors manipulated:* Experiment 1 – Text: ST-R and ST-S (B-P) – Secondary Task: ST, AS, and CC (W-P) Experiment 2 Texts: NS, ST-R, and ST-S (B-P) – Secondary Task: S-seq, S-sim, and CC (W-P) Texts: auditory presentation Dependent variables: FR and VT	Experiment 1 Spatial: yes for ST-R Verbal: yes for ST-S Experiment 2 Spatial: ST-R: S-seq > S-sim ST-S: S-seq = S-sim	Effects on secondary tasks S-seq > S-sim

Notes
Texts: NST, Nonspatial text; SR-R, Spatial text in route perspective; SR-S, Spatial text in survey perspective; VT, Visual text.
Secondary Tasks: ST, Spatial Tapping; AS, Articulatory Suppression; DVN, Dynamic visual noise; BJ, Brightness Judgement; S-seq, Spatial sequential; S-sim, Spatial simultaneous; Vi, Visual task; Ve, verbal task; CC, control condition – no secondary task.
Dependents variables: FR, Free recall; VT, Verification Test; MD, Map drawing.
Experimental design: W-P, within participant; B-P, between-participants; >, better performance; <, lower performance.

texts (spatial, visual, or abstract texts). They found a facilitating effect of the use of an imagery-based strategy over a repetition strategy in processing visual and spatial passages, but not abstract passages, when text presentation was oral, but not when visual. The authors interpret their results in the light of Baddeley's working memory model, considering interference effects between encoding and processing modalities: that is, reading and imagery strategies both stressed visuospatial working memory, whereas listening and rehearsing both stressed verbal working memory.

Gyselinck, De Beni, Pazzaglia, Meneghetti, and Mondoloni (2007) carried out a more systematic investigation of the relation between mental imagery instructions, spatial text processing, and working memory storage components. Subjects were presented with texts describing locations from a route perspective, and had either to imagine themselves moving along a route in surroundings or to rehearse verbal information. Concurrently they had to perform a spatial tapping task, an articulatory task, or no secondary task. Performance on a verification test used to assess the product of comprehension clearly showed that instructions prompting subjects to use a strategy based on mental imagery are more efficient for processing spatial texts than those prompting use of a verbal strategy based on repetition of information. Results showed that concurrent spatial tapping and articulatory tasks impaired spatial text comprehension. However, these interference effects were modulated by the instructions participants received. The concurrent tapping task impaired performance in the imagery instructions group but not the repetition instructions group, and caused the beneficial effect of imagery instructions to vanish. This result was not observed with the articulatory task, where interference effects were similar in both groups, thus indicating that imagery instructions prompt subjects to form mental images (which help them form a spatial model) and that these processes involve both verbal and visuospatial working memory. In the case of the repetition instructions, however, participants appeared to rely only slightly on their visuospatial working memory for performing the comprehension task.

In addition, high spatial span subjects, i.e., individual with high visuospatial working memory capacity, benefited from the imagery instructions and were selectively disturbed by the concurrent tapping task, whereas low spatial span subjects did not show this pattern of results. This finding is in line with the results of Gyselinck et al. (2002), who found that storage capacity, as assessed by spatial and verbal spans, defines the extent to which participants benefit from illustrations and the extent to which verbal and visuospatial working memory are involved in the integration of texts and illustrations. One interpretation of these converging results is that participants with high capacity rely heavily on their visuospatial working memory. When they have to perform tasks that disrupt the functioning of their visuospatial working memory concurrently with those that exercise it (e.g., processing illustrations or imagining themselves at the location described), their performance declines. In contrast, participants with a low span (whether cause or effect) make little use of their visuospatial working memory, as assessed by the lack of benefit derived from illustrations or imagery instructions. In this case, an interfering spatial task would have nothing to compete with and thus no decrease in performance arises.

Spatial ability and imagery in spatial text processing

In the encoding of environmental descriptions, a number of studies reported in this chapter found that working memory systems and in particular the visuospatial component is specifically involved in spatial text processing. In parallel, other studies showed that spatial ability plays a significant role in environmental learning (e.g., Hegarty, Montello, Richardson, Ishikawa, & Lovelace, 2006) even when spatial information is presented verbally (e.g., Bosco, Filomena, Sardone, Scalisi, & Longoni, 1996; de Vega, 1994; Pazzaglia, 2008). Spatial ability is the ability to generate, retain, and transform abstract visual images (Lohman, 1979) and includes several factors such as visuospatial perceptual speed, spatial visualization, and mental rotation abilities (Linn & Petersen, 1985).

Together, these two lines of research recognize that spatial ability and visuospatial working memory are cognitive aspects important in the construction of spatial mental representations derived from environmental descriptions. However, to date very little research has made systematic exploration of the simultaneous role of working memory systems and spatial ability in spatial text processing.

In a study by Gyselinck, Meneghetti, Pazzaglia, and De Beni (2009), participants were trained to use either imagery or verbal strategies to process route spatial texts, and their spatial ability characteristics were examined. These findings confirmed the beneficial effect of using a strategy based on mental images on spatial text processing. When imagery strategies were used, a concurrent articulatory task and a spatial tapping task produced interference effects on performance of primary tasks. Instead, when repetition strategies were used, only the articulatory task produced interference effects, underlining the role of the verbal working memory. To clarify how the involvement of the visuospatial component might differ in relation to visuospatial abilities, comparison was made of participants with good or poor ability in generation of visual images (using the Vividness of Visual Imagery Questionnaire; Marks, 1973) and spatial manipulation of objects (using the Mental Rotation Test; Vandenberg & Kuse, 1978). The benefit of using imagery strategies was found in both groups, but whereas low visuospatial-imagery participants were sensitive to spatial interference, their high-ability counterparts were not. These results provide evidence that individuals with high spatial ability perform well in spatial text processing even when their working memory components are loaded by performance of secondary tasks. They also question the role of imagery processes in the construction of spatial models and their relation to visuospatial working memory.

To clarify whether skills developed in spatial ability do indeed allow participants to process specifically large-scale spatial information easily, rather than this being simply due to the intervention of more general central ability, a subsequent study was carried out by Meneghetti, Gyselinck, Pazzaglia, and De Beni (2009), investigating how individual differences in spatial ability are related to working memory subcomponents during spatial text processing. Two groups with different spatial ability selected on the basis of Mental Rotation Test performance were presented with spatial and nonspatial descriptions (similar to those used by De Beni et al., 2005) and concurrently performed a articulatory suppression and a spatial tapping task. Both experiments showed impairment of spatial text recall in individuals with poor mental rotation ability with both concurrent tasks, the verbal task having a stronger effect than the spatial task. In individuals with high spatial ability, however, the involvement of the working memory systems in spatial text processing occurs in a different way. This group of individuals were able to efficiently process a spatial text even when performing a spatial tapping task, but the load produced by the dual task changed spatial secondary task performance. However, the spatial and nonspatial recall of individuals with high spatial ability – but also of their lower-ability counterparts – was impaired by the verbal concurrent task. These results suggests that the higher spatial resources of high spatial ability individuals are supported at least partially by the visuospatial working memory system, but that this higher ability is specifically spatial, given that they are subject to verbal interference effect.

In addition, this study indicates that the storing and processing functions of working memory are related to the ability of individuals with high spatial ability to process spatial descriptions. Indeed, this group performed better than individuals with low spatial ability in spatial span (CBT) but not in verbal span (digit span task), confirming that spatial span and spatial ability yield the same factor (e.g., Shah & Miyake, 1996). The difference in favour of high mental rotation individuals was found in the backward version but not in the forward version. The backward version tests the storing and processing functions of visuospatial working memory requiring a certain level of control of central executive functions (Cornoldi & Vecchi, 2003) probably sharing, at least partially, the same functions involved in spatial mental transformation ability tested with mental rotation tasks (Miyake, Friedman, Rettinger, Shah, & Hegarty, 2001). Working memory studies showed that complex span tasks, such as the backward CBT, require additional executive processes in order to cope with interference (see also Vandierendonck, Kemps, Fastame, & Szmalec, 2004; for a review see Kane, Conway, Hambrick, & Engle, 2007); thus individuals with high abilities in such tasks proved able to handle dual-task performance. It follows that the ability of high mental rotation individuals to maintain good spatial text processing while simultaneously performing a secondary task could be ascribable to their larger spatial working memory resources (not only spatial specific but also more central).

General conclusions

This review of the present status of research is clear confirmation that working memory is a relevant cognitive aspect involved in complex activities such as understanding and memorizing texts conveying spatial information, even if only verbally described. The distinction between verbal and visuospatial working memory systems originally proposed by Baddeley and Hitch (1974) still offers a good theoretical framework for approaching the question of the relationship between working memory and the processing of spatial information. Until recently, however, very few data or satisfactory explanations were available to account for how the verbal and the visuospatial working memory work together.

We have presented a series of experiments based on both the dual-task paradigm and the individual differences approach, to assess the role of the verbal and the visuospatial working memory in the processing of texts conveying visuospatial information. The findings summarized here open a useful window onto the question of the interaction between verbal and spatial processing, although it should be recalled that there is a continuing debate about the limitations (if not the usefulness) of what can be inferred from double dissociations (see e.g., Dunn & Kirsner, 2003; Baddeley, 2003; Vandierendonck & Szmalec, Chapter 1, this volume). Indeed, the debate highlights the methodological precautions that should be taken when designing dual-task experiments and the limits of the possible interpretations; in particular, special attention should be paid to the possible role of general executive functions, or of verbal strategies (at least in visuospatial tasks). In addition, a crossed double dissociation that results in interaction effects is considered a good guarantee for inferring separable resources (see Klauer & Zhao, 2004). In most of the experiments presented here, the design precautions have been applied and the interaction effects are certain. First, we presented studies focused on analysis of the role of working memory systems in processing texts containing iconic information illustrating the processes or mechanisms described in the text itself; we then described research work based on texts conveying spatial information only verbally.

The robust and consistent finding of these two complementary veins of research is the involvement of the visuospatial working memory system during the processing of visuospatial information conveyed either by illustrations or by texts alone (in the spatial texts), while no involvement of visuospatial working memory is found when nonspatial texts (and without illustration) were presented. The verbal working memory is however involved in the processing of texts. Some central components seem also to be involved in the interpretation and integration processes of visuospatial and verbal information. It nevertheless appears to be the case that the simple storage capacities of individuals deserve consideration, even in cases where complex material is processed, given that these capacities – while not explaining performance – may at least influence the strategies used and thus modify the obtained performance patterns. It has been recognized that the relationships between visuospatial working memory, executive functions, and spatial abilities are strong but complex (Miyake et al., 2001). However, taking the whole corpus of findings from studies of the role of spatial ability and working memory systems in spatial text processing, it might be postulated that visuospatial working memory is a cognitive system implied in the mediation between spatial ability and spatial text processing. Also relevant alongside the use of imagery strategy is ability, which intervenes in this processing and requires the involvement of the visuospatial working memory component.

Overall, research findings to date all point to the conclusion that verbal and spatial resources are relevant in processing and in maintaining spatial mental representations in memory. This contrasts with the new version of the Baddeley model (2000), which proposes the addition of an episodic buffer; this was incorporated into the model to allow for temporary storage of information held in a multimodal code, capable of binding information from the subsidiary systems and from long-term memory into a unitary episodic representation. To date, however, there has been little mention of how this might take place, and how it might be tested experimentally without any confounding between the peripheral systems and the episodic buffer.

The role played by working memory components in the comprehension and memorization of descriptions thus confirms the value of the working memory construct in investigating mechanisms involved in complex cognitive tasks. In addition, imagery and visuospatial abilities participate in this processing and interact with working memory components.

References

Baddeley, A. D. (1986). *Working memory*. Oxford: Oxford University Press.

Baddeley, A. D. (2000). The episodic buffer: A new component of working memory? *Trends in Cognitive Sciences, 4,* 417–423.

Baddeley, A. D. (2003). Working memory: Looking back and looking forward. *Neuroscience, 4,* 829–839. *Nature Reviews Neuroscience, 4,* 829–839.

Baddeley, A. D., Elridge, M., & Lewis, V. J. (1981). The role of subvocalization in reading. *Quarterly Journal of Experimental Psychology, 33,* 439–454.

Baddeley, A. D., & Hitch, G. (1974). Working memory. In G. H. Bower (Ed.), *The psychology of learning and motivation* (Vol. 8, pp. 47–89). New York: Academic Press.

Baddeley, A. D., & Logie, R. (1999). Working memory: The multiple-component model. In A. Miyake, & P. Shah (Eds.), *Models of working memory: Mechanisms of active maintenance and executive control* (pp. 28–61). New York: Cambridge University Press.

Bosco, A., Filomena, S., Sardone, L., Scalisi, T. G., & Longoni, A. M. (1996). Spatial models derived from verbal descriptions of fictitious environments: The influence of study time and the individual differences in visuo-spatial ability. *Psychology Beitrage, 38,* 451–464.

Brünken, R., Plass, J. L., & Leutner, D. (2003). Direct measurement of cognitive load in multimedia learning. *Educational Psychologist, 38,* 53–61.

Brünken, R., Plass, J. L., & Leutner, D. (2004). Assessment of cognitive load in multimedia learning with dual-task methodology: Auditory load and modality effects. *Instructional Science, 32,* 115–132.

Brunyé, T. T., Rapp, D. N., & Taylor, H. A. (2008). Representational flexibility and specificity following spatial descriptions of real-world environments. *Cognition, 108,* 418–443.

Brunyé, T. T., & Taylor, H. A. (2008). Working memory in developing and applying mental models from spatial descriptions. *Journal of Memory and Language, 58,* 701–729.

Brunyé, T. T., Taylor, H. A., Rapp, D. N., & Spiro, A. B. (2006). Learning procedures: The role of working memory in multimedia learning experiences. *Applied Cognitive Psychology, 20,* 917–940.

Cornoldi, C., & Vecchi, T. (2003). *Visuo-spatial working memory and individual differences.* Hove, UK: Psychology Press.

Corsi, P. M. (1972). *Human memory and the medial temporal region of the brain.* Unpublished doctoral dissertation, McGill University, Montreal, Canada.

Daneman, M., & Carpenter, P. A. (1980). Individual differences in working memory and reading. *Journal of verbal learning and verbal behaviour, 19,* 450–466.

Daneman, M., & Merickle, P. M. (1996). Working memory and language comprehension: A meta-analysis. *Psychonomic Bulletin & Review, 3,* 422–433.

De Beni, R., & Moé, A. (2003). Presentation modality effects in studying passages. Are mental images always effective? *Applied Cognitive Psychology, 17,* 309–324.

De Beni, R., Palladino, P., Pazzaglia, F., & Cornoldi, C. (1998). Increases in intrusion errors and working memory deficit of poor comprehenders. *The Quarterly Journal of Experimental Psychology, 51,* 305–320.

De Beni, R., Pazzaglia, F., Gyselinck, V., & Meneghetti, C. (2005). Visuo-spatial working memory and mental representation of spatial descriptions. *European Journal of Cognitive Psychology, 17,* 77–95.

Denis, M. (1996). Imagery and the description of spatial configurations. In M. de Vega, M. J. Intons-Peterson, P. M. Johnson-Laird, M. Denis, & M. Marschark (Eds.), *Models of visual-spatial cognition* (pp. 128–197). London: Oxford University Press.

Denis, M. (1997). The descriptions of routes: A cognitive approach to the production of spatial discourse. *Cahiers de Psychologie Cognitive/Current Psychology of Cognition, 16,* 409–458.

Denis, M., Daniel, M. P., Fontaine, S., & Pazzaglia, F. (2001). Language, spatial cognition, and navigation. In M. Denis, R. H. Logie, C. Cornoldi, M. de Vega, & J. Engelkamp (Eds.), *Imagery, language and visuo-spatial thinking* (pp. 137–160). Hove, UK: Psychology Press.

de Vega, M. (1994). Characters and their perspectives in narratives describing spatial environments. *Psychological Research, 56,* 116–126.

de Vega, M., Cocude, M., Denis, M., Rodrigo M. J., & Zimmer, H. D. (2001). The interface between language and visuo-spatial representation. In M. Denis, R. H. Logie, C. Cornoldi, M. de Vega, & J. Engelkamp (Eds.), *Imagery, language and visuo-spatial thinking* (pp. 137–160). Hove, UK: Psychology Press.

Deyzac, E., Logie, R. H., & Denis, M. (2006). Visuo-spatial working memory and the processing of spatial descriptions. *British Journal of Psychology, 97,* 217–243.

Dunn, J. C., & Kirsner, K. (2003). What can we infer from double dissociations? *Cortex, 39,* 1–7.

Gathercole, S. E., & Baddeley, A. D. (1993). *Working memory and language*. Hove, UK: Lawrence Erlbaum Associates Ltd.

Glenberg, A. M., & Langston, W. E. (1992). Comprehension of illustrated text: Pictures help to build mental models. *Journal of Memory and Language, 31,* 129–151.

Gyselinck, V., Cornoldi, C., Dubois, V., De Beni, R., & Ehrlich, M. F. (2002). Visuo-spatial memory and phonological loop in learning from multimedia. *Applied Cognitive Psychology, 16,* 665–685.

Gyselinck, V., De Beni, R., Pazzaglia, F., Meneghetti, C., & Mondoloni, A. (2007). Working memory components and imagery instructions in the elaboration of a spatial mental model. *Psychological Research, 71,* 373–382.

Gyselinck, V., Ehrlich, M. F., Cornoldi, C., De Beni, R., & Dubois, V. (2000). Visual-spatial working memory in learning from multimedia systems. *Journal of Computer Assisted Learning, 16,* 166–176.

Gyselinck, V., Jamet, E., & Dubois, V. (2008). The role of working memory components in multimedia comprehension. *Applied Cognitive Psychology, 22,* 353–374.

Gyselinck, V., Meneghetti, C., Pazzaglia, F., & De Beni, R. (2009). The role of working memory in spatial text processing: What benefit of imagery strategy and visual spatial ability? *Learning and Individual Differences, 19,* 12–20.

Gyselinck, V., & Tardieu, H. (1999). The role of illustrations in text comprehension: What, when, for whom, and why? In H. van Oostendorp & S. R. Goldman (Eds.), *The construction of mental representations during reading* (pp. 195–218). Mahwah, NJ: Lawrence Erlbaum Associates, Inc.

Hegarty, M., & Just, M. A. (1993). Constructing mental models of machines from text and diagrams. *Journal of Memory and Language, 32,* 717–742.

Hegarty, M., Montello, D. R., Richardson, A. E., Ishikawa, T., & Lovelace, K. (2006). Spatial ability at different scales: Individual differences in aptitude-test performance and spatial-layout learning. *Intelligence, 34,* 151–176.

Johnson-Laird, P. N. (1983). *Mental models: Towards a cognitive science of language, inference, and consciousness*. Cambridge, MA: Harvard University Press.

Just, M. A., & Carpenter, P. A. (1992). A capacity theory of comprehension: individual differences in working memory. *Psychological Review, 99,* 122–149.

Kane, M. J., Conway, A. R. A., Hambrick, D. Z., & Engle, R. W. (2007). Variation in working memory capacity as variation in executive attention and control. In A. R. A. Conway, C. Jarrold, M. J. Kane, A. Miyake, & J. N. Towse (Eds.), *Variation in working memory* (pp. 21–48). New York: Oxford University Press.

Klauer, K. C., & Zhao, Z. M. (2004). Double dissociations in visual and spatial short-term Memory. *Journal of Experimental Psychology: General, 3,* 355–381.

Kruley, P., Sciama, S. C., & Glenberg, A. M. (1994). On-line processing of textual illustrations in the visual-spatial sketchpad: Evidence from dual-task studies. *Memory and Cognition, 22,* 261–272.

Lecerf, T., & de Ribaupierre, A. (2005). Recognition in a visuo-spatial memory task: The effect of presentation. *European Journal of Cognitive Psychology, 17,* 47–75.

Linn, M. C., & Petersen, A. C. (1985). Emergence and characterization of sex differences in spatial ability: A meta-analysis. *Child Development, 56,* 1479–1498.

Logie, R. H. (1986). Visuo-spatial processing in working memory. The *Quarterly Journal of Experimental Psychology, 38,* 229–247.

Logie, R. H. (1995). *Visuo-spatial working memory*. Hove, UK: Lawrence Erlbaum Associates Ltd.

Lohman, D. F. (1979). *Spatial ability: A review and reanalysis of the correlational literature* (Tech. Rep. No. 8). Stanford, CA: Stanford University School of Education.

Mammarella, I. C., Pazzaglia, F., & Cornoldi, C. (2008). Evidences for different components in children's visuo-spatial working memory. *British Journal of Developmental Psychology, 26,* 337–355.

Marks, D. F. (1973). Visual imagery differences in the recall of pictures. *British Journal of Psychology, 64,* 17–24.

Mayer, R. E. (2001). *Multimedia learning*. New York: Cambridge University Press.

Meneghetti, C., Gyselinck, V., Pazzaglia, F., & De Beni, R. (2009). Individual differences in spatial text processing: high spatial ability can compensate for spatial working memory interference. *Learning and Individual Differences, 19,* 577–589.

Miyake, A., Friedman, N. P., Rettinger, D. A., Shah, P., & Hegarty, M. (2001). How are visuo-spatial working memory, executive functioning, and spatial abilities related? A latent-variable analysis. *Journal of Experimental Psychology: General, 130,* 621–640.

Noordzij, M. L., van der Lubbe, R. H. J., Neggers, S. F. W., & Postma, A. (2004). Spatial tapping interferes with the processing of linguistic spatial relations. *Canadian Journal of Experimental Psychology, 58,* 259–271.

Oakhill, J. V., Yuill, N., & Parkin, A. J. (1986). On the nature of the difference between skilled and less-skilled comprehenders. *Journal of Research in Reading, 9,* 80–91.

Pazzaglia, F. (2008). Text and picture integration in comprehending and memorizing spatial descriptions. In J. F. Rouet & R. K. Lowe (Eds.), *Understanding multimedia documents,* (pp. 43–59). New York: Springer-Verlag.

Pazzaglia, F., & Cornoldi, C. (1999). The role of distinct components of visuo-spatial working memory in the processing of texts. *Memory, 7,* 19–41.

Pazzaglia, F., De Beni, R., & Meneghetti, C. (2007). The effects of verbal and spatial interference in the encoding and retrieval of spatial and non spatial texts. *Psychological Research, 71,* 484–494.

Pazzaglia, F., Meneghetti, C., De Beni, R., & Gyselinck, V. (2009). Working memory components in survey and route spatial text processing. *Cognitive processing, 11,* 359–369.

Perrig, W., & Kintsch, W. (1985). Propositional and situational representations of text. *Journal of Memory and Language, 24,* 503–518.

Pickering, S. J., Gathercole, S. E., Hall, M., & Lloyd, S. A. (2001). Development of memory for pattern and path: Further evidence for the fractionation of visuo-spatial memory. *The Quarterly Journal of Experimental Psychology, 54,* 397–420.

Quinn J. G., & McConnell, J. (1996). Irrelevant pictures in visual working memory. *Quarterly Journal of Experimental Psychology, 49,* 200–215.

Richardson, J. T. E. (1998). The availability of effectiveness of reported mediators in associative learning: a historical review and an experimental investigation. *Psychonomic Bulletin and Review, 5,* 597–614.

Rinck, M., Hahnel, A., Bower, G. H., & Glowalla, U. (1997). The metrics of spatial situation models. *Journal of Experimental Psychology: Learning, Memory and Cognition, 32,* 506–515.

Schnotz, W. (2005). An integrated model of text and picture comprehension. In R. E. Mayer (Ed.), *The Cambridge handbook of multimedia learning* (pp. 49–69). New York: Cambridge University Press.

Shah, P., & Miyake, A. (1996). The separability of working memory resources for spatial thinking and language processing: An individual differences approach. *Journal of Experimental Psychology: General, 125,* 4–27.

Sweller, J., van Merrienboer, J. J. G., & Paas, F. (1998). Cognitive architecture and instructional design. *Educational Psychology Review, 10,* 251–296.

Tardieu, H., & Gyselinck, V. (2003).Working memory constraints in the integration and comprehension of information in a multimedia context. In H. van Oostendorp (Ed.), *Cognition in a digital world* (pp. 3–24). Mahwah, NJ: Lawrence Erlbaum Associates, Inc.

Taylor, H. A., & Tversky, B. (1992). Spatial mental models derived from *survey* and *route* descriptions. *Journal of Memory and Language, 31,* 261–292.

Vandenberg, S. G., & Kuse, A. R. (1978). Mental rotation, a group test of three-dimensional spatial visualization. *Perceptual and Motor Skills, 47,* 599–604.

Vandierendonck, A., & De Vooght, G. (1997). Working memory constraints on linear reasoning with spatial and temporal contents. *Quarterly Journal of Experimental Psychology, 50,* 803–820.

Vandierendonck, A., Kemps, E., Fastame, M. C., & Szmalec, A. (2004). Working memory components involved in the Corsi block test. *British Journal of Psychology, 95,* 57–79.

Waters, G. S., Komoda, M. K., & Arbuckle, T. Y. (1985). The effects of concurrent tasks on reading: Implications for phonological recoding. *Journal of Memory and Language, 24,* 27–45.

Zwaan, R. A., & Radvansky, G. A. (1998). Situation models in language comprehension and memory. *Psychological Bulletin, 123,* 162–185.

Author Index

Abrahams, S., 37–38
Abrams, R. A., 48, 50–51, 78, 91, 136
Adams, A., 148–149
Adlam, A., 152
Agazzi, D., 68, 108
Agid, Y., 91
Ahmad, S. A., 113
Aizawa, H., 90
Alain, C., 55
Alberoni, M., 31
Alexander, A., 95
Allamano, N., 2, 27, 29, 47, 58, 68, 79, 107, 124–125, 128–129, 133–134, 149
Allen, R. J., 36–37, 52, 154–155
Alloway, T. P., 110
Amedi, A., 92
Amil, N., 113
Andersen, R. A., 54
Anderson, A. W., 56
Anderson, J. R., 3
Anderson, R., 19
Andrade, J., 72, 74–75, 134, 136, 139, 151
Andrés, P., 51, 70–71, 79
Ang, S. Y., 134
Anllo-Vento, L., 89
Antal, A., 93
Arbuckle, T. Y., 160
Armstrong, K. M., 50, 88–89
Arnott, S. R., 55
Ashley, C. T., 112
Aslan, A., 92
Atkinson, R. C., 3
Attneave, F., 135, 145
Avons, S. E., 56, 60, 69–70, 75, 135
Awh, E., 50, 50, 78, 88–89, 91, 125–126, 128, 135, 137, 139

Baddeley, A. D., 2–3, 3–4, 7, 10–11, 13, 13–14, 20–21, 23–27, 27–29, 31, 31–32, 35–36, 36–37, 46–50, 52, 57–58, 67–68, 68, 71–72, 74–76, 79, 91, 104–111, 122–125, 128–129, 131–132, 137, 139, 145–147, 149, 151–152, 154–155, 159–161, 172, 175–176
Bailleux, C., 150
Bajric, J., 57
Bajszar, Jr. G., 74
Barnard, P., 38
Barnes, M., 111
Barrouillet, P., 4, 9, 23, 29–30, 136–138
Barry, C., 75
Bassani, C., 104
Bauml, K. H., 92
Baylis, G. C., 145
Bayliss, D. M., 110
Beck, D. M., 92
Becker, S., 19, 47, 58
Belacchi, C., 112
Bellucci, S., 130–131
Belopolsky, A., 49, 87, 91
Belotti, M., 106–107
Berch, D. B., 2, 47, 74, 127
Berger, H., 92
Berman, J. V. F., 20–21, 51, 67, 76, 91
Bernardin, S., 4, 23, 29
Berto, R., 104
Beschin, N., 22–23
Bestmann, S., 89
Biederman, I., 59
Bishop, D., 25
Bisiach, E., 22
Bjoertomt, O., 89
Bjork, R.A., 70
Blanco, M. J., 91
Blankenburg, F., 89
Bleckley, M. K., 104

Bliss, T. V. P., 73
Bloise, S. M., 37
Boduroglu, A., 56
Bohan, T. P., 111
Bollimunta, A., 93
Bor, D., 54, 75, 77
Bornstein, M., 150
Bosch, V., 55
Bosco, A., 173
Botvinick, M. M., 76
Bower, G. H., 72, 163
Bozzali, M., 38
Bradley, D. C., 54
Braga, C., 106–107
Brandimonte, M. A., 19, 25
Bressi, S., 31
Broadbent, D. E., 30, 69
Broadbent, M. H. P., 30, 69
Broadway, J. M., 33
Brockmole, J. R., 36–38, 52
Brodbeck, V., 92
Brooks, L. R., 3, 11, 20–21, 26–28, 35
Brookshire, B. L., 111
Brown, G. D. A., 3, 5, 75
Brown, L. A., 135
Brown, P., 94
Brunyé, T. T., 162, 165, 167–168, 170
Bryden, M. P., 102
Brünken, R., 162
Bull, R., 115
Bunton, L. J., 103
Burgess, A. P., 92
Burgess, N., 3, 5, 19, 47, 58, 71
Busch, N. A., 92
Busch, R. M., 53
Buxton, R. B., 78, 89
Buzsaki, G., 93
Bylsma, L. M., 76
Byrd, D., 127
Byrne, P., 19, 47, 58
Bédard, M. J., 72
Büchel, C., 19
Bülthoff, H.H., 145

Cacace, A. T., 70
Caltagirone, C., 37, 108, 112
Calvanio, R., 68, 108
Camos, V., 4, 9, 23, 29, 29–30, 136–138
Campbell, J. I. D., 5
Canoune, H., 37
Cantagallo, A., 12, 28, 130
Caplan, D., 36
Carlesimo, G. A., 37, 108, 112, 130–131
Caroli, M. G., 106–107
Carpenter, P. A., 5, 56, 102–103, 106, 114, 160
Carretti, B., 107, 111–112
Case, R., 5
Cattaneo, Z., 139
Caulo, M., 55
Caviola, S., 115
Cesa-Bianchi, M., 68, 108
Chafee, M. V., 90
Chaleb, L., 93
Chalmers, P., 25
Chang, M. H., 89
Chater, N., 3, 5
Chelazzi, L., 88
Chen, Y., 93
Cherubini, A., 38
Chiang, C., 93
Chincotta, D. M., 152
Chipman, S. F., 135
Chizk, C. L., 49, 90
Christie, D. F. M., 30, 69, 122, 124, 137
Chua, T. C., 38
Chun, M. M., 49, 55, 139
Claeys, K., 11
Clark, J. J., 146
Clark, W. H., 147
Coates, R. O., 108, 124, 131–132, 134, 136, 138, 153
Cocchini, G., 22–25, 31–32
Cocude, M., 169
Cohen, J. D., 8
Cohen, R. G., 5
Collette, F., 153
Collins, D. W., 113
Colnaghi, A., 23
Coltri, S., 115
Conway, A. R. A., 104, 112, 174
Conway, C. M., 5
Conway, J. A., 111
Cooper, N. R., 92
Corballis, M. C., 145
Corbetta, M., 89
Corley, R. P., 33
Cornish, K. M., 112–113
Cornoldi, C., 4, 12, 19, 57, 68, 102–107, 109–115, 122–123, 125–127, 129, 131–133, 140, 160–161, 164, 166, 168, 171–172, 174
Corsi, P. M., 2, 11, 67, 74–76, 161
Courtney, S. M., 68
Couture, M., 7, 72, 76
Cowan, N., 4, 14, 23–25, 29, 33, 55, 125, 127, 132, 155
Crevits, L., 11

Crivello, F., 57
Croft, R. J., 92
Crone, E. A., 131
Cross, G., 112–113
Crowder, R. G., 70–71
Culpin, V., 71
Cumming, N., 72
Cunitz, A. R., 13
Curtis, C. E., 49, 90

Dale, H. C. A., 123, 126
Dalla Vecchia, R., 107, 114–115
Daneman, M., 5, 36, 106, 114, 160
Daniel, M. P., 163
Darling, S., 12, 22, 28, 123, 128–130, 134, 139
Dascola, I., 88
Davidson, K. C., 111
Davis, H. P., 74
De Beni, R., 106–107, 111, 160–161, 164, 166–174
De Franchis, V., 107
de Haan, E. H. F., 54–55, 79, 123–124, 126–127, 135, 140, 152
De Liberto, S., 112
De Meo, T., 106–107
De Renzi, E., 67, 70
de Ribaupierre, A., 109, 150–151, 168
de Vega, M., 169, 173
De Vooght, G., 11, 160
Dean, G. M., 123, 139
Deary, I. J., 35
DeFries, J. C., 33
Deichmann, R., 89
Del Gratta, C., 55
Delis, D. C., 74
Delius, J. D., 145
Della Sala, S., 2, 12, 19, 22–29, 31–32, 36–38, 47–48, 57–58, 60, 68, 79, 91, 106–108, 123–125, 128–130, 133–134, 136, 139, 149
Denis, M., 22, 111, 163, 166–170
Dent, K., 54, 139
Depoorter, A., 5–7, 14, 52, 69, 73
Derrick, B. E., 73
Desimone, R., 88
Desmond, J. E., 34
Dewhurst, S. A., 75, 123, 139
Deyzac, E., 167–168, 170
Di Matteo, R., 55
Di Salle, F., 57
Dierks, T., 57
Ding, M., 93
Diwadkar, V., 56
Dixon, M. J., 146
Dominey, S. J. J., 92
Donadello, E., 109, 111
Donderi, D. C., 135
Doppelmayr, M., 94
Drigo, S., 107, 113
Driver, J., 89, 113, 145–146
Dubois, J., 92
Dubois, V., 161–162, 164–165, 172
Dulberg, C., 111
Duncan, J., 54, 75, 77, 88, 149, 152
Dunn, J. C., 13, 175
Duroe, S., 69
Duyck, W., 5, 8
D'Esposito, M., 8, 49–50, 89, 139
d'Ydewalle, G., 150

Eals, M., 123, 127
Ecker, U. K. H., 52
Egan, G. F., 56
Egly, R., 146
Ehrlich, M. F., 161, 164, 172
Eichmann, B., 145
Elford, G., 11, 13, 51, 53–54, 70–71, 77
Ellsasser, R., 94–95
Elridge, M., 160
Elsley, J. V., 52
Emerson, M. J., 137
Emslie, H., 149, 152
Engle, R. W., 4–5, 33, 103–106, 112, 174
Esposito, F., 57
Espy, K. A., 115
Ester, E. F., 126, 139
Estes, W. K., 70
Eusebio, A., 94
Evans, F. J., 28

Fabi, K., 38
Fabiani, M., 92
Fallah, M., 88–89
Farah, M. J., 68, 103, 108
Farmer, E. W., 20–21, 51, 67, 76, 91
Farrand, P., 2, 51–52, 69–70, 72, 77, 79
Farrell, K., 53
Farrell, S., 75
Fastame, M. C., 10, 28, 51–52, 72, 134, 152–153, 174
Fein, D., 74
Ferdinandsen, K., 150
Feredoes, E., 95
Fernandez, G., 37
Ferrarelli, F., 95
Ferretti, A., 55

Ferrier, I. N., 52, 54, 123–125, 130, 136, 138–139
Filomena, S., 173
Finke, R. A., 103
Fisher, C., 150
Fisk, J. E., 52, 134, 153
Fletcher, J. M., 111
Fletcher, Y. L., 20–21, 51, 67, 76, 91
Flude, B., 72
Fogarty, G. J., 103
Fontaine, S., 163
Forbes, D., 135
Formisano, E., 57
Fougnie, D., 52
Fox, H. C., 35
Foxe, J. J., 92
Francis, D. J., 111
Frank, L. R., 78, 89
Frankish, C. F., 70–71
Freeman, E., 89
Freudenthaler, H. H., 94
Freund, L., 112
Friederici, A. D., 55
Friedman, N. P., 33, 110, 112, 137, 174–175
Funahashi, S., 37
Fuster, J. M., 73
Fürst, A. J., 149, 152

Gabrieli, J. D. E., 34
Gagnon, S., 72
Gajewski, D. A., 36, 52
Gallagher, P., 127
Garuti, M., 113
Gathercole, S. E., 27, 68–69, 108, 110, 148–149, 160, 168
Gauthier, I., 56
Gaymard, B., 91
Gaynor, L.D., 94
Gerloff, C., 94, 96
Gilliam, F., 56
Girelli, L., 68, 107
Giurfa, M., 145
Glanzer, M., 13, 147
Glenberg, A. M., 161, 164
Glencross, D. J., 72
Glover, G. H., 34
Glowalla, U., 163
Gmeindl, L., 78, 89
Godijn, R., 91
Goebel, R., 57
Goldberg, J., 5
Goldman-Rakic, P. S., 8, 88, 90, 153
Goldowsky, B., 145
Golomb, J. D., 49
Gordon, R. D., 10
Gore, J. C., 8, 56, 153
Gould, J. H., 72
Grady, C. L., 55
Grafman, J., 37
Graham, S., 55
Grant, S., 3, 11, 47, 67
Gratton, G., 92
Gray, C., 2, 27, 29, 47, 58, 68, 79, 106–108, 124–125, 128–129, 133–134, 149
Gray, J. M., 52, 54, 123–125, 127, 130, 136, 138–139
Greene, R. L., 70–71
Greenlee, M. W., 57
Grimoldi, M., 109, 115
Gross-Tsur, V., 113
Grossi, D., 57
Gruzelier, J. H., 92
Guariglia, C., 22
Gunn, D. M., 110
Guérard, K., 48, 50–51, 69, 71–73, 78
Gyselinck, V., 10, 159, 161–162, 164–174

Hagerman, R. J., 113
Hahnel, A., 163
Hale, S., 48, 51, 91
Hall, M., 27, 68–69, 108, 168
Halligan, P.W., 22
Hambrick, D. Z., 33, 174
Hamidi, M., 9, 91, 94–96
Hamilton, C. J., 13, 26, 52, 54, 58, 108, 122–125, 127, 130–132, 134, 136, 138–139, 153
Hamilton, P., 72
Hamilton, S., 127
Hamker, F. H., 88
Hammond, K. M., 68, 108
Hanley, J. R., 67
Hannon, B., 36
Hannula, D. E., 37
Hanslmayr, S., 92
Harris, I. M., 56
Harrison, S. A., 139
Hartwich–Young, R., 90
Haxby, J. V., 68
Hayman-Abello, B. A., 113
Hayman-Abello, S. E., 113
Haynes, J. D., 89
Hayword, W. G., 56
Hebb, D. O., 7–8, 72, 76
Hecker, R., 28
Heffernan, T., 108, 124, 131–132, 134, 136, 138, 153

Hegarty, M., 13, 19, 51, 102, 110, 112, 161, 173–175
Heil, M., 57
Heinke, D., 91
Heitz, R. P., 33
Helstrup, T., 19
Hennighausen, E., 57
Henson, R. N. A., 4–5
Hermann, C. S., 92
Heslenfeld, D. J., 139
Hevenor, S. J., 55
Hewes, A. K., 111
Hewitt, J. K., 33
Higgins, J. A., 37
Hillyard, S. A., 88–89
Hitch, G. J., 3, 3–5, 10, 13, 25, 36, 36, 46, 52, 69, 71, 71–72, 75, 104, 122, 131, 148–149, 152, 154–155, 175
Hockey, R., 72
Hollingworth, A., 52
Horwitz, G., 127
Howerter, A., 137
Hughes, R. W., 71
Huha, E. M., 2, 47, 74, 127
Huitson, M., 70, 72
Hull, A., 71
Hulme, C., 3, 74–75
Humphreys, G. W., 91
Huston, J. P., 127
Hyun, J. S., 52

Idzikowski, C., 48–49, 91, 136
Ikkai, A., 90
Inhelder, B., 102
Intons-Peterson, M., 19
Ishikawa, T., 173
Istvan, P. J., 90
Izendoorn, R., 123–124, 126–127, 135, 140

Jalbert, A., 48, 50, 78
James, W., 155
Jamet, E., 162, 165
Jarrold, C., 7, 110–111
Jax, S. A., 5
Jenkins, R., 71
Jensen, O., 73, 92, 96
Jiang, Y., 55
Johnson, D. J., 113
Johnson, J. S., 52, 95–96
Johnson, M. K., 37, 139
Johnson, M. R., 139
Johnson, R. Jr., 37
Johnson-Laird, P. N., 161
Jones, D. M., 2, 51–52, 69–72, 76–77, 79
Jonides, J., 8, 37, 50, 68, 78, 89, 91, 128, 135
Josephs, O., 89
Just, M. A., 56, 102–103, 160–161

Kaila, K., 93
Kaiser, J., 96
Kanai, R., 93
Kane, M. J., 4, 33, 104–106, 174
Kantowitz, B. H., 75
Kaplan, E., 74
Kappelle, L. J., 79
Karmiloff-Smith, A., 113
Kassubek, J., 57
Kastner, S., 49
Kaufmann, K., 19
Keehner, M., 51
Keil, K., 68
Kemps, E., 10, 12, 28, 51–53, 75–77, 134, 136, 139, 146–147, 149, 151–154, 174
Kessels, R. P. C., 37, 79
King, T., 127
Kinnunen, L. H., 94–95
Kinsbourne, M., 22
Kintsch, W., 163
Kirk, J. W., 113
Kirsner, K., 13, 175
Klauer, K. C., 13, 29, 51–52, 107, 125, 128, 133–134, 136–137, 152, 154–155, 168, 175
Klimesch, W., 92, 94, 96
Knauff, M., 57
Koenig, P., 93
Koeppe, R. A., 128
Koffka, K., 145
Kolodny, J., 149, 152
Komoda, M. K., 160
Kosslyn, S. M., 58, 124, 127
Kover, S. T., 113
Krikorian, R., 2, 47, 53, 74, 127
Krinsky, S., 150
Kriz, S., 51
Kruley, P., 161, 164
Kruse, A. R., 102
Kurland, D. M., 5
Kuse, A. R., 173

Lachaux, J.-P., 96
Laiacona, M., 25
Landry, S. H., 111
Lanfranchi, S., 107, 111–113
Langston, W. E., 161
Larsen, J. D., 74–75

Latter, J., 111
Laughlin, J. E., 112
Law, A., 6, 26, 34
Lawrence, A., 74
Lawrence, B. M., 48, 50–51, 78, 91, 136
Laws, G., 111
Lecerf, T., 104, 109, 150–151, 168
Lee, K., 134
Lehnert, G., 50, 55–56
Lepsien, J., 139
Leung, H. C., 8, 153
Leutner, D., 162
Levine, D. N., 68, 108
Levy, E. I., 69
Lewandowsky, S., 75
Lewis, V. J., 160
Lezak, M. D., 152
Lieberman, K., 20–21, 26–27, 35, 47, 50, 67, 91
Liesefeld, H. R., 4, 46, 90, 123
Lima, B., 93
Linden, D. E. J., 57
Linn, M. C., 102, 173
Lisanby, S. H., 94–95
Lisdahl–Medina, K., 53
Lisman, J. E., 73, 73
Lloyd, S. A., 27, 68–69, 108, 168
Logan, G. D., 10
Logie, R. H., 3–6, 11–14, 19–28, 31, 31–32, 34–39, 47–49, 51–52, 54, 57–58, 60, 67–68, 91, 104, 107–108, 122–125, 128–132, 134–139, 147, 154, 159, 167–168, 170
Lohman, D. F., 173
Loncke, M., 8
Longoni, A. M., 173
Loomis, J. M., 19
Lopera, F., 38
Love, T., 78, 89
Lovelace, K., 173
Luber, B., 94–95
Lucangeli, D., 113, 115
Luck, S. J., 36, 46, 52, 88, 127, 146, 146, 154, 154–155
Luzzatti, C., 22, 68, 108
Luzzi, S., 38
Lømo, T., 73

Macken, W. J., 69, 72
Mackin, P., 52, 54, 123–125, 130, 136, 138–139
MacPherson, S. E., 23–24, 31
Magnussen, S., 125
Maguire, M., 56
Mahrer, P., 70–71
Maljkovic, V., 127
Mammarella, I. C., 12, 57, 68, 102, 104, 106, 109–110, 113–115, 123, 125, 127, 132, 168
Mammarella, N., 104, 106, 109, 111
Manning, S. K., 70–71
Manor, O., 113
Manos, C. S., 145
Mapperson, B., 28
Marchetti, C., 51, 68, 91, 107, 123–125, 128, 134, 139
Marconato, F., 113–114
Marks, D. F., 173
Marois, R., 52, 139
Mars, R. B., 37
Martinez, J. L., 73
Marzocchi, G. M., 106–107
Massimini, M., 95
Mata, B., 5
Mathewson, K. E., 92
May, J., 134, 136, 139, 151
Maybery, M. T., 11, 13, 51, 53–54, 70, 70–72, 77
Mayer, R. E., 162
Mayer, S., 51
Mazard, A., 57
Mazer, J. A., 49
Mazzocco, M. M., 113
McComas, J., 111
McConnell, J., 27, 107, 135, 139, 151, 154, 167
McFarland, D. J., 70
McGee, M. G., 102
McGeorge, P., 23
McGivern, R. F., 127
McMains, S., 56
McNabb, W. L., 70
McNeil, A. M., 72
Mecklinger, A., 55
Meeter, M., 91
Meijer, F., 91
Meiser, T., 51–52, 152
Melling, L., 70, 135
Melloni, L., 93
Meneghetti, C., 10, 159, 166–174
Menor, J., 31
Menzel, R., 145
Mercer, R., 75
Merickle, P. M., 160
Merten, H., 91
Mesulam, M. M., 113
Metzler, J., 56
Michel, C. M., 92, 92

Miles, C., 70–71
Miller, E. K., 8, 88, 96
Miller, G. A., 75
Milner, B., 27, 106, 108, 123, 127
Miner, M. E., 111
Miniussi, C., 56, 93
Minoshima, S., 128
Mishkin, M., 37
Mitchell, K. J., 37, 139
Miyake, A., 3, 13, 33, 103, 110, 112, 135, 137, 174–175
Miyatsuji, H., 52
Molin, A., 113–114
Mondoloni, A., 172
Montello, D. R., 173
Monticelli, M. L., 107
Montinari, C., 113–114
Moore, T., 50, 88–89
Morey, C. C., 24–25, 29
Morita, A., 6, 26, 34
Morris, N., 2, 51–52, 67, 69–70, 72, 77, 79
Morris, R. G., 38
Morris, R., 74
Morton, J., 71
Mosse, E. K., 7
Moé, A., 169
Muir, C., 74
Mulack, T., 57
Munir, F., 112–113
Munneke, J., 139
Munoz, D. P., 90
Murray, A., 76
Myerson, J., 48, 50–51, 78, 91, 136
Méndez, L. G., 38

Nairne, J. S., 70
Neath, I., 3, 5, 69, 75
Neave, N., 127
Neggers, S. F. W., 166
Neubauer, A., 94
Neuenschwander, S., 93
Ng, H. L. H., 71
Nichelli, P., 67, 70, 113
Nicholls, A. P., 51, 71–72
Nikolic, D., 93
Nobre, A. C., 139
Noordzij, M. L., 166
Norris, D., 4–5, 72
Nowak, B., 145

Oakhill, J. V., 160
Oberauer, K., 4, 14, 46
Oh, S.-H., 50, 135
Ojemann, J. G., 56
Oleksiak, A., 125
Olivers, C. N. L., 49, 87, 90–91
Olivetti Belardinelli, M., 55
Olson, I. R., 37, 55
Oonk, H. M., 48, 51, 91
Oostenveld, R., 92
Orme, E., 137–139
Ornstein, P. A., 75
Owen, A. M., 54, 75, 77
O'Regan, J. K., 146

Paas, F., 162
Pachinger, T., 94
Padovani, A., 22
Page, M. P. A., 4–5, 8, 14, 72, 72
Paivio, A., 25
Palladino, P., 106, 160
Palmer, S. E., 59, 146
Palmer, S., 152
Palva, J. M., 93, 96
Palva, S., 93, 96
Pantano, P., 22
Papagno, C., 72
Pare, M., 88
Parkin, A. J., 160
Parmentier, F. B. R., 4, 11, 13, 51–54, 67, 70–72, 77, 79, 146
Parra, M. A., 36–38
Pascual-Leone, A., 92, 95, 139
Pashler, H., 145, 150
Passolunghi, M. C., 112
Pauls, A. C., 57
Paulus, W., 93
Paxinos, G., 56
Payne, T. W., 33
Pazzaglia, F., 106, 109–110, 115, 125, 127, 160, 163, 166–174
Peaker, M., 108
Pearson, D. G., 27–28, 48–49, 52, 54, 68, 78, 91, 108, 130–131, 134–135, 138–139, 153
Pearson, N. A., 51, 67, 78, 91
Pelky, P. L., 51
Pelleiter, P. M., 113
Pendleton, L. R., 27, 35, 51, 67, 78, 91
Penney, C. G., 71
Pennington, B. F., 113
Perri, R., 37, 108
Perrig, W., 163
Petersen, A. C., 102, 173
Peterson, M. J., 95
Petersson, K. M., 37
Pfeifer, E., 55
Pfurtscheller, G., 94

Phillips, L., 124, 138
Phillips, W. A., 30, 56, 69, 122, 124–125, 135, 137
Piaget, J., 102
Pickering, S. J., 27, 68–69, 108, 110, 168
Piekema, C., 37
Pieroni, L., 10, 76, 135, 145–147, 149, 151–152, 154
Pierrot-Deseilligny, C., 91
Pinker, S., 103
Pipa, G., 93
Pisoni, D. B., 5
Pitt, M. A., 70
Pizzamiglio, L., 22
Plass, J. L., 162
Plaut, D. C., 76
Podgorny, P., 56
Poggio, T., 145
Pogosyan, A., 94
Poirier, M., 72
Posner, M. I., 88, 92
Postle, B. R., 4, 8–9, 13–14, 48–50, 73, 87, 89, 91, 94–96, 136
Postma, A., 54–55, 79, 123–127, 135, 140, 152, 166
Potter, M. C., 69
Power, K. G., 2, 27
Prabhakaran, V., 34
Preece, T., 3
Prvulovic, D., 57

Quinn, J. G., 27, 27, 35, 50–52, 54, 60, 91, 107, 123–125, 130, 136, 138–139, 151, 154, 167

Radvansky, G. A., 163
Rafal, R. D., 145–146
Rakitin, B. C., 94–95
Ralston, G. E., 27, 35, 51, 91
Ranganath, C., 37, 139
Rao, V. Y., 49
Rapp, D. N., 162, 165, 167
Raven, J. C., 103
Raye, C. L., 139
Re, A. M., 107
Redick, T. S., 33
Rees, G., 89
Reilly, J., 127
Reisberg, D., 19
Reiss, A. L., 112
Rensink, R. A., 146
Rettinger, D. A., 110, 112, 174–175
Reuter-Lorenz, P. A., 50, 89, 91, 135
Rhee, S. H., 48, 51, 91
Richardson, A. E., 173
Richardson, J. T. E., 107, 169
Riggall, A. C., 90
Riggio, L., 88
Rigoni, F., 107, 114
Rihs, T. A., 92
Rinck, M., 163
Ripper, B., 94
Ritter, W., 37
Rivaud, S., 91
Rizzolatti, G., 88
Ro, T., 92
Robertson, I. H., 22
Rock, I., 145–146
Rodrigo, M.J., 169
Rogers, T., 111
Roitblat, H., 145
Roldan, C. E., 145
Romani., G., 55
Romei, V., 92
Roodenrys, S., 75
Rosen, V. M., 103
Rosenbaum, D. A., 5
Roskos-Ewoldsen, B., 19
Ross, E. D., 21
Rossi-Arnaud, C., 10, 76, 135, 145–147, 149, 151–152, 154
Rothstein, P., 91
Roulin, J. L., 104
Rourke, B. P., 111, 113
Rowe, E. J., 70–71
Rowe, W. G., 70–71
Ruchkin, D. S., 37
Rudkin, S. J., 28, 52, 54, 134–135, 138
Ruff, C. C., 89
Rusconi, M. L., 23
Rypma, B., 34
Rösler, F., 57

Sachdev, P. S., 38
Sack, A. T., 57
Sahraie, A., 48–49, 78, 91
Saiki, J., 52
Saint-Aubin, J., 48, 50, 69, 72, 78
Saito, S., 6, 26, 34
Salih, H. R., 57
Salthouse, T. A., 10
Salway, A. F. S., 11, 28, 51, 91
Samuel, A. G., 70–71
Santa, J. L., 55
Sardone, L., 173
Saults, J. S., 25, 29, 55
Sauseng, P., 94, 96
Scalisi, T. G., 173

Scerif, G., 113
Schiller, P. H., 88
Schmidt, B. K., 146
Schnotz, W., 162
Schoffelen, J. M., 92
Scholey, K. A., 35, 48, 50–51, 70, 74–75
Schreier, H., 70–71
Schroeder, C. E., 93
Schulze, R., 46
Schumacher, E. H., 128
Schumann-Hengsteler, R., 77, 145
Schwartz, M., 75
Sciama, S. C., 161, 164
Scolari, M., 125–126, 137, 139
Scott, J. H., 2, 27
Seamon, J. G., 28, 68, 124–125
Sebastian, M. V., 31
Sechler, E. S., 72
Seidler, B., 51–52, 56, 60, 78, 123
Selemon, R. D., 88, 90
Selfridge, J. A., 75
Serences, J. T., 89, 126, 139
Sestieri, C., 55–56, 60
Shah, P., 3, 13, 33, 56, 103, 110, 112, 135, 174–175
Shalev, R. S., 113
Shallice, T., 22
Sharp, C. A., 52, 134, 153
Shepard, R. N., 56
Shiffrin, R. M., 3
Shulman, G. L., 89
Siegel, L., 107
Siegel, M., 96
Siegle, G. J., 127
Silvanto, J., 139
Silverman, I., 123, 127
Simpson, G. V., 92
Singer, W., 93
Sinnamon, H. M., 28, 68, 124–125
Skudlarski, P., 56
Slagter, H. A., 95–96
Slavin, M. J., 38
Smirni, P., 53, 74, 76
Smith, E. E., 8, 37, 50, 78, 89, 128
Smyth, M. M., 27, 35, 48, 50–51, 54, 67, 70, 74–75, 78, 91
Snyder, L. H., 54
Sommer, M. A., 88, 90
Sonkkila, C., 56
Soto, D., 91
Spanò, G., 111–112
Sparks, D. L., 90
Speiser, H. R., 51–52, 56, 60, 78, 123
Sperling, J. M., 57
Spinnler, H., 31
Spiro, A. B., 162, 165
Squire, L. R., 74
Srimal, R., 90
Starr, J. M., 35
Staudigl, T., 92
Stegmaier, R., 52, 134
Stern, Y., 94–95
Stiles-Davis, J., 150
Strobl, M., 77, 145
Stuart, G., 2, 51–52, 69–70, 72, 75, 77, 79
Stuyven, E., 11
Suardi, A., 6
Surprenant, A. M., 70
Swanson, H.L., 107
Sweller, J., 162
Szmalec, A., 1, 5, 8, 10, 12, 23, 28, 51–52, 69, 72, 134, 136, 139, 151–153, 174–175
Süß, H. M., 46

Takeda, K., 37
Tardieu, H., 161–162
Tarr, M. J., 56
Tartaro, A., 55
Taylor, H. A., 162–163, 165, 167–168, 170
Theeuwes, J., 49, 87, 90–91, 139
Thompson, J. M., 52, 54, 123–125, 130, 136, 138–139
Thompson, W., 127
Thomson, N. M., 111
Thomson, N., 3, 11, 47, 67, 74
Thurstone, L. L., 103
Thurstone, T. G., 103
Thut, G., 92–93
Tochon-Danguy, H. J., 56
Todd, J. J., 139
Tomaiuolo, F., 37, 108
Tong, F., 139
Tononi, G., 9, 94–96
Toso, C., 109, 115
Towse, J. N., 71
Treisman, A., 52
Tremblay, S., 7, 48–51, 69, 71–73, 76, 78
Tresch, M. C., 28, 68, 124–125
Tressoldi, P. E., 107, 114–115
Treue, S., 88
Trojano, L., 57
Tuholski, S. W., 4, 33, 105–106, 112
Tuiten, A., 126
Turcotte, J., 72
Turk, J., 112
Turner, M. L., 5
Turriziani, P., 37, 108

Tversky, B., 163
Tzourio–Mazoyer, N., 57

Uhlhaas, P. J., 93
Umiltà, C., 88
Ungerleider, L. G., 37, 49, 68
Unsworth, N., 33, 104

Vallar, G., 22
Van der Goten, K., 11
van der Ham, I. J. M., 125
Van der Linden, M., 153
van der Lubbe, R. H. J., 166
van der Meulen, M., 19–20, 39, 57, 60, 122, 132, 139
van der Molen, M. W., 131
Van der Stigchel, S., 91
van der Wel, R., 5
van Dijk, H., 92
Van Gool, L., 150
van Honk, J., 126
Van Leijenhorst, L., 131
van Merrienboer, J. J. G., 162
van Wezel, R. J., 125
van Zandvoort, K. J. E., 79
Vandenberg, S. G., 102, 173
Vandierendonck, A., 1, 5–7, 10–12, 14, 23, 28, 51–52, 69, 72–73, 134, 152–153, 160, 174–175
VanRullen, R., 92
Vargha-Khadem, F., 37
Vecchi, T., 4, 12, 35, 57, 68, 103, 105–111, 114–115, 122–123, 125–126, 129, 131–133, 139–140, 174
Vecera, S.P., 146, 154
Venneri, A., 113–114
Vergani, C., 68, 108
Vergauwe, E., 9, 29–30, 136–138
Vetter, T., 145
Vianello, R., 107, 112–113
Vicari, S., 112, 130–131
Villardita, C., 74, 76
Villardita, G., 53
Vio, C., 107, 109, 114–115
Vogel, E. K., 36, 46, 50, 125–127, 135, 137, 139, 146, 154–155
von Fersen, L., 145
von Stein, A., 93
Voyer, D., 102
Voyer, S., 102

Wagar, B. M., 146
Wagemans, J., 146, 150, 153
Wager, T. D., 137
Walker, P., 69
Waller, A., 51
Waller, D., 102
Walsh, V., 93, 95
Wang, N., 92
Ward, G., 70, 135
Warden, M., 96
Warren, S. T., 112
Warriner, E. M., 113
Warrington, E. K., 22
Watanabe, Y., 37
Waters, G. S., 36, 160
Watkins, M. J., 72
Watson, J. D. G., 56
Weintraub, S., 113
Weiss, C. S., 48, 51, 91
Weiss, D. J., 5
Wen, W., 38
Wenderoth, P., 145, 150
Werniers, Y., 134, 136, 139, 151
Wertheimer, M., 146
Whalley, L. J., 35
Whiteman, M. C., 35
Whittaker, A., 123, 139
Whitten, W.B., 70
Wickens, C. D., 10
Wiebe, S. A., 115
Wight, E., 3, 11, 47, 67
Wilding, J., 112–113
Wilhelm, O., 33, 46
Willcock, G. K., 31
Wilson, J. T. L., 2, 27
Wilson, L., 2, 27, 29, 47, 58, 106–108, 124–125, 128–129, 133–134, 149
Wilson, N., 68, 79
Winkel, J., 126
Winzenz, D., 72
Wiseman, R. J., 54, 75, 77
Wittmann, W. W., 46
Witzki, A. H., 137
Wolbers, T., 19
Wong, E. C., 78, 89
Woodman, G. F., 52, 146, 146, 154, 154–155
Worden, M. S., 92
Wurtz, R. H., 88, 90
Wynn, V., 25–26, 57

Xing, J., 54
Xu, Y. D., 139, 146

Yantis, S., 89
Young, A. H., 52, 54, 123–125, 130, 136, 138–139

Young, A. W., 67
Young, S. E., 33
Yuill, N., 160

Zacks, J. M., 56
Zanella, F. E., 57
Zappalà, G., 53, 74, 76
Zhang, J. X., 37
Zhao, Z. M., 13, 29, 107, 125, 128, 133–134, 136–137, 154–155, 168, 175
Zimmer, H. D., 4, 46, 50–53, 55–56, 59–60, 78, 90, 123, 132, 138, 140, 169
Zoelch, C., 77, 145
Zucco, G. M., 3, 20–21, 31, 67

Subject Index

abstract codes, 3, 8
ADHD, 107
alpha-band, 92–96
Alzheimer disease, 31–33, 38
angular variation, 80
arithmetic, 5, 113
articulatory suppression, 6, 10–11, 25–26, 52, 67, 69, 149, 151, 153, 160, 165–167, 174
attention deficit hyperactivity disorder, *see* ADHD

binding, 3–4, 36–39, 52–53, 55, 126, 153, 155, 176
bipolar disorder, 130
Brightness Judgement Task, 167

central executive, 3, 7, 52, 54, 104, 147, 149, 151, 153, 155, 160, 174
change-detection, 46, 55, 89, 124
cognitive load, 21, 136, 162–163
complex span, 104–107, 109–110, 174
complexity, 23, 30, 73, 75–77, 79–80, 122–123, 126–127, 135, 137, 145, 149, 151, 159
continuity framework, 12–13, 105, 107, 109–111, 113–116
Corsi Blocks Test, 2, 10–11, 27–28, 46–49, 51–54, 58–60, 67, 70, 74, 77–79, 106, 108–109, 111, 114, 123, 127–131, 133–137, 145, 147, 149, 151, 161, 174
cross-modal, 6–7, 13, 55, 72–73, 134

development, 9, 14, 27, 37, 68, 73, 102–103, 107–108, 113, 115, 129–131, 159
domain-generality, 8–9, 23, 28–29, 31, 33–37, 134
domain-specificity, 9, 23–24, 28, 31, 33–36, 38–39, 104, 106, 110
dorsolateral prefrontal cortex, 8, 49, 94–95
Dots Task, 2, 77–78
double dissociation, 12–14, 21, 58, 115, 130, 175
Down syndrome, 111–112, 115
Dual-task, 6, 10, 13, 20, 23–25, 28, 31, 33, 36, 124, 128, 133, 136–138, 145, 147, 151, 159, 161–164, 166, 169–170, 174–175
DVN, dynamic visual noise, 129, 139, 170–171
dyslexia, 8, 107

EEG, electroencephalography, 89, 91–92, 94–96
electrophysiology, 56, 88
encoding format, 3, 14
endogenous, 89, 91, 95–96, 132, 134
episodic buffer, 3, 7, 36–38, 176
ERP, event–related potentials, 55, 89
executive control, 10–11, 28–29, 37, 132, 134–139, 153, 155
executive function, 28, 36, 38, 107, 110, 175
exogenous, 95–96, 132, 134
eye movements, 48–50, 53–54, 78–80, 87–91, 136

fMRI, 13, 34, 37, 55, 77, 89–90, 95
focus of attention, 26, 29, 33, 104
fragile X, 112–113, 115
frontal eye fields, 49, 88–91, 94–95
functional magnetic resonance imaging, *see* fMRI

generalization gradient, 70, 76
genetic syndrome, 106, 111, 115
Gestalt, 135, 145, 153, 155

Hebb learning, 7–8, 14
Hebb repetition effect, 7, 72
hemispheric specialization, 8
hippocampus, 37, 58

illustrated text, 159–161
imagery, 60, 68, 103, 123, 159, 169, 172–173, 175–176
individual differences, 33–35, 39, 91, 96, 103–104, 106, 115, 122–123, 127, 129–130, 159, 174–175
inner scribe, 5, 47, 57–59, 107, 168
intellectual disability, 107, 112
intraparietal sulcus, 49, 56–57, 94–95
irrelevant pictures, 21, 27, 68, 107, 125, 128, 133–134

just-noticeable difference, 133, 138

kanji, 6, 26

language, 5, 7, 35, 112–113, 163, 166–167
left hemisphere, 8, 91, 130
lesion, 130
limited capacity, 10, 23, 26, 33, 162
long-term memory, 4–5, 7–8, 13–14, 36, 56, 58, 73, 76, 104, 125–126, 128, 133–134, 137–140, 145, 147, 153, 159, 176

memory span, 2, 34, 67, 70, 74, 76, 104–106, 109, 162
mental model, 14, 57, 111, 159, 161, 163, 167, 169
mental rotation, 56–57, 94, 102–103, 173–174
modality effect, 71, 162
modality-specific, 4, 7–8, 10, 52, 73, 80, 132, 134, 139
motor planning, 5
multicomponent model, 4–5, 7, 23, 47, 131–132, 153
multimedia learning, 162–163

neglect, *see* spatial neglect
neuroimaging, 8–9, 14
nonverbal learning disability, 107, 113–115

oculomotor control, 90, 96
order information, 5, 7–8, 10, 14, 51, 58, 69–70, 72

parietal cortex, 47, 55–57, 87–88, 93–94
path complexity, 67, 74, 77–80
path crossing, 77–80
path encoding, 109, 168
path length, 53, 75, 77–80
performance IQ, 111, 113
phonological loop, 3–5, 68, 104, 160
phonological similarity, 6, 25–26, 74–75
position coding, 7
postcentral gyrus, 95
posterior dorsal stream, 89
prefrontal cortex, 8–9, 55, 90, 153
primacy model, 5
process dissociation, 12
proximity, 75, 103, 145
pursuit tracking, 11

random generation, 10, 28, 52, 135, 153, 162
reading span, 106, 160
reasoning, 10, 51, 108–109, 160
recency effect, 71
recognition, 2, 6, 19, 59, 69–70, 87, 91, 96, 112, 124, 127, 130, 138, 145, 149, 151
regularity, 145, 147, 153
rehearsal, 21, 26–27, 29, 33, 36, 48–50, 53, 58–60, 71, 74, 78–80, 88–89, 105, 107, 136, 168
right hemisphere, 8, 22, 113
route description, 166–169, 171–172

saccade, 49, 90–91
selective interference, 10–12, 23, 52, 67–68, 72, 107, 128, 138, 160–161, 166
sequential presentation, 28, 30, 127, 137–138, 147, 149, 151, 153
serial position, 51, 69–71
serial recall, 5–8, 10, 13, 71–72, 76–78, 135, 137, 151, 153
set shifting, 137
short-term memory, 3, 6–8, 14, 19, 25, 37, 46, 48, 56, 67, 69, 80, 87–89, 91–92, 94–96, 123
short-term recall, 147, 151, 153
simple span, 105–107
simultaneous presentation, 28, 147, 149, 151, 153, 155

spatial description, 159, 163, 168
spatial location, 1, 21–22, 27–29, 35, 37, 70, 126, 130–131, 135–136, 139, 153
spatial modality, 6–7
spatial movement, 5, 51
spatial neglect, 22–23
spatial orientation, 102, 114, 123
spatial path, 2, 10–11, 67, 76, 80
spatial processing, 10–11, 51, 94, 109, 128, 153
spatial representations, 22, 46–47, 49, 57, 59, 103, 166–167
spatial tapping, 10–11, 49, 51, 57, 128–129, 134, 136, 139, 145, 149, 153, 155, 161, 165–168, 172–174
spatial working memory, 1–2, 5, 8, 11, 13–14, 19–20, 22, 29–31, 33, 38–39, 46–47, 49, 51–52, 54–55, 57–58, 60, 87, 90–91, 96, 102–104, 107–115, 122–125, 127, 131, 134–139, 145, 147, 151, 153, 155, 159–161, 163, 166–169, 172–175
spatial-sequential, 28, 50, 57, 109, 111, 115–116, 123, 127, 130, 136, 169, 171
spina bifida, 111, 115
static-active, 68, 129–130
strategies, 2, 11, 26, 30, 33–34, 38, 59, 93, 109, 124–125, 151, 169, 172–173, 175
suffix effect, 71
superior colliculus, 49, 87–88, 90
superior parietal cortex, 89
superior parietal lobule, 94–96
supplementary eye fields, 91
survey description, 166–168, 171
symmetry, 53, 76, 145, 147, 149, 151, 153, 155

temporal grouping, 71
text comprehension, 111, 159–161, 163, 169
TMS, 13, 56–57, 92, 94–96
Trails Task, 149, 151
transcranial magnetic stimulation, *see* TMS
transition, 67, 73, 75–76, 80, 89

updating, 19, 49, 112, 137

verbal IQ, 111, 113
verbal modality, 6
verbal processing, 3, 20, 25, 27, 29, 34, 92, 145, 155, 168
verbal representations, 1, 22, 27, 139
verbal span task, 2, 67, 70, 74
visual cache, 36, 47, 58–59, 107, 139, 168
visual cortex, 92–93, 139
Visual Pattern Test, 2, 27, 106, 108–109, 111, 114, 125, 128, 130–131, 133–137, 139
visual representations, 50
visualization process, 122
visuo-spatial sketch pad, 67–68, 122–123, 132, 139
visuospatial representations, 1, 7, 67, 72
VPT, *see* Visual Pattern Test

Williams syndrome, 111, 130
working memory architecture, 3, 9, 13